The Theory and the Practice of Market Law in Medieval Islam

A Study of Kitāb Niṣāb al-Iḥtisāb

of

ᶜUmar b. Muḥammad al-Sunāmī
(fl. 7th–8th/13th–14th Century)

by

M. Izzi Dien

E.J.W. GIBB MEMORIAL TRUST

British Library Cataloguing-in-Publication Data
A catalogue record of this book is available from the British Library

ISBN 0906094 33 X

Contents

Foreword

The appearance of this welcome addition to the list of works published in the time-honoured "E.J.W. Gibb Memorial" series marks the culmination of a research project that was to prove far more demanding and time-consuming than could have been foreseen at the time of its conception. The first fruit of the project was the completion and publication, in 1983, of a much-needed critical edition of the Arabic text of the Ḥanafite manual of *ḥisba* that is the *Niṣāb al-iḥtisāb*. In view of the particular relevance of the latter to the history of Islam and Ḥanafite law on the Indian subcontinent, and, given the great number of extant manuscripts of the work – bespeaking an importance worthy of scholarly attention – one's first reaction is one of surprise at how little is said of it in modern works of reference. It is only when we learn, as we do in this volume, of the problems confronting Dr Izzi Dien from the moment he embarked on a study of the *Niṣāb* that the reasons why it is accorded scant space in our reference works become clear: the provenance of the work and the identity of its author as well as questions of dating turn out to have been nothing if not highly problematic. Now, thanks to a masterly study based on percipient evaluation of evidence relevant to these and other matters of importance, there are no longer any serious obstacles in the way of scholarly exploitation of the content of the *Niṣāb*.

J. Derek Latham
11 August 1997

Preface

This study is an attempt to throw some light on the work entitled *Niṣāb al-iḥtisāb*, a treatise on Ḥanafī *iḥtisāb* which has largely been neglected and forgotten due to a lack of comprehension of its importance and value. Nevertheless, the large number of extant manuscripts of the text hint at the significance which should be attached to it. The study comprises an introduction which investigates both the author and his book, and furnishes sufficient evidence, I believe, to show that he was a native of India, not of Egypt, as some previous scholars have suggested. Then follows an analysis of selected practices mentioned in the *Niṣāb* and an attempt to explain them with reference to the social atmosphere. I have also included a chapter which explains the *Niṣāb* with respect to the general theory of *ḥisba*. The various manuscripts used in editing the Arabic text which was published in 1983[1] have been carefully reviewed by me in the course of my work on the translation. The published book page numbers are also incorporated in the text in bold type. In order to simplify the task of referring to notes, all the relevant biographies, books referred to in the text and glossary, and the glossary index are placed immediatly after the translation. There then follows a description of the manuscripts used and a general biography.

I must thank the publishers for the help they have given; above all I am grateful to Professors J. Derek Latham and Rex Smith who saved me from errors. I would also like to record my deepest gratitude to Elizabeth Huda Bladon for her help and patient assistance.

M.I.D.

---

1 *Niṣāb al-iḥtisāb* by ᶜUmar b. ᶜIwaḍ al-Sunāmī, ed. Mawil Izzi Dien, Dar al-ᶜUlūm, Jeddah, 1983/1403.

Method of Transliteration

All transliterated words (except proper names) are printed in italics.

Consonants

ا	'	ز	z	ق	q
ب	b	س	s	ك	k
ت	t	ش	sh	ل	l
ث	th	ص	ṣ	م	m
ج	j	ض	ḍ	ن	n
ح	ḥ	ط	ṭ	ه	h
خ	kh	ظ	ẓ	و	w
د	d	ع	ᶜ	ي	y
ذ	dh	غ	gh	ة	a (in construct state-at)
ر	r	ف	f		

The article is written as al- even when used before sun letters and after vowels e.g. Abū al-Salt (not Abū' s-Salt, or Abū' l-Salt. However, wa-al- is written as wa-l-.

Vowels

Short:		Long		Doubled	iyya
َ	a	ى	ā		(final form : ī)
ُ	u	و	ū	Dipthongs و	aw
ِ	i	ي	ī	ي	ay

Exceptions

1. The names of well known places e.g. Makkaa, Madina, Iraq.

2. The following words have been written as indicated (without italics): amir, Arab, caliph, dhimmi, dirham, faqih, hadith, Hanafi, Hanbali, ᶜId, imam, Islam, jihad, Kaaba, Maliki, qadi, qibla, Quran, Quranic, Ramadhan, Shafiᶜa, Shariᶜa, Shaykh, Sufi, sultan, sura, ulama, sunna, Shaᶜban.

I
Niṣāb al-iḥtisāb and its author

Authorship

In the introduction to Ibn al-Ukhuwwa's *Maᶜālim al-qurba*, R. Levy refers to the manuscripts of *Niṣāb al-iḥtisāb*,[1] a critical study which forms a major portion of the present work. The name of the author he gives as ᶜUmar b. ᶜIwaḍ al-Shāmī and, after noting that there are manuscripts of the work in the India Office Library and elsewhere, he says nothing further of either the work or the author. In the *Encyclopaedia of Islam* (New edition), the authors of the first section (iii: 486–89), C. Cahen and M. Talbi, draw attention to *Niṣāb* in the following terms: 'in Central Asia, [was written] *Niṣāb fi ʾl-iḥtisāb* of al-Sinämī(?), the title of which refers to the author's own position as *muḥtasib* (7th/13th century), and which, to judge by the number of manuscripts ... must have had a considerable success in Irano-Turkish countries'. In his study, *El 'Señor del zoco' en España*, Pedro Chalmeta speaks of the work as one which he had occasion to consult and gives the author's name as ᶜUmar al-Sināmī, without saying anything further.[2] Brockelmann in his *Geshchichte der arabischen Litteratur* provides no accurate information about the author apart from the fact that he was Ḥanafī.[3]

As we shall see, none of the authorities mentioned can have had anything but a superficial acquaintance with the work. Not a single one of them appears to be aware that *Niṣāb al-iḥtisāb* was published by Sprenger in Calcutta as long ago as the 1830s. A copy of this text, which is completely devoid of critical apparatus, is preserved in the British Museum (No. 14528 b.19), the author's name being given as Muḥammad b. ᶜUmar ᶜIwaḍ Al-Shāmī.[4] Although better than one might have expected, the Calcutta text is not free from errors, and it carries certain unusual features such as فح for فحينئذ.[5] Because of the large number of manuscripts extant, a critical edition was obviously called for, and this is sufficient justification for the translation forming part of this work.

---

1 R. Levy's introduction to Ibn al-Ukhuwwa, *Maᶜālim*, xvi.

2 Chalmeta, *Zoco*: 300.

3 Brockelmann's information about Sunāmī reads as follows: 'ᶜUmar b. Muḥammad b. ᶜIwaḍ al-Shāmī (al- Sunāmī)al-Ḥanafī Ḍiyā' al-Dīn, died c. 993/1585 in Bukhārā', *GAL*: Suppl. 2:427.

4 A. Gallis, *Catalogue of Arabic Books in the British Museum* (London, 1901): 2:718.

5 *Niṣāb*, Calcutta edition: 52.

If Levy, Cahen, Talbi and Chalmeta are unclear about our author and his work, so also were others who studied the work and the manuscripts somewhat more closely. The man's name presents an obvious problem since the extant manuscripts present all kinds of variations ranging from 'Shāmī',[6] 'Sh.nnāmī',[7] and 'S.nāmī',[8] to 'Shāfiᶜī',[9] this last representing the most distorted form of the name. Quite obviously, any attempt to arrive at the correct form of the author's name would be furthered if we had some idea of where and when he lived, so that the appropriate biographical dictionaries might be searched.

As to the period in which the man lived, a contemporary scholar by the name of Muḥyī Hilāl Sirḥān has suggested, after studying the *Niṣāb*, that our author flourished in the sixth/twelfth century.[10] This suggestion is based on a remark made by our author that al-Ghazālī disapproved of a certain practice at the time. From this observation Sirḥān inferred that the author of the *Niṣāb* and al-Ghazālī were contemporaries.[11] There may, quite clearly, be some truth in this idea, but since our author may well have lived fifty years or more after al-Ghazālī, more conclusive evidence is required to substantiate it, and this is certainly not adduced by Sirḥān. From internal evidence we can certainly say that the man cannot have died prior to the period 617/1220–1 – 628/1230–1 since there is a point of reference for that date.[12] Equally, he must have written his work not later than 912/1506–7, for that is the earliest date written on any manuscript of my acquaintance.[13] It is not impossible, therefore, for him to have flourished around the lifetime of al-Ghazālī (450–505/1058–1111). As we shall see, we can pinpoint our author's lifetime somewhat more closely than those suggested by our *ante quem* and *post quem* noted above, but we must first take a look at the biographical sources.

Ḥājjī Khalīfa has nothing whatever to say about where and when the *Niṣāb* was written,[14] but, according to Ismāᶜīl Bāshā al-Baghdādī (d.1339/1920), the *Niṣāb* was the work of one ᶜIzz al-Dīn ᶜUmar b. Muḥammad b. ᶜIwaḍ, whose *nisba* was in fact

---

6 MS no. 1417 Wetzstein.

7 MS no. 89 Ijtimāᶜ Taymūr.

MS no. 1775 Princeton University. MS no. 707 Mingana, Birmingham.

MS no. 1884 Nūr ᶜUthmāniyya (cited by ᶜAwwāḍ *Niṣāb*, in *RAAD* 17, 434).

10 *Majallat al-risāla al-Islāmiyya* 29–30 (1970): 15.

11 *Niṣāb*: 82A.

12 This is one of the dates which we have for ᶜAṭṭār, the author of *Tadhkirat al-awliyā'*, Some suggest that he may have lived until 628/1230–1. I have not referred to some of the other books mentioned in the text such as *al-Ṣārim al-maslūl* or *Tafsīr al-Bayḍāwī*. The reason for this is that they were mentioned in a chapter about which there is some doubt as to the true author see pp. 220–1.

13 MS no. 2846 Hyderabad State Central Library (Fiqh Ḥanafī).

14 *Ibid.*

Maqdisī or Muqaddasī. Noting that he was a Ḥanbālī *qāḍī al-quḍāh*, he indicates that this man lived in Egypt and died in 696/1296–7.[15] It would, however, seem that our ᶜUmar b. ᶜIwaḍ has been confused with another man of the same name and period. Many of our historical sources dealing with Egypt of the thirteenth century note that there was an ᶜUmar b. ᶜIwaḍ who lived in the time of the Sultan Badr al-Dīn Salāmish (Sulemish), son of Baybars, and who was appointed *qāḍī al-quḍāh* in 678/1279, remaining such until his death in 696/1296–7.[16] One main respect in which al-Baghdadī differs from these historians is that he alone attributed *Niṣāb* to this man. Before proceeding further, it is obviously important either to confirm or to refute the idea that our ᶜUmar b. ᶜIwaḍ was an Egyptian Ḥanbalī *qāḍī al-quḍāh* as suggested by al-Baghdadī and accepted over twenty years ago by ᶜUmar Kaḥḥāla in his *Muᶜjam al-mu'allifīn.*[17]

In the *Niṣāb al-iḥtisāb* we are told by the author that he practised *iḥtisāb* in a *sūq* the name of which was *sūq N.w.h.t.h.*[18] a name not far different from Nabtūha, the name of a place near Cairo, on the west bank of the Nile.[19] Moreover, in the *Niṣāb* we can plainly see that its author was acquainted with the duties of the *qāḍī al-quḍāh.*[20] On the other hand, it is equally clear from the *Niṣāb* that he was by no means a Ḥanbalī since his sources and views[21] and notably his reference to the Iraqi school as 'our school' (*madhhabuna*) show him to have been a Ḥanafī. Furthermore, there is no record of any book attributed to the al-Maqdisī of whom al-Baghdadī speaks. Last but by no means least, the whole tone of the book and its entire ethos militate against its having been written in Egypt or indeed any Arab country. Everything points to its having been written on the Indian sub-continent. The most obvious indication of this is the fact that there are repeated references to Hindus (*Hunūd*). In particular, the author deplores the fact that Muslims have to purchase liquids and semi-liquids from Hindus.[22] We may add to this the fact that the *Niṣāb* was well known in India; indeed, many Indian authors refer to the work.[23] More

---

15 *Hadiyyat al-ᶜārifīn*: 2:788.

16 Maqrīzī, *al-Sulūk li maᶜrifat duwal al-mulūk* (Cairo, 1957/1970): I/2,657; I/3,830.

17 Kaḥḥāla, *Muᶜjam*: 7:317.

18 *Niṣāb*: 29A.

19 Ibn Ẓahīra, *al-Faḍā'il al-bāhira* (Cairo, 1969): 102.

20 See *Niṣāb*: Chapter 12.

21 *Ibid*: 55A.

22 *Ibid*: 15A.

23 See, for example al-Sahrānpūrī, *Kitāb Bayān al-amr bi-al-maᶜrūf wa-l-nahy ᶜan al-munkar*, MS. no. 1697 in *Catalogue of Arabic MSS India Office Library*, 1, folio 3, 15.

importantly, the author of the *Akhbār al-akhyār* (written in 996/1587–8, according to MS no. Or 221, in the *Catalogue of Persian MSS. in the BM*, 355) notes that a 'Sunāmī' lived and died in India,[24] while Nadwī, in quoting this source, notes that the *Tārīkh-i Fīrūz Shāhī* mentions Sunāmī and also reports that he lived in India.[25]

At this point we must ask ourselves: if our author lived in India, to what place does his *nisba* refer? This presents no difficulty. In the Punjab there exists a town called Sunām situated 30° 8' N and 75° 52' E, forty-three miles south-west of the town of Patala.[26] So far, so good. But what of *N.w.h.t.h.*? Where was this town or village of whose *sūq* Sunāmī speaks? It is my submission that the scribe or copyist misread the consonants /n/ and /t/ as /t/ and /n/ – in other words, he misread the consonantal ductus of the village Tuhana (*T.w.h.n.h.*) – a place also situated in the Punjab not very far from the place from which Sunāmī took his *nisba*, the precise bearing being 29° 43' N and 75° 54' E.

All these facts fall very neatly into place, but they do not tell us much about the place in which Sunāmī flourished. None of the works I have been able to consult provide a conclusive solution to the problem. The author of the *Akhbār al-akhyār* speaks of Sunāmī as a contemporary of Niẓām al-Dīn Muḥammad al-Badā'ūnī (d. 725/1324–5). He records that Sunāmī was a bitter opponent of Badā'ūnī because of the latter's practice of *samā*ᶜ[27] and this accords well with Sunāmī's stand against the *sama*ᶜ in the *Niṣāb*.[28] Badā'ūnī is said to have respected Sunāmī and visited him when the latter was dying. Sunāmī, however, refused to see him because he was an 'innovator'. But, in the end, Badā'ūnī was received when he said he had come to repent of his *bida*ᶜ.[29]

Al-Nadwī (d. 1341/1923), quoting al-Dahlawī, gives a somewhat different account in that he maintains that Sunāmī died in Dawlatabad, which only became a Muslim city after Badā'ūnī's death (727/1327).[30] Unfortunately, al-Nadwī does not substantiate his claim with clear references or any other evidence.

Be that as it may, there is material enabling us to suggest an approximate date for Sunāmī's death. In Chapter 36 he says that his teacher saw Ḥamīd al-Dīn al-Ḍarīr

---

See also MS no. 1225, *Catalogue of Arabic and Persian MSS in the Public Oriental Library of Bankipur*, 1925.

24 Dahlawī, *Akhbār*: 182B.

25 *Nuzha*: 2:93.

26 *Imperial Gazeteer of India* (Oxford, 1908) XXIII: 139; *Times Atlas* (London, 1975): 29.

27 Dahlawī, *Akhbār*: 182B.

28 *Niṣāb*: 9A.

29 Dahlawī, *Akhbār*: 182B.

30 Nadwī, *Nuzha*: 2:93.

preaching in the pulpit.[31] It could be, then, that Ḥamīd al-Dīn was the teacher of Sunāmī's teacher or that he was a much older contemporary. However, al-Ḍarīr is known to have died in 666/1267-8.[32] It is possible, then, that if Sunāmī flourished in the second generation following al-Ḍarīr, he lived around the period 670/1271–2 – 740/1339–40.

Despite what has been said so far, there are nevertheless grounds for doubt as to whether our author predeceased al-Badā'ūnī (d. 725/1324–5). If he did, he must have died in the reign of Ghiyāth al-Dīn Tughluq Shāh, who died in the same year as al-Badā'ūnī. But did he in fact die in this sultan's reign? We have already noted that Sunāmī is said to have died in Dawalatabad. This in itself makes us wonder whether Sunāmī lived in, or into, the reign of Tughluq Shāh's son and successor, Muḥammad b. Tughluq, for it was the latter who decided that what had hitherto been called Deogiri should be renamed Dawlatabad and that this city should become his capital. This event is known to date from 727/1327.[33] At this point, then, it becomes important to consider whether there is any evidence for the view that Sunāmī was alive during the reign of Muḥammad b. Tughluq.

In Chapter 26, where he deals with the matter of currency, Sunāmī seems to be addressing himself not to a hypothetical situation but to an actual problem when he denounces the iniquitous practice, described as commonplace among sultans (*al-ẓulm al-mᶜrūf min al-salāṭīn*) of putting into circulation money to which they assigned their own value. He comments, 'when they are no longer in power, the money in circulation is then devalued to its true worth'.[34] Who, may we ask, are the *salāṭīn* whom our author has in mind? During the reign of ᶜAlā' al-Dīn Muḥammad Shāh (695–715/1295–1315) the expenses of the army caused him to contemplate reducing the silver *tanka* from 175 to 140 grs., but gold *tankas* remained at the nominal 175grs. often crudely struck, with no attempt to bring them up to the standard of the northern mints.[35] This was we may note, around the time that the future Dawlatabad (then Devagiri, or Deogiri) appears as a mint town (c.1314–15).[36] As regards Ghiyāth al-Dīn, we know that he struck a coin on his expedition to Bengal in 724/1324, but this money appears to have caused no particular scandal. When we come to Muḥammad b. Tughluq, however, the position changes: great innovations come in, to the extent that this sultan earned himself the nickname 'prince of moneyers'.[37] The Delhi coinage was, amongst other things, broken up into

31 *Niṣāb*: 44B.

32 *GAL* Suppl: 519; Quṭlubughā: 46; Luknawī: 125; H.Kh., *Kashf*: 2031.

33 *EI*²: 2:179.

34 *Niṣāb*: 37B.

35 *EI*²: 2:120.

36 *Ibid.*

37 *Ibid.*

a number of subdivisions. Without going into all the details, which need not concern us in this context, we should, however, note one or two points that seem relevant. In the first place, the new *dīnār* exchanged at 8 old silver *tankas* or 10 *ᶜadalīs*, *a fictitious rate in terms of the relative value of gold and silver.* The complete scheme of the sub-divisional currency was later conflated to mix silver and copper in arbitrary proportions to produce coins of similar size but different intrinsic values; this brought in the 'black *tanka*', containing only 16.4 grs. silver.[38] At this point we may pause to consider whether it is not the black *tanka* that Sunāmī has in mind when he speaks of dirhams as being *mukaḥḥal*.[39] This black *tanka* is reported to have been minted of mixed silver and copper in arbitrary proportions.[40] It seems probable that Sunāmī is rejecting exactly the same type of coins, especially when we know that in the black *tanka* the amount of silver mixed with the copper was arbitrary.[41] This fits in very well with Sunāmī's prohibition of *mukaḥḥal* coins in which the amount of silver is unknown.[42]

Whatever we may think of this last suggestion, we cannot fail to be struck by the fact that in 731–2/1330–1, Muḥammad b. Tughluq produced his 'forced currency'. These were brass tokens valued at one *ᶜadalī*. The experiment was a disaster because precautions against forgery were inadequate. The result was described by John Burton-Page: ' Tokens were turned out in their thousands by local artisans, but after three years all were called in and redeemed. The whole operation thus became virtually a temporary loan from the sultan's subjects which was repaid at a swingeing rate of interest.' [43]

However, this would not seem to be the whole story. In *Tārīkh-i Firshita* (1550 – 1611) the story is related in the following terms:

> Muḥammad b. Tughluq ... minted copper coins which were issued with a notional value. These were accepted throughout Hindustan... Bankers acquired large fortunes in this coinage... The great calamity consequent upon this debasement of the coinage arose from the known instability of the government. Public credit could not exist for long in a state so liable to revolutions as Hindustan... From these evils discontent became universal, and the ruler was finally obliged to call in all the copper currency. So great were the abuses that had occurred in the mint, however, that after the copper money had been exchanged for gold or silver the treasury was empty. But there still remained huge debts which

---

38 *Ibid.*

39 *Niṣāb*: 37B.

40 *EI²*: 2:120.

41 *Ibid.*

42 *Niṣāb*: 37B.

43 *EI²*: 2:120.

were written off by the ruler, and in consequence, thousands were ruined.[44]

It is, it seems to me, this tampering with coinage by Muḥammad b. Tughluq which was at the forefront of Sunāmī's mind. True, he speaks of *salāṭīn* and not of *a* sultan in the singular; but this we can readily put down to caution, for Muḥammad b. Tughluq can scarcely be expected to have taken kindly to direct criticism of his policy. Scholars such as al-Baranī, for instance, preferred to give their approval of un-Islamic practices adopted by the ruler on the basis of *ḍarūra* (unavoidable necessity) rather than to risk his ire. He was in fact prepared to go as far as declaring that sovereign power is divinity on earth![45]

Be that as it may, we have one further indication, this time in Chapter 17 (24B–25A), that we are dealing with Muḥammad b. Tughluq: the styles and titles of the sultan (note the use of the singular) which are considered by Sunāmī to be unlawful are those considered elsewhere to be those borne by Muḥammad b. Tughluq alone.[46]

Finally, it is worth noting Sunāmī's reference to the prostration of subjects before the sovereign and his condemnation of it.[47] This abasement was sometimes taken to the ridiculous extreme of kissing the hoof of a horse which the sultan had presented to a subject.[48] We know for certain that this custom was observed in Muḥammad b. Tughluq's reign, but, of course, we are bound to acknowledge that this mark of excessive deference was not exclusive to this ruler.

The last question to occur to us is this: Why, if Muḥammad b. Tughluq is, as seems likely, the ruler in whose time Sunāmī died, were there no reactions on his part to criticisms which were directly applicable to him? On this point we can only speculate. The sultan may not have been aware of the existence of the *Niṣāb*, or, if he was aware of it, he preferred to do nothing about it so long as the views expressed in it were not widely and publicly canvassed, especially if its author was an old and respected figure. That he cannot have been a young man we know from the *Niṣāb* itself;[49] that he was a respected figure is clear from the story of al-Badā'ūnī.

While one is bound to admit that circumstantial evidence is absolute proof of nothing, we are, on balance, left with the suspicion that Sunāmī did live into the reign of Muḥammad b. Tughluq, that he did live to see the introduction of his 'forced currency' in 731–2/1330–2 and its recall three years later with all its consequences, and that he did die in Dawlatabad somewhere around or after 734–4/1333–4.

---

44 *Tarīkh-i Firshita*: 238–9.

45 Afsar ud-Din, *Indian Islam*: 347.

46 Nadwī, *Nuzha*: 133.

47 *Niṣāb*: 58A.

48 *Ibid*: 18A.

49 *Ibid*: 83A.

Sunāmī's Life, Education and Works

Very little is known about Sunāmī's life. All we can be certain of is that he was born and lived in India. There he remained, residing in his native town Sunām, from which he derived his *nisba*. It was during this period that he received his educational training.

His first teacher was his father, Muḥammad b. ᶜIwaḍ al-Sunāmī, who was also a religious scholar.[50] We know little about Sunāmī's other teachers, but there is one person mentioned in *Nuzhat al-khawāṭir*[51] who seems to fit the description we have of the teacher who is named in the *Niṣāb*[52] as Kamāl al-Dīn al-Sāmānawī. This man, who is reported to have been one of the most eminent teachers of his age, worked in Delhi during the reign of Muḥammad b. Tughluq and moved to Dawlatabad about 729/1338–9,[53] on the orders of the sultan.[54] Among his students was one Shaykh Muḥammad al-Shīrāzī (701–771/1301–2 – 1369–70), a stubborn opponent of the Sufis whom he criticised vigorously, particularly for the practice known as *samāᶜ*. Among the chief parties whom he subjected to attack was Shaykh Burhān al-Dīn al-Hānsawī,[55] the father of Shaykh Quṭb al-Dīn Munawwar (d.760/1358–9), who was the second in succession to Burhān al-Dīn Gharīb (d. 741/1340–1) as head of the Chishtiyya *silsila*.[56]

Sunāmī's teacher lived during the same period as the persons just named. Moreover, we know that he met Ḥamīd al-Dīn al-Ḍarīr(d. 666/1267–8) and that he was still alive at the time *Niṣāb* was written[57] because Sunāmī prays to God to grant his teacher a long life.[58] The similarity between Sunāmī's opposition to Shaykh Gharīb for the latter's practice of *samāᶜ*, and Shīrāzī's criticism of Shaykh Gharīb's successor, Shaykh Munawwar, is very strong. This similarity, if linked with the period and place (Delhi) in which Sunāmī, Shīrāzī, and Kamāl al-Dīn al-Sāmānawī all lived, leads us to suspect that Sunāmī's teacher was one and the same as al-Shīrāzī's.

---

50 Nadwī, *Nuzha*: 95.

51 *Ibid*: 93.

52 *Niṣāb*: 44B.

53 The exodus to Dawlatabad took place during this year. Nizami, *Delhi Sultanate*: 512. also see *EI*²: 2:179 s.v. ᶜDihlī.

54 Nadwī, *Nuzha*: 114.

55 *Ibid*: 40.

56 The Chistiyya is one of the most popular and influential mystic orders (*silsilāt*). It was brought to India by Shaykh Muᶜīn al-Dīn al-Chishtī (d. 633/1235–6). The real founder of the *silsila* was Khawāja Abū Isḥāq Maḥmūd from Syria. *EI*²: 2:50.

57 Probably during the first years of Muḥammad b. Tughluq's reign (725/1325 – 752/1351).

58 *Niṣāb*: 44B.

The name Kamāl al-Dīn al-Sāmānawī occurs in the well known debate between Niẓām al-Dīn al-Badāūnī, or Badā'ūnī, and the ulama of his time – a debate that took place during the reign of Sultan Ghiyāth al-Dīn Tughluq and in his presence and which was arranged by the ulama in order to discredit al-Badā'ūnī's predilection for a *samā*^{c}.[59]

In the course of the debate discussion arose concerning *samā*^{c} which, in Badā'ūnī's submission, was lawful, a submission contrary to that of the ulama, who tried to prove that it was unlawful. Neither succeeded in proving the case conclusively. However, two main questions were put to Badā'ūnī. Of these, the first was put by Shaykh Zāda Ḥusām al-Dīn, *viz* 'Do you practise *samā*^{c} in your assemblies during which people dance, shout and clap?' To this Shaykh Niẓām al-Dīn responded with another question: What do you know about *samā*^{c}?' Ḥusām declared that he knew only that it was prohibited by the ulama. Al-Badā'ūnī then rejoined, 'If you know nothing then there is no point in discussing the matter with you!'.

Another discussion was started by Qadi Kamāl al-Dīn at the same time, in which he stated, 'Abū Ḥanīfa declared *samā*^{c} to be *ḥarām*'. Al-Badā'ūnī refuted the authenticity of such a declaration, and quoted the Tradition in which it is reported that *samā*^{c} is allowed to those who have understanding.[60] The ulama refused to accept this reference to Tradition, as al-Badā'ūnī had no recognised qualification in this field, and gave preference in this case to the words of Abū Ḥanīfa.

This debate gives us some idea of contemporary thinking with regard to *samā*^{c}. While we cannot be certain that Qadi Kamāl al-Dīn is the same person as Sunāmī's teacher, we can nevertheless, see what appears to be a pattern of opposition between successive members of the ulama, including Sunāmī, and the leaders of the Chishtiyya *silsila* Sufis. If we are right, then, Sunāmī's teacher would have been a contemporary critic of al-Badā'ūnī. The line of such opposition would seem to follow the pattern now indicated:

Muḥammad al-Shīrāzī (701–771/1301–2 – 1369–70)	v	Quṭb al-Dīn (d. 760/1358–9)
Sunāmī	v	Burhān al-Dīn Gharīb (d.741/1340–1)
Kamāl al-Dīn	v	Niẓām al-Dīn al-Badā'ūnī al-Sāmānawī

59 Nizami, *Delhi Sultanate*: 481. Also see Nadwī, *Nuzha*: 2:123.

60 This is not hadith but an opinion of Ghazālī in his *Iḥyā'*. Nadwi, *Tārīkh*: 17.

Sunāmī's Works

Apart from *Niṣāb al-iḥtisāb*, the works *al-Fatāwa al-ḍiyā'iyya* and *Tafsīr Sūrat Yūsuf*[61] are also attributed to Sunāmī. *Nuzhat al-khawāṭir* quotes a few lines of the second work in its commentary on the following part of the Sūrat Yūsuf, viz:

يا أبآنا مالك لأتأمنا على يوسف:

الأية دلت على ان اولآد الأنبياء مثل اولآد غيرهم يدعون آبآئهم بأسم الأبوة لأن اخوة يوسف قالوا لابيهم ياابانا كما يدعو كل واحد اباه "يا ابتي" . ويتفرع على هذا فضل اولاد النبي صلى الله عليه وسلم عن سائر الناس.

This style leaves little doubt that it was written by the same author. There is a great similarity between this analogy and the analogies made by Sunāmī in Chapter 54 of the *Niṣāb*.

Some observations on Sunāmī's Presentation

When we read the text, the feature that is most striking is that the author has paid no attention to the systematic arrangement of the text. It resembles a note-book, and indeed Sunāmī himself states that he wrote his book as a guide for *muḥtasib*s,[62] which might explain his continuous reference to the Ḥanafī books of *fiqh*. He states that his book is a manual.[63] Many points in the book are discussed briefly, and he suggests further reading.[64] Elsewhere, he suggests that certain points should be memorised.[65] He describes the practical aspects of *ḥisba*.[66] One of the principal characteristics of the text is that the author repeatedly changes his subject, as, for example, in Chapter 10, where bread is discussed. Here he suddenly leaves the subject for discussion of another subject, *viz.* eating in a recumbent position. Returning to the subject of bread, he informs us that putting a salt-cellar on bread is reprehensible. He then writes: 'This is what concerns bread' as though in conclusion to the subject, but he then goes on to discuss other matters, returning eventually to the subject of bread only at the end of the chapter. A similar case is his discussion concerning the exhumation of a corpse and the transfer of a corpse to another grave.[67] This tendency to change subjects is also found in his chapters' classification. Discussions of death and funerals are scattered throughout three chapters.[68]

---

61 Nadwī, *Nuzha*: 95.

62 *Niṣāb*: 1B.

63 *Ibid*: 70A.

64 *Ibid*: 9B and 70A.

65 *Ibid*: 13B.

66 *Ibid*: 64B, 65A & B.

67 *Ibid*: 52A.

68 *Ibid*: Chapters 13,16 and 42.

Sunāmī evidently does not commence by planning each subject and its position in the book, and it is also possible that he wrote the text and later decided to add additional material which had occurred to him.

Sunāmī's Legal Mentality

Sunāmī seems to have acquired a sound legal knowledge, and that to a degree where he feels able to deliver *fatwa*s and reject other eminent jurists' opinions such as he does in the case of *Hidāya*.[69] Some of his quotations from other works are word for word as, for example the quotation from *al-Kifāya al-Shaʿbiyya*.[70] In other references to works he does give a full quotation but just the meaning.[71] Where there is more than one opinion, Sunāmī gives his own view.[72] When he quotes, he often does so to demonstrate his own analysis of the references. Thus in Chapter 21 he looks to *al-Mughrib* for the definition of *tamā'im*. *Al-Mughrib* offers two contradictory views, and Sunāmī takes one of them, and in support of it he presents quite sound and logical reasons.[73] The numerous cases with which he deals suggests that they were not all products of his imagination. They seem to be cases which he actually encountered during the course of his work as a judge or *muḥtasib*. We do not know with certainty whether Sunāmī was an appointed *muḥtasib* or whether he had volunteered for the task. It seems, however, from his description of the methods of a duly appointed *muḥtasib* that he was himself one.[74] His directions for the disposal of wine and the slaughter of pigs[75] reinforce this view, since Sunāmī allows only an official *muḥtasib* to carry out these practices.

The *Niṣāb* and its Author's Social Milieu

The *Niṣāb* is a particularly rich source of information for those whose main interest centres on popular practices in Indian Islam during the medieval period. In his approach to the subject of *ḥisba* Sunāmī had first to describe many social innovations, manners, customs and ceremonies. In his description he was not writing as an historian as both Firshita and Baranī were in their works,[76] nor was he writing as a traveller like Ibn Baṭṭūṭa in his *Riḥla* or Marco Polo in his *Travels*. Sunāmī's chief aim was to draw a clear distinction between what is lawful and what is

---

69 *Ibid*: 45A.

70 *Ibid*: 36B, 53A.

71 *Ibid*: 34A, 25B.

72 *Ibid*: 25B.

73 *Ibid*: 42.

74 *Ibid*: 64B, 38B.

75 *Ibid*.

76 *Tārīkh-i Firshita*. See also *Tārīkh-i Fīrūz Shāh*.

unlawful according to Islam. He seeks to assist the *muḥtasib* in the disharge of his duty – a duty which, in the context of India, was far from easy. India possessed many racial groups, and was a land of many creeds. In Islam, moreover, there had been a proliferation of innovatory practices, contrary to the purity of the original faith. The author states very clearly that his text is a guide for those upon whom was placed the burden of *iḥtisāb*.[77]

We may consider some aspects of the society in which Sunāmī lived and which he sought to reform.

Sufism Sufis and *Samāᶜ*: Sufism reached India in the second half of the twelfth century A.D.,[78] and by Sunāmī's time it seems to have gained widespread popularity amongst the mass of the people. Sunāmī does not concern himself with Sufi practices which are not contrary to the Sharīᶜa; he opposes only those customs and practices which do not accord with the directives of the sacred laws of Islam. Far from disapproving of mysticism which sought to harmonise itself with the orthodox precepts of Islam, he even praises such an approach.[79] His main concern was rather of those 'who imitate Sufis'.[80] The mendicants seem to have been confused with the original Sufis whom he praised such as Junayd.[81] The mendicants whom Sunāmī mentions[82] appear to be similar to the Hindu mendicants reported by Dubois. They are called devotees of Vishnu.[83] They always carry a bronze gong and a conch shell called a *sangu* when they are travelling or begging. Both of these objects are used to make a noise and thus announce their approach. With one hand they strike the gong with a small drumstick producing a bell-like sound; with the other they hold the *sangu* to their mouths and blow through it. To ask for alms is looked upon by these mendicants as a right and even as an inherent duty.[84]

Sunāmī's strictures, in fact, largely centre on the practice of *samāᶜ*. *Samāᶜ* is one of the Sufi methods of inducing ecstasy.[85] The previously mentioned Shaykh Niẓām al-Dīn al-Badā'ūnī (636–725/1238–1325) was an eminent Sufi who became the leader of the Chishtiyya *silsila* in (664/1265)[86] and was one of the strongest

---

77 Introduction to the *Niṣāb*: 1B.

78 Schimmel, *Mystical Dimensions*: 345.

79 *Niṣāb*: 9A.

80 *Ibid*: 9A–10A.

81 *Ibid*: 9B.

82 *Ibid*.

83 Vishnu is one of the two great divinities which Hindus profess to pay equal honour. The other is named Shiva. Dubois, *Hindu Manners*: 111.

84 Dubois, *Hindu Manners*: 112–3.

85 Ḥujwīrī, *Kashf*: 405; see also Schimmel, *Dimensions*: 178–180.

86 Husain, *Indian Islam*: 45–46.

supporters of *samāᶜ*. His involvement with the leading supporters of the practice drew him into a great dispute with the theologians of his age,[87] in which, as previously stated,[88] neither Shaykh al-Badā'ūnī nor the ulama were able to prove the lawfulness or otherwise of *samāᶜ*. In this respect Sunāmī's concern with *samāᶜ* was most probably a reaction to the social atmosphere. From *Niṣāb* it would appear that Sunāmī's opposition to *samāᶜ* was based on an objective approach and did not emerge from personal animosity.

The Wearing of Iron: This was another unorthodox Sufi practice which Sunāmī strongly opposed. In so doing he presumably has the Qalandarīs and their sub-divisions such as the Ḥaydarīs in mind, for they are reported to have worn iron rings on their hands, around their necks, in their ears and even in the area of their sexual parts, so that they were unable to practice sexual intercourse.[89] The Ḥaydarīs constituted a Qalandarī order founded by Quṭb al-Dīn Ḥaydar of Nīshāpūr[90] or Nishawur.[91] Sunāmī describes Ḥaydar as follows: 'A man enraptured with thoughts of God (*maghlūb*) who lived in the mountains' – a description that accords with a report by Maqrīzī,[92] who quoted from *al-Sawāniḥ al-adabiyya fī madā'iḥ al-qunnabiyya* by al-Ḥasan b. Muḥammad.[93]

The Use of Banj (Hemp): Maqrīzī's description of the hemp which the Ḥaydarīs of Khurāsān used does not differ a great deal from Sunāmī's own description, especially when he says it is dry, cold [94] and avoided by animals.[95] It also describes how oil is taken by the consumer in order to nullify the effect of the drug.[96] Maqrīzī tells us that one of the Qalandarīs informed him that Shaykh Ḥaydar himself shunned the use of hemp and that its use is attributed to him only because his followers used it.[97]

---

87 Nizami, *Delhi sultanate*: 481; Nadwī, *Nuzha*: 2:123.

88 Pp. 18–19 of this book.

89 Ibn Baṭṭūṭa, *Riḥla*: 389. See also Bosworth, *Islamic Underworld* 1. 113; Trimingham, *Sufi*: 39, 268.

90 Maqrīzī, *Khiṭaṭ*: 3:205; Ibn Baṭṭūṭa, *Riḥla*: 388–9. Sauvaire, 'Description de Damas', *Journal Asiatique*, ix (1985): 399.

91 Yāqūt, *Muᶜjam*: 5:331.

92 Maqrīzī, Khiṭaṭ: 3:205.

93 H.Kh., *Kashf*: 2:1009.

94 Maqrīzī, *Khiṭaṭ*: 3:207; cf. *Niṣāb*: 121/21.

95 Maqrīzī, *Khiṭaṭ*: 3:208; cf. *Niṣāb*: 2/4.

96 Maqrīzī, *Khiṭaṭ*: 3:208.

97 *Ibid*: 3:207. See also Rosenthal, *Herb*: 45.

Sunāmī's story concerning the prohibition of hemp[98] must have had a great impact on society. The drug was probably very popular, for he is at pains to demonstrate the authenticity of his report (*riwāya*), indicating that it was personally narrated by his teacher. This *riwāya* transmitted by Sunāmī is the only record we have of the Ḥanafī consensus during the time of Ḥamīd al-Dīn al-Ḍarīr, so undoubtedly, considerable importance ought to attach to it. Muḥammad b. ᶜAbd Allāh (745–794/1344–5 – 1391–2) was a Shāfiᶜī scholar who, realizing the importance of the issue of hemp, wrote a treatise about it. He wrote in his introduction, 'There are points dealing with *ḥashīsh* that require comment at this time because so many lower-class people are affected by it and because many scholars hesitate to pronounce themselves on the legal situation concerning it'.[99] Having been unable to find any discussion of it by the ancients (*salaf*) Sunāmī's description of Ḥamīd al-Dīn al-Darīr's hesitation to give a legal decision concerning *banj* accords with the above statement by Zarkashī.[100] Zarkashī, however, does not appear to be aware of the Ḥanafī consensus which prohibits *banj*, and this may be due to the distance between his own country, Egypt, and India. Alternatively, he may not have been interested in it since he was Shāfiᶜī and not Ḥanafī.

The Veneration of Saints: Sunāmī's reference in Chapter 24, to those people who display fake tombs and liken cemeteries to the Kaaba together with his description of their practices may be considered a direct criticism of the innovation of venerating the tombs of the dead, sometimes verging on actual saint-worship. Indeed, this practice was so popular in India, during Sunāmī's time that the Muslim masses venerated not only their own saints, but also those of other religions,[101] or even the supposed occupants of empty tombs.[102] S.M. Husain describes as many as fourteen major shrines to which Muslims paid homage.[103]

Protected People: The term *ahl al-dhimma* has, in Muslim usage, a very specific meaning: it denotes certain the free non-Muslim subjects living under Muslim jurisdiction, who, in return for payment of poll tax, enjoy protection and safety.[104]

---

98 *Niṣāb*: 44A.

99 Rosenthal, *Herb*: 102.

100 *Niṣāb*: Chapter 36.

101 Marco Polo visited India during the thirteenth Century A.D. found Muslims at the shrine of St. Thomas. Yule, *The Book of Ser Marco Polo* (London, 1903): 2:353.

102 Shaykh Sirāj al-Dīn ᶜUthmān buried a few clothes from his *murshid* in Lakhanuti and gave it the appearance of a grave. S.M. Husain, *Indian Islam*: 200.

103 *Ibid*: 201–13.

104 *Lisān al-ᶜArab*: 15, 112; Zaydān, *Aḥkām al-dhimmiyīn*: 22.

The word *dhimma* alone means protection.[105] Originally only Jews and Christians were accepted as subjects of this protection. Later it became necessary to consider the Zoroastrians and some other minor faiths (particularly in Central Asia) as dhimmi despite there being no mention of them in the Quran.[106] Furthermore, Ḥanafī law accords all non-Muslim subjects the rights and status of dhimmis, with the single exception of the pagan Arabs.[107]

Following the conquest of Sind by Muḥammad b. Qāsim, the question of idolatry was one of the major ensuing problems. In the tolerant and catholic atmosphere of the Ḥanafī school, however, the difficulty was quickly resolved, and the Hindus were accordingly recognised as dhimmis.[108] This recognition, however, was not easily accepted by the Shāfiᶜī jurists.[109]

Dhimmis are not bound to abide by laws relating to the fulfilment of the religious duties of Islam, and they are free to practice their own religion. Moreover, they are allowed to go about their business unhindered, albeit that such business may involve their dealing in forbidden commodities.[110] The poll tax (*jizya*) is levied upon dhimmis solely as a cash alternative to military service in defence of the state.[111]

Sunāmī, while not disputing dhimmis' rights, nevertheless finds himself forced to define the limits of these rights. Knowledge of these limits is necessary for the *muḥtasib* whose work includes the control of dhimmis.[112] Realizing the problem Sunāmī attempted to define the cases in which a *muḥtasib* should interfere. The cases include wine-drinking; consumption of pork; marriage within degrees prohibited by Islam and the worship of deities other than God.

Sunāmī prohibited the building of new churches, synagogues,[113] and places of fire-worship. The Hindus had many temples dedicated to fire-worship, including Shrjvālāmukhī (the flame-mouthed), which was an ancient site of pilgrimage. It is as famous as the site of a shrine dedicated to the Hindu mother-goddess Devī Bajrēshrī or the goddess of thunderbolts. It is situated at Lat. 31° 51' N., Long. 77° 20' E. in the Baharan suburb of the town Kāngrā Nagarkot or Kotkingra in the Kangrā district of the Punjab. It was ruined by an earthquake in A.D. 1905. The temple was a centre of Hindu fire-worship. Muḥammad b. Tughluq was accused of

---

105 Wehr, *Dictionary*: 312.

106 *EI*²: 2:227. See also Zaydān, *Aḥkām al-dhimmiyīn*: 25.

107 Zaydān, *Aḥkām al-dhimmiyīn*: 27.

108 S.M. Husain, *Studies in Islam*: 33; S.M. Husain, *Sultans*: 6; Afsar ud-din, *Fatāwā*: 510.

109 *Ibid*: 35.

110 *Ibid*: See also Hamilton, *Hidāya*: 309–10.

111 Qureshi, *Administration of the Sultanate of Delhi* (Karachi, 1958), Pakistan Historical Society Publication no. 10.

112 *EI*²: 2:228.

113 *Niṣāb*: 38A.

having visited this temple and honoured its goddesses.[114] Sultan Fīrūz Shāh reports that the dhimmis were encouraged to build temples during the reigns of the previous sultans, and he records in his *Futūḥ al-salāṭīn* that he put an end to the practice.[115]

Other practices which Sunāmī mentions include display of the cross, and bell-ringing, which leaves us in no doubt that he was dealing with Christians. As regards to Jews, it should be noted that Sunāmī only mentions them while quoting another work.[116] This leaves us in some doubt as to whether he did actually encounter them or included them in the chapter on dhimmis solely on a theoretical basis. However, he mentions the synagogues as places of religious worship which can be distinguished from the churches and places of fire-worship.[117] Another point worth noticing here is his view with regard to permitting dhimmis to marry within the prohibited degrees. Since this would not be applicable to Jews or Christians, whose prohibited degrees are similar to those of Muslims, he must have been referring to Hindus. Hindus always aim at marrying their children into families allied to them and the nearer the relationship, the more easily the marriage is contracted. An example of this is a man marrying his niece.[118] It can be concluded, therefore, that when Sunāmī refers to dhimmis he has in mind Jews, Christians, Zoroastrians and Hindus.

Sunāmī's approach to the dhimmis seems to have been conditioned by theories and practices developed by rulers and jurists from the time of early Islam down to his own day. It should also be noted that when Sunāmī discusses a problem, he does so on the basis of an actual case which he himself might have dealt with. Thus when he rejects the construction of new religious buildings for dhimmis, he does so as a result of practical experience.

Ceremonies Associated with Deaths and Marriages etc: The social form of these fundamental aspects of life had, in India, as elsewhere, been shaped and influenced by the interaction of several different cultural and spiritual perspectives. Evidently Sunāmī tried very hard to eradicate non-Islamic practices prevalent amongst Muslims in India at the time.

Death: Sunāmī devotes four chapters[119] to this subject, and there are also several scattered references throughout his work. This suffices to illustrate the importance attached to death and the events surrounding it. Nowhere do we find greater

114 Hastings (ed.), *Encyclopedia of Religion and Ethics*: 7:579–80 (Edinburgh, 1914).

115 M. Nadwī, *Tārīkh*: 37.

116 *Niṣāb*: 38B.

117 *Ibid*: 38A.

118 Dubois, *Hindu Manners*: 20–21.

119 *Niṣāb*: Chapters 13, 16, 24 and 42.

evidence of the Hindu influence on the great human experience of life among the Muslims of India than in the event of death.

Uncontrolled wailing and weeping are one of the first targets of Sunāmī's criticism.[120] In this connection he carefully narrates the story about ᶜUmar and his beating of a wailing woman with his *dirra* (whip).[121] Professional mourning of the deceased, was common in India, just as it had been with the Greeks and Romans. Abbé Dubois describes for us such women: they arrive with dishevelled hair and only half-clothed, and wearing their scanty garments in a disordered fashion.[122] It is against the behaviour and demeanour of such women that Sunāmī inveighs.

He also deals with the problem of actual relatives of the deceased rending their clothes or scratching their faces (Chapter 42).[123] Similarly, he draws attention to many interesting practices, and his evidence is of great value to us since it is that of a native eye-witness. In the chapter on funerals (Chapter 42) he speaks of the body washer and the fee charged for the service given, and then goes on to declare such a fee to be illegal. On the other hand, he observes that donating a shroud for the dead person is a voluntary meritorious act.[124]

Carrying the dead through the streets is another popular practice noted by Sunāmī, who goes on to describe the conditions under which it is allowed, and by implication communicates to posterity the unorthodox ways of contemporary society:

(a) no public proclamation is to be made in the market; (b) the mourners are not to precede the bier *en masse*; (c) no fire should be allowed to follow the bier; (d) no one is to rise on seeing the bier; (e) the mound over the grave is to be raised but not squared.

This last custom was very popular in India during Sunāmī's time.[125] He also describes the niche (*laḥd*), and the attire with which the corpse is to be clothed. He forbids the carrying of the corpse from town to town, and also describes in detail the laments used. Noting that the common laments in his town are reprehensible because they exaggerate the sorrow, he offers us a description that accords with that given by Ibn Baṭṭūṭa, particularly on the following points: (a) eulogizing of the deceased;[126] (b) laments in cemeteries;[127] (c) covering the grave with vegetation[128]

---

120 *Ibid.*

121 *Niṣāb*: 12A.

122 Dubois, *Hindu Manners*: 352.

123 This act is also described in *Fawā'id al-fawā'id*, 21, cited by S.M. Husain, *Indian Islam*: 249.

124 *Niṣāb*: 53B.

125 *Tuḥfat-i-nasī'in*: 24 cited by S.M. Husain, *Indian Islam*, cf. *Niṣāb* 52B–53A and what Sunāmī has to say about covering the graves.

126 *Niṣāb*: 23A, 52A and Ibn Baṭṭūṭa, *Riḥla*: 506.

and silk garments;[129] (d) eating food and drinking sherbet;[130] and (e) chanting the Quran. [131]

To appreciate the significance of Sunāmī's observations we must bear in mind his critical attitude, which differs greatly from that of certain other scholars such as Ibn Baṭṭūṭa. Ibn Baṭṭūṭa aimed at recording the attractive features of life in foreign lands which would interest his readers, while Sunāmī was attempted to establish a correct way of life complying with the Sharīᶜa as he saw it. It is for this reason that we find him noting many practices never before associated with Muslims in India. His reference to the practice of exhumation[132] is an excellent example. The measure of his preoccupation with the practice may be judged from the fact that he raises the matter four times in the same chapter (Chapter 42). The custom seems to have been Hindu in origin. It is described by Abbé Dubois in the following terms:

> 'Burial is refused to persons who die of wounds or eruptive diseases such as small-pox or measles; also to those whose bodies have white marks on them; to a pregnant woman who died before the birth of her child; and above all to the many who fall victims to tigers. In the case of a pregnant woman the Brahmins usually take the foetus from the dead woman and burn it separately.[133] In consequence of this absurd superstition, whenever the country has been a long time without rain, the inhabitants think that drought can be attributed to the fact that someone must have surreptitiously infringed this unwritten law. Accordingly the magistrates give immediate orders that all bodies that had been buried in the course of a year should be exhumed and become food for the birds of prey.[134]

Indeed, this problem was no minor affair, and like so many Hindu practices, it had evidently survived for many hundreds of years. Moreover, such a survival is only natural within the framework of Hindu customs and traditions; for as Beauchamp says in his introduction to Abbé Dubois' book, '...with them the same ancestral traditions and customs are followed nowadays that were followed hundreds of years ago at least by the vast majority of the population'.[135]

Finally, we can say that even if Sunāmī's records, for the reasons indicated earlier, are not as detailed as those of some of the other medieval writers such as Ibn

---

127 *Ibid*: Chapter 6 and Ibn Baṭṭūṭa, *Riḥla*: 506.

128 *Ibid*: 22B and Ibn Baṭṭūṭa, *Riḥla*: 506.

129 *Ibid*: 23B and Ibn Baṭṭūṭa, *Riḥla*: 506.

130 *Ibid*: 23B and Ibn Baṭṭūṭa, *Riḥla*: 506.

131 *Ibid*: 22B and Ibn Baṭṭūṭa, *Riḥla*: 506.

132 *Ibid*: 53A.

133 Compare this case of a pregnant woman with what Sunāmī has to say in *Niṣāb*, 52B.

134 Dubois, *Hindu Manners*, 319.

135 *Ibid*: editor's introduction, p. 43.

Baṭṭūṭa or even modern scholars like S.M. Husain in his thesis, he has provided us with some important fresh ideas about his age.

Wedding Ceremonies: Innovations in this sphere are not as numerous as one might expect when compared with those associated with death and funerals. Sunāmī's objections are general, and he criticises only such things as could have been criticised in any Muslim country. Examples are the use of gold vessels, musicians and entertainers, and the *jilwa*, or uncovering of the bride's face to the groom and the others in the wedding procession. On the other hand, we can detect some interesting observations of customs he rejects. An example of such practices is the riding of horses in the wedding procession. This seems to be a Hindu tradition, although it is possible to find the custom in other Muslim countries as well. Abbé Dubois reports how attached Hindus are to the tradition of the wedding procession, and that to the extent that they would fight to preserve the custom.[136] He adds that they sometimes fight amongst themselves for the privilege of being escorted by musicians at public ceremonies.[137]

The other interesting observation is concerned with the wedding contract. This contract contains certain vows which Sunāmī attacks because the name of God is not invoked.[138] These vows normally bind the groom to pay the woman a certain amount of money in the event of a divorce, which seems to be further insurance for the wife, in addition to her receiving her deferred dowry (*mahr 'ājil*).[139] Sunāmī also denounces the judges for accepting more money than normal for recording the marriage in the register. This information might imply, of course, that they did not receive any payment for their services from the state. The following statement from Sunāmī is rather vague and deserves examination: 'There is a practice in Muslim countries in respect of a marriage after which the marriage can be executed.'[140] The meaning of this pronouncement seems to be that the actual payment is not made to the qadi himself to perform the marriage, since marriage can take place without a *walī*, according to Ḥanafī law.[141] The *walī* is represented here by the qadi; therefore the only way in which this statement can be interpreted is that Sunāmī is actually referring to permission for a marriage or for a licence.

Muslim life was apparently greatly affected by contempory superstitions. In marriage, as in other aspects of life, superstition has its role, and to maintain love between the married couple, a thread equal to the height of the groom was given to a

136 *Ibid*: 26.

137 *Ibid*.

138 *Niṣāb*: 16B.

139 Ibn ᶜĀbi dī n, *Baḥr*: 3:117.

140 *Niṣāb*: 17A.

141 Marghinānī, *Hidāya*: 1:196; Sarakhsī, *Mabsūt*, 5, 10; Ibn ᶜĀbi dī n, *Baḥr*, 3:117.

magician, who then cast a spell on the young man and woman, in the general belief that the bond between the couple would thereby be strengthened. This was supposed to be brought about by granting the woman power over the man by magical means.[142] It is a practice connected with the cure for the disease scrofula.[143]

Sunāmī's strictures on the wearing of silk by men are another good example of Islamic social practices in Muslim society. Early in the history of Islam an ascetic tendency was expressed in a group of Traditions, as a result of which all schools of religious law forbid men to wear garments made entirely of silk next to the skin. The Shāfiᶜīs and Ḥanbalīs, in addition, forbid sitting or leaning on silk as material in cushions. Since the Ḥanafīs permit lying or sleeping on silk,[144] however, it may well be that Sunāmī is reacting to Hindu practice; for the Hindus were greatly attracted by silk. Thus Sunāmī's refusal to allow a bridegroom to sit on silk may well be a rejection of a Hindu custom, and in fact, Dubois' description of a Hindu marriage ceremony is instructive in this respect: 'Then follows the ceremony called *mangaleshta*. The bride and bridegroom are seated facing one another and a sheet of silk is spread in front of them'.[145]

Sunāmī always followed the directives of the Sharīᶜa. Very often the Hindu customs he attacked were contrary to the Sharīᶜa, such as the wearing of silk, and in his attacks he sought to enlighten Muslims on the Sharīᶜa, by pointing to a Hindu habit which contradicted it. It might be useful to remark here that we should be careful not to associate all the practices Sunāmī rejects with Hindus, as in the case of *jilwa*. The practice was also widespread in Arabic countries: Ma'mūn, the son of Hārūn al-Rashīd is reported to have practised it.[146] A similar practice can be seen in India. S.M. Husain describes it to us as follows: 'The groom is not allowed to see the bride before the *jilwa* which takes place after the wedding (*nikāḥ*) ceremony. He would be seated near his bride, her veil would be removed and the bridegroom would thus be able to see the face of his bride; at this moment the bride gives the groom betel leaf'.[147]

The Position of Women in Society: While men have been able to exercise their functions in society either for good or ill, women in contrast have not always had the same degree of freedom. We find many implications in Sunāmī's work that women were treated unjustly and with suspicion by their husbands.[148] It is difficult not to

---

142 *Niṣāb*: 81B.

143 S.M. Husain, *Indian Islam*: 236.

144 *EI*[2]: 3:209 *s.v. harīr*.

145 Dubois, *Hindu Manners*: 223.

146 Shibībī, *Ibn al-Fūwaṭī*: 99.

147 S.M. Husain, *Indian Islam*: 247.

148 See what S.M. Husain has to say about women in *Indian Islam*: 170–1.

see in what he has to say some connection between the Hindu and Muslim attitudes towards women and their respective treatment of them.

Abbé Dubois describes women's position as follows: 'A real union with sincere and mutual affection or even peace is very rare in Hindu households. The moral gulf between the two sexes is so great that in the eyes of a native the woman is simply a passive object who must be abjectly submissive to her husband's will and fancy'.[149] It is true to say that even after Islam entered India, women did not enjoy as many rights as their sisters in the Arab countries.[150] It is noteworthy that Sunāmī fails to encourage Muslims to treat their womenfolk with the kindness and respect enjoined by Islam.[151]

One of the commonest female practices condemned by Sunāmī is the visiting of relatives' graves or the tombs of saints.[152] This practice is also mentioned by Fīrūz Shāh in the *Futūḥ Fīrūz Shāh*:

> 'One of the innovations that was common before my reign was the practice whereby women visited the graves or the tombs of saints on festivals and celebrations. This practice is prohibited by the Sharīᶜa. It is even more reprehensible for women to go out of their homes in crowds, either walking or riding, fully made-up or veiled. The reprobates who follow them avail themselves of any opportunity to exploit these women. We have enacted a royal decree in order to prevent women from continuing this practice and to apply *taᶜzīr* to any woman violating this command'.[153]

Miscellaneous Incidents: Sunāmī describes certain mendicants whose innovations consisted in allowing their hair to grow very long, leaving it unwashed and ungroomed until it became filthy and lice-ridden. It was an innovation because it

---

149 Dubois, *Hindu Manners*: 231.

150 Some women in the Middle East in Sunāmī's time reached high positions, for example, Zaynab al-Maqdisiyya 646–740/1248–9 – 1339–40. This lady is reported to have been one of the most eminent scholars in hadith and she taught many male scholars including Ibn Baṭṭūṭa, Kaḥḥāla, *Aᶜlām*: 2, 46; Ibn Baṭṭūṭa *Riḥla*: 110. Another woman who could be mentioned is Sharjarat al-Durr, who was the actual ruler of Egypt for a time. She died in 655/ 1257–8. Kaḥḥāla, *Aᶜlām*: 286–90; Raḥmat-Allāh, *Ḥāla*: 124–31.

151 See Quran iv: 19: 'You who believe, you are forbidden to inherit women against their will nor should you treat them with harshness. On the contrary, live with them on a footing of kindness and equality'. See also Prophetic Traditions: 'I recommended to you [the care of] the women'. Ibn Māja, *Sunan*: 1:594); 'You have rights over your women and they have rights over you'. Albānī, *Ādāb al-zifāf* (Damascus, AH 1358): 153.

152 *Niṣāb*: 2B, 11A, 13A–13B, 43, 46, 47, Chapter 4.

153 M. Nadwī, *Tārīkh*: 38.

was the practice of certain Indian fakirs, and also contrary to the personal cleanliness enjoined by Islam.[154] The Indians whom Sunāmī may had in mind, were perhaps of the same caste as the Sudras, or cultivators whom Dubois describes as follows:

> 'The various classes of cultivators, Sudras who dwell in the hills of Carantic, observe during their life a practice as peculiar as it is disgusting. Both men and women pass their lives in a state of uncleanliness, never washing their clothes. Having once put on a set of clothes fresh from the loom they do not remove them until the material falls apart due to rot. One can imagine the filthy condition of these garments after they have been worn day and night for several months soaked with perspiration and soiled with dirt'.[155]

Fīrūz Shāh in his *Futūḥ Fīrūz Shāh* records many practices, prevalent before his reign, which he rejected and stopped because of their irreligious nature. One of these was the use of gold and silver vessels to eat or drink from.[156] Sunāmī in Chapter 37 mentions the same practice and criticises it.[157] Fīrūz Shāh also tells us that he put an end to the custom of making food- and drinking-vessels and horse-saddles, in the shape of animals, and even drawing pictures of living things on clothes.[158] As already noted, Sunāmī also criticises the custom of wearing silk clothes,[159] although silk was a popular material with the sultans.

Another subject worth considering is the caste system. Dubois describes the caste system in India as follows: 'The word caste is derived from the Portuguese and is used in Europe to designate the different tribes or classes into which the people of India (Hindus) are divided. The most ordinary and ancient classification divides them into four main castes. The first and most distinguished group are the *Brahmins*; the second in rank are the *Kshatriyas* or *Rajahs*; the third are the *Visyas* (landholders and merchants) and the fourth group are the *Sudras* or cultivators. The functions of each of these main four castes are: for *Brahmins* priesthood and its various duties; for *Kshatriyas*, military service in all its branches, for *Visyas*, agriculture, trade and cattle breeding; and for *Sudras* general servitude. Each of the four main castes is subdivided into many others, the number of which it is difficult to determine'.[160]

Sunāmī writes in several places to criticise the practice of distinguishing between people according to their birth, profession or wealth.[161] He does, however, permit

---

154 *Niṣāb*: 10.

155 Dubois, *Hindu Manners*: 19.

156 M. Nadwī, *Tārīkh*: 37.

157 *Niṣāb*: 45.

158 *Ibid*: 36B; M. Nadwī, *Tārīkh*: 37.

159 M.Nadwī, *Tārīkh*: 37.

160 Dubois, *Hindu Manners*: 15.

161 *Niṣāb*: 17B, 22B, 49B.

some social distinction, to which he occasionally refers. For example, he mentions the Hindus who specialise in selling liquids and semi-liquids.[162] He also writes about religious scholars as though they are a group of people with distinctive clothes.[163] Nevertheless, he does not appear to take a social view which pays great attention to class distinction as was the case in Hindu society. In fact, Sunāmī's attitude does not appear greatly different from that which would be found in the Arab society of his time.

Analysis of Innovations

It is important to realise in examining the practices mentioned in the *Niṣāb* that some of them may have been neither Islamic nor Hindu, but were perhaps a·result of the interaction which inevitably took place between the two cultures. An example of this is the custom which Sunāmī condemns at the end of Chapter 9: administering wine to a son and the scattering of money and sweetmeats.'[164] There can be no doubt about the prohibition of intoxicating liquor in Islam. The use of alcohol is also condemned by almost all Hindus. However, it is permitted amongst the Sudras, who allow even their women and children to drink *ᶜaraq.*[165] The practice of scattering money and sweetmeats (*nithār*) was common in Iraq on certain festive occasions, such as weddings[166], but it is interesting to note that the custom disappeared from Iraq after the Mongol invasion, for the Mongols had no taste for the life of luxury which was associated with such practices.[167] The custom, however, must have survived as it is, is still in evidence today in Iraq, though it goes under various local names. The *nithār* must also have existed in India, since Sunāmī describes it.[168] The Hindus share a custom similar to *nithār*, although in their case they scatter money and rice. This is the practice of *chaula*, which takes place when a child is three years old.[169] The practice which Sunāmī condemns of offering the child intoxicating liquor to drink may have been an influence traceable to Sudras, who permit it to children, but at the same time the practice is a type of *nithār* amongst all Muslims. The fact that many innovations, or *bidaᶜ*, exist in the Arabo-Muslim countries may explain why similar innovations occur in India. Not only the masses, but sometimes certain scholars appear to respect and venerate an Arab custom and

---

162 *Ibid*: 15A.

163 *Ibid*: 6B.

164 *Ibid*: 14B.

165 Dubois, *Hindu Manners*: 158–9 cf. *Niṣāb* 39/1, 40/18–9.

166 Shibībī, *Ibn al-Fūwaṭī*: 97–105.

167 *Ibid.*

168 *Niṣāb*: 14B. This custom is also mentioned as having been very common in India by S.M. Husain, *Indian Islam*: 179.

169 Dubois, *Hindu Manners*: 158–9.

mistake it for an Islamic custom.[170] Many of the customs and practices which Sunāmī criticises or rejects in Indian society were also current among the Arabs. Some of these innovations have already been mentioned such as *samāᶜ*, and revealing the bride's face (*jilwa*), but many others could equally well have been mentioned.

Ṭurṭūshī, an Andalusian Muslim (c. 451–520/1059–60 – 1126) who died in Egypt, records the following innovations which were also noted by Sunāmī: chanting the Quran;[171] decorating the mosque;[172] storytelling in the mosque;[173] general etiquette and conduct in the mosque, covering such matters as cleanliness, the prohibition of spitting on the floor, the position of beggars in the mosque, and whether certain occupations can or cannot be undertaken in the mosque (e.g. the copying of books, the teaching of children, and tailoring);[174] the unorthodox practice of celebrating the middle of Shaᶜbān;[175] laments and similar innovations;[176] and the attendance of women at funerals.[177]

---

170 During the controversy over *samaᶜ*, one method which the sultan used to decide its legality was to enquire whether it was current in Arabic countries such as Baghdad and Syria. S.M. Husain, *Indian Islam*: 135.

171 Ṭurṭūshī, *Ḥawādith*, 81–86, cf. *Niṣāb*: 22A.

172 Ṭurṭūshī, *Ḥawādith*, 97; cf. *Niṣāb*: 20A.

173 Ṭurṭūshī, *Hawādith*, 99–103; cf. *Niṣab*: 20B–21A.

174 Ṭurṭūshī, *Ḥawādith*, 103–112; cf. *Nisāb*: Chapter 15.

175 Ṭurṭūshī, *Ḥawādith*, 117–12; cf. *Niṣāb*: 3A.

176 Ṭurṭūshī, *Ḥawādith*, 162; cf. *Niṣāb*: 49B–50A.

177 Ṭurṭūshī, *Ḥawādith*: 163; cf. *Niṣāb*: 13A–13B.

II
The Value of the *Niṣāb*

Niṣāb al-iḥtisāb and the general theory of ḥisba

In this chapter no attempt will be made to study the theory of *ḥisba* itself. My main aim will be to present a bird's-eye view of the concept of *ḥisba* as it has developed in the Muslim world. Thus, the actual value of *Niṣāb* in comparison with other treatises of *ḥisba* will be made apparent.

The institution of *ḥisba* is one of the administrative institutions that developed within the framework of Islamic law. The origin of the institution and the reason for its name have caused great controversy amongst scholars. There are those who associate the institution with the Hellenistic *agoranomos.*[178] However, Cl. Cahen and M. Talbi suspect the authenticity of this view as there is no record of the *agoranomos* in Greek inscriptions during the three hundred years prior to the Arab conquest.[179] Be that as it may, the first indication of the position of *muḥtasib* which has been found relates to the first half of the 2nd/8th century.[180] This does not mean that the institutions started then, for indeed it was practised by the Prophet Muḥammad and his companions from the beginning of Islam. He is also reported to have appointed Saᶜīd b. Saᶜīd b. al-ᶜĀṣ to supervise the market in Makka.[181] Between the simple duties of policing markets and preventing fraud, and the established office of *muḥtasib*, there were several stages. *Al-ᶜāmil ᶜalā al-sūq* or *ᶜarīf al-sūq* are the predominant names for the *muḥtasib*, while in the West the most remembered name is *ṣāḥib al-sūq.*[182]

The connotations of the word *ḥisba* have broadened rapidly through the ages to cover much more than it did originally. Māwardī (d.450/1058) defined it as the duty imposed on Muslims by the Quran of enjoining good and forbidding evil actions.[183] Ghazālī's description was that of a bridge between the qadi and the *wālī al-maẓālim.*[184] Sunāmī defines it as every legal action practised in order to comply with

---

178 See for example N. Ziyāda, *al-Ḥisba wa-l-muḥtasib fī al-Islām* (Beirut, 1962), 31.

179 *EI²*: 3:487.

180 See M. b. Khalaf Wakīᶜ, *Akhbār al-Quḍāt* (1947): 1:303.

181 See Muḥammad al-Dasūqī al-Shahawī, *al-Ḥisba fī al-Islām* (Cairo, 1962): 103–104.

182 *EI²*: 3:487.

183 H. Amedroz, 'The *ḥisba* jurisdiction', *JRAS* (April 1916): 77.

184 Ghazālī, *Iḥyā:* 2:274.

God's commandments.[185] Ibn Khaldūn (d.808/1406) defines it as a part of the religious institution of ordering good deeds and remonstrating against bad deeds.[186]

In the time of Tāshköprüzāde d. AH 962, *ḥisba* was defined as dealing with the affairs of urban civilization by applying what is good and preventing what is bad, day and night. The *muḥtasib* was described as the sultan's hands and limbs.[187] During the time of Ḥājjī Khalīfa it was 'the science of civil relationships which is essential for civilization'.[188]

The *ḥisba* or *iḥtisāb* had an important role in the Ottoman Empire.[189] The orders which regulate the duties of the *muḥtasib* were quantified in the *iḥtisāb qānūnnāmelerī.* The importance of *iḥtisāb* may be recognised in the popularity of the *Niṣāb* in Turkey. The work was written according to Ḥanafī law, which was the current *madhhab* of Ottoman Turkey.[190] The last existing form of *iḥtisāb* was abolished in 1271/1874 in Turkey[191] when the office of *ḥisba* was replaced by *majālis al-baladiyya* (local councils).[192]

Kurd ʿAli classified *ḥisba* of his day into (i) civil, and (ii) religious. He added that the latter disappeared from Muslim countries with the abolition of Islamic government.[193]

Ibn Khaldūn's definition of *ḥisba* seems to be the preferred definition among *ḥisba* scholars.[194] However, this is a general definition not describing precisely the office of *muḥtasib*. An alternative definition is suggested as follows: '*ḥisba* is an administrative supervision applied by an officer appointed by the government. This supervision covers the deeds and actions of individuals in order to harmonise them with the Islamic Law'. As for *iḥtisāb*, it can be defined as 'the application of such supervision which is authorised by the government.'

The following definitions of the word *ḥisba* can be found in the two editions of *EI*:

---

185 *Niṣāb*: 1B.

186 'Abd al-Raḥmān Ibn Khaldūn, *Muqaddima* (Beirut, 1967): 1:77.

187 Tashköprüzāde, *Miftāḥ al-saʿāda* ed. K. Bakrī and A. Abū al-Nūr (Cairo, c. 1965): 414.

188 H.Kh, *Kashf:* 1:15–16.

189 *EI²*: 3:409.

190 The *Niṣāb* is represented by 14 copies in Turkey (see also the chapter on comparison of the various Mss used.

191 *EI²*: 3:409.

192 See Muḥammad Kurd ʿAlī, al-Ḥisba fī al-Islām, *Muqtabas*, 9 (October, 1908): 538.

193 *Ibid.*

194 A. Murshid, *Niẓām al-ḥisba fī al-Islām*, M.A. Thesis. University of Muḥammad b. Saʿūd, Riyad, 1393/1973: 15.

(1) A technical term in administrative law, the meaning of which is, act of counting, office of *muḥtasib*. The word then acquired the special meaning of police, and finally the police in charge of the markets and public morals. It is in this latter, the narrowest, meaning that *ḥisba* is used by those authors who deal with Muslim law, etc.'[195]

(2) A non-Quranic term which is used to mean on the one hand the duty of every Muslim to 'promote good and forbid evil' and, on the other, the function of the person who is effectively entrusted in a town with the application of this rule in the supervision of moral behaviour and more particularly of the markets; this person entrusted with the *ḥisba* was called the *muḥtasib*. There seems to exist no text which states explicitly either the reason for the choice of this term or how the meanings mentioned above have arisen from the idea of 'calculation' or 'sufficiency' which is expressed by the root.[196]

---

195 *EI*[1]: 2:317.

196 *EI*[2]: 3:485.

A Chronological List of Known *ḥisba* Treatises

(* An asterisk indicates a work not devoted exclusively to *ḥisba*).

1.	Author	:	Yaḥyā b. ᶜUmar. (213–289/828–901)
	School	:	Mālikī
	Title	:	*Aḥkām al-sūq* [197]
2.	Author	:	Abū al-ᶜAbbās Muḥammad b. Aḥmad al-Sarakhsī (d. 286/899)
	School	:	Rāfiḍī
	Title	:	*Kitāb ghishsh al-ṣināᶜāt wa-l-ḥisba*[198]
3.	Author	:	Nāṣir al-Ḥasan b. ᶜAlī al-Aṭrūsh (d. 304/917)
	School	:	Zaydī
	Title	:	*Kitāb al-iḥtisāb*[199]
4.	Author	:	ᶜAbd al-ᶜAzīz b. Aḥmad b. Jaᶜfar b. Yazdād b. Bakr. (d. 373/983–4)
	School	:	Ḥanbalī
	Title	:	*Mukhtaṣar al-ḥisba*[200]
5.	Author	:	Abū al-Ḥasan ᶜAlī b. Muḥammad al-Māwardī (d. 450/1058)
	School	:	Ḥanbalī
	Title	:	(a) **Al-aḥkām al-sulṭāniyya*[201]
			(b) *Al-aḥkām fī al-ḥisba*
			(c) *Al-rutba fī al-ḥisba*[202]
6.	Author	:	Muḥammad b. al-Ḥusayn al-Farrā'. (380–458/990–1066)
	School	:	Ḥanbalī
	Title	:	**Al-aḥkām al-sulṭāniyya*[203]

197 Yaḥya, *Aḥkām*: 10.

198 Ibn Ḥajar, *Lisān*: 1:189–190. See also Chalmeta, *Zoco*: 304.

199 Serjeant, 'A Zaydī manual of ḥisba', *RSO*, 18 (1953): 1–34.

200 ᶜAwwād, *Ḥisba*: 422.

201 Māwardī, *Aḥkām*.

202 ᶜAwwād, RAAD, 419. Two of these works were cited by ᶜAwwād from an article by Aḥmad Sāmiḥ al-Khālidī in *Majallat al-thaqāfa*: 7:18.

203 Farrā', *Ṭabaqāt*: 2:193–230. See also *GAL*: 1: 502.

7.	Author	:	Abū Ḥāmid Muḥammad b. Muḥammad al-Ghazālī (450–505/1058–1111)
	School	:	Shāfiᶜī
	Title	:	**Iḥyā' ᶜulūm al-dīn*[204]
8.	Author	:	ᶜAbd al-Raḥmān b. Naṣr al-Shayzarī (d. 589/1193)
	School	:	Shāfiᶜī
	Title	:	*Nihāyat al-rutba fī ṭalab al-ḥisba*[205]
9.	Author	:	ᶜAbd al-Raḥīm b. Abū Bakr Jamāl-Din al-Dimashqī al-Jawbarī
	School	:	Shāfiᶜī
	Title	:	*Al-mukhtār fī kashf al-asrār*[206] (written between 629/1232 and 644/1248–9)[207]
10.	Author	:	Muḥāmmad b. Ibrāhīm b. Jamāᶜa 639–733/1241–1333.
	School	:	Shāfiᶜī
	Title	:	*Taḥrir al-aḥkām fī tadbīr ahl al-Islām*[208]
11.	Author	:	Aḥmad b. ᶜAbd al-Ḥalīm b. ᶜAbd al-Salām b. ᶜAbd Allāh b. Taymiyya. (661–728/1263–1328)
	School	:	Ḥanbalī
	Title	:	*Al-ḥisba fī al-Islām*[209]
12.	Author	:	Aḥmad b. Muḥammad b. Rifᶜa (645–710/1247–1310)
	School	:	Shāfiᶜī
	Title	:	*Al-rutba fī al-ḥisba*[210]

---

204 Badawī, *Mu'allafāt*: 21:98.

205 Shayzarī, *Nihāyat al-rutba fī ṭalab al-ḥisba* ed. al-Bāz alᶜArīnī (Cairo, 1946), editor's intro. p.9. See also *GAL*: 1:832.

206 *GAL*, Suppl.: 1:910. See also H.Kh., *Kashf*: 1623; M.J. de Goeje, 'Gaubari's "entdecktle Geheimnisse" ', *ZDMG* 20: (1866): 485–510.

207 See *EI*²: 2: Suppl.: 250.

208 *GAL*, Suppl.: 2:80; Ziriklī: 6:188; Ibn Ḥajar, *Durar*: 3:268.

209 *Ibid*: 1:159–171; Ziriklī: 1:140.

13. Author : ᶜAbd al-Laṭīf b. ᶜAbd al-Raḥmān al-Maqdisī
School : Shāfiᶜī
Title : *Kitāb al-amr bi-l-maᶜrūf wa-l-nahī ᶜan al-munkar*[211]

14. Author : Yūsuf b. ᶜAbd al-Hādī Ibn al-Mubarrad (840–909/1436–1503)
School : Ḥanbalī
Title : *Kitāb al-ḥisba* [212]

15. Author : ᶜIṣmat Allāh b. Muḥammad Aᶜẓam al-Sahāranpūrī (d. 1039/1629)
School : Ḥanafī
Title : *Kitāb bayān al-amr bi-l-maᶜruf wa-l-nahī ᶜan al-munkar*[213]

16. Author : Aḥmad b. Saᶜīd al-Mujaylidī (d. 1094/1683)
School : Mālikī
Title : *Al-taysīr fī aḥkām al-tasᶜīr* [214]

17. Author : Aḥmad b. ᶜAbd Allāh b. ᶜAbd al-Ra'ūf (fl. c. 4th/10th cent.)
School : Mālikī
Title : *Risāla fī ādāb al-ḥisba*[215]

18. Author : Muḥammad b. Aḥmad b. ᶜAbdūn (fl. c. 5th/11th cent.)
School : Mālikī
Title : *Risāla fi al-qaḍā' wa-l-ḥisba*[216]

---

210 Ibn Ḥajar, *Durar*: 303–306. See also Ziriklī: 1:213.

211 H.Kh., *Kashf*: 2:265. See also Kaḥḥāla, Muᶜjam: 6:10.

212 *Ibid*: 13:289. See also ᶜAwwād, *Ḥisba*: 421.

213 Levy, *Catalogue*: 276.

214 Liqbāl, *Ḥisba*: 11. See also Ziriklī: 1:126.

215 Chalmeta, *Zoco*: 302, 381. See also Lévi-Provençal, *Trois traités hispaniques de ḥisba* (Cairo, 1955): 5:70.

216 Chalmeta, *Zoco*, 302, 381.

19.	Author	:	Abū ᶜAbd Allāh Muḥammad al-Saqaṭi al-Mālaqī (fl. c. 7th/13th cent.)
	School	:	Mālikī
	Title	:	*Kitāb fī ādāb al-ḥisba*[217]
20.	Author	:	Muḥammad b. al-Ukhuwwa (d. 729/1329)
	School	:	Shāfiᶜī
	Title	:	*Maᶜālim al-qurba fī aḥkām al-ḥisba*[218]
21.	Author	:	ᶜUmar b. ᶜUthmān al-Jarsīfī (fl. 7th/13th or 8th/14th cent.)
	School	:	Mālikī
	Title	:	*Risāla fī al-ḥisba*[219]
22.	Author	:	Muḥammad b. Aḥmad b. Bassām (fl. 8th/14th–9th/15th cent.)
	School	:	Shāfiᶜī
	Title	:	*Nihāyat al-rutba fī ṭalab al-ḥisba*[220]
23.	Author	:	Abū ᶜAbd Allāh Muḥammad Aḥmad al-ᶜUqbānī al-Tilimsānī (d. 871/1467)
	School	:	Mālikī
	Title	:	*Tuḥfat al-nāẓir wa-ghunyat al-dhākir fī ḥifẓ al-shaᶜā'ir wa-taghyīr al-manākir*[221]

There are also several short discourses on *ḥisba* and *muḥtasib* scattered through various works, for example the *Khiṭaṭ* of al-Maqrīzī (845–766/1365–1441),[222] the

217 *Ibid.* Lévi-Provençal and Colin state that the author might have lived in the 11th–12th century; see Saqaṭī, *Kitāb*, intro. p.ix.

218 Ibn al-Ukhuwwa, *Maᶜālim*, intro. xiii – xvii; see also Chalmeta, *Zoco*, 305.

219 Chalmeta, *Zoco*, 307.

220 *Ibid.* 308; Ibn Bassām, *Nihāya*.

221 *BEO*, xix, 1965–1966 (1967): 133–340.

222 Maqrīzī, *Khiṭaṭ*; 343.

Subḥ of al-Qalqashandī (d.820),[223] or the *Muqaddima* of Ibn Khaldūn (d. 808/1406).[224]

Before concluding this list of treatises dealing with the subject of *ḥisba*, I should add that Ḥajjī Khalīfa lists a work entitled *Niṣāb al-iḥtisāb*. He then quotes the introduction to Sunāmī's work, but he does not give the author's name. However, the editor of *Kashf al-ẓunūn* notes in the margin that this *Niṣāb al-iḥtisāb* is not the one by Shāmī.[225] The statement is quite clearly inaccurate, since the quotation may be quite definitely traced in the work by Sunāmī.

Various definitions of *ḥisba*

Some long encyclopaedic works define the terms *ḥisba* and *muḥtasib* generally with some details. The *Nihāya* of al-Nuwayrī (d. 733/1333) is one such work.[226] A similar work was written by Muḥammad b. Muḥammad Ibn al-Ḥājj al-ᶜAbdarī al-Fāsī, who died in Cairo in the year 737/1336 at the age of 80.[227] We know from his *Madkhal al-sharᶜī al-sharīf* that he belonged to the Mālikī school.[228] His treatment of the concept of *ḥisba* is even slighter than Sunāmī's. He concentrates on the notion of enjoining good and prohibiting evil.[229] He deals with *ḥisba* from a moral point of view, but gives some details of different fraudulent practices. The information which he furnishes could be utilised by anyone in charge of the practical administration of the justice in a city, including the *muḥtasib*. It is interesting to note that the social climate which Ibn al-Ḥājj criticises is very similar in many aspects to that criticised by Sunāmī. This similarity can be seen in spite of the great differences that arise from geographical location. The similarity may be due not only to Sunāmī's being contemporary with this author and the interrelations existing between different parts of the Islamic world; it could also be due to the alien atmosphere in which both works were written,[230] as well as the unifying force of Islam.

The following chapters are worth noting in a comparision of the two texts: the visiting of graves[231]; Sufis of the day; festivals of the dhimmis.[232] In this last-

---

223 Al-Qalqashandī classifies the *muḥtasib* among 'men of the pen' (*aṣahāb al-aqlām*). This designation also includes the qadi and the state clerk *Subḥ al-aᶜshā* (Cairo, 1915): 5:451.

224 ᶜAbd al-Raḥmān b. Khaldūn, *Muqaddima* (Beirut, 1967): 1:398.

225 H.Kh., *Kashf*: 16.

226 *Nihāyat al-arab fī funūn al-adab* (Cairo, 1926): 6:219–315.

227 H.Kh., *Kashf*, 1643. See also *GAL*, Suppl.: 2:92.

228 Ibn al-Ḥājj, *Madkhal* (Cairo, 1291/1874): 1:262.

229 *Ibid*: 169.

230 Cf. ᶜUqbānī, *Tuḥfa*.

231 Ibn al-Ḥājj, *Madkhal* (Cairo, 1291/1874): 1:262.

mentioned chapter Ibn al-Ḥājj notes that dhimmis on some of their festivals collect flowers and trees and after boiling them make them into a bath. He adds that Mālik sees no harm in this practice if followed by Muslims; the name for this practice is the same as Sunāmī uses, namely *nashra*. The aim of the custom is curative.[233] In the section dealing with visits to tombs of saints [234] and the Sufi practice of *samāᶜ*, the conditions are almost identical to those depicted by Sunāmī.[235] We even find the story of al-Junayd and his reason for forbidding *samāᶜ*.[236] Also worthy of comparison is the section dealing with paper which should be used for writing.[237]

Comparison of *Niṣāb al-iḥtisāb* with Other Treatises on *Ḥisba* written by Representatives of the Various Schools of Law.

When we compare *Niṣāb* with other works on *ḥisba* several observations can be made. The *Niṣāb's* unique character seems to consist in its being a Ḥanafī treatise. Numerous authors have written works on *ḥisba*, but their primary concern has been with the general history of *ḥisba*, as embodied within the general framework of governmental theory in Islam. Examples of this can be found in the works *al-Aḥkām al-sulṭāniyya* of both al-Māwardī (d. 450/1058) and al-Farrā' (d. 458/1065). The basic principle according to these scholars is the idea of specialization of the institution. In addition, there should be no interaction between the various state institutions.[238] Accordingly the police as an instituition should have its own framework, which should not be associated with any other institution. *Ḥisba* should also be separate from well-defined institutions like all the other institutions. The fact that it serves as a link between the institutions of *qaḍā'* and *maẓālim* is not inconsistent with the fact that it is still a separate institution.[239] Other authors, such as Ibn Taymiyya (661–728/1263–1328), had a completely different view. He believes that all governmental institutions are interconnected in such a way that the duty of each individual institution cannot be strictly defined.[240] He also believes that, according to Islamic law, the general scope of the institution should be unlimited. It is, therefore, very feasible that what may be considered as part of the

232 *Ibid*: 298.
233 *Ibid*: 306–7.
234 *Ibid*: 16–21.
235 *Ibid*: 279–281.
236 *Ibid*:
237 *Ibid*: 135–8.
238 Māwardī, *Aḥkām*: 240; Farrā', *Aḥkām*: 268.
239 Māwardī, *Aḥkām*: 169; Farrā', *Aḥkām*: 241.
240 Ibn Taymiyya, *Ḥisba*: 7.

judicial apparatus can then be considered as part of the military apparatus. The same applies to the institutions of *ḥisba* and finance.[241]

Although Sunāmī is silent about the position of *ḥisba* vis-à-vis other governmental apparatus, he does not forget to mention that the judicial apparatus is said to be a branch of *ḥisba* or *iḥtisāb*.[242] On the other hand, he discusses the function of the *muḥtasib* as a distinct one from that of a judge (qadi).[243] Be that as it may, every author on *ḥisba*, be he a lawyer like Ibn Taymiyya or practical *muḥtasib* like al-Saqaṭī (7th/13th cent.)[244], has incorporated in his writings the flavour of his school. The school to which he belongs may be a result of his education or his own declaration. A striking point about the treatises on *ḥisba* that have come down to us is that they represent almost every Muslim school of law, apart from the Ḥanafī, on which the only available works would seem to be *Niṣāb al-iḥtisāb*, and Sahāranpūrī's rather late, short book.[245] It might be useful at this point to comment that no one appears to have written a comparative study of *ḥisba* of these various schools; the only author to have attempted anything of this kind was Mūsā Liqbāl, who restricted himself solely to the Muslim West.[246] *Niṣāb al-iḥtisāb* would thus appear to provide a very important link in such a study due to the lack of any other well-defined text on the subject of *ḥisba* according to Ḥanafī law, or a least written by a Ḥanafī lawyer or *muḥtasib*. The duality of our author's personality as a result of being a practical *muḥtasib* and also a lawyer seems to be rather important for the study of Ḥanafī *ḥisba*. His life in a society which respected, followed, and even venerated Abū Ḥanīfa's opinions may have resulted in his receiving a great amount of credit for his book. The unorganised lay-out and inconsistency in some parts of the text may indicate that Sunāmī was writing from basic and rough notes.

Sunāmī's View of Certain Legal Points as Compared with the Views of Other Jurists.

Although the previous chapter provides a bird's-eye view on some points which Sunāmī discussed, many still remain useful to modern analysis of *ḥisba*. One of the points to which many lawyers attempt to give an adequate answer was the problem of what kind of knowledge is required of a person before he can be appointed as *muḥtasib*. Is a knowledge of what is generally considered to be evil adequate? Or should this knowledge be accompanied by more specialised legal knowledge?

241 *Ibid*: 8.

242 *Niṣāb*: 2A.

243 *Niṣāb*: 4B, 10B–11.

244 See list on p. 31.

245 See list on p. 30.

246 Liqbāl, *Ḥisba*.

Al-Farrā' gave his opinion with some uncertainty when he wrote, 'perhaps knowledge of obviously unlawful acts is adequate'.[247] Māwārdī reports two conflicting legal opinions on this point. He observes that Abū Saᶜīd al-Iṣṭakhrī (d. 328/939–40) holds the view that he,(the *muḥtasib*) should be a man competent to decide in cases on which the law is doubtful. The alternative view is that all he requires is a knowledge of what is generally reputed to be evil.[248] The main reason for this question is a result of the *muḥtasib*'s right to enforce his own view of what is right and wrong when the general opinion is not unanimous. Shāfiᶜī jurists, for example, gave two contrary views when answering this question. According to Abū Saᶜīd al-Iṣṭakhrī, the *muḥtasib* can enforce his own opinion, even if some jurists disagree. The other Shāfiᶜī opinion is opposite to this.[249] Māwardī does not concede to the *muḥtasib* the right to enforce his own opinions. Sunāmī's views are very clear as to what qualifications a *muḥtasib* requires: he is of the opinion that it is to know *ᶜālim* good (*maᶜrūf*) and evil (*munkar*).[250] According to this, it would seem that the *muḥtasib* is not allowed to enforce any legal decision unless it is unanimous. In fact, in the case of chess, played by a Shāfiᶜī, Sunāmī seems very certain that the *muḥtasib* has no right to prevent him playing since it is permitted by the Shāfiᶜī school of law.[251]

Many legal opinions are expressed in *Niṣāb*. It would appear to be Sunāmī's aim to solve many of the most common problems which face the *muḥtasib*. He does this in accordance with Ḥanafī law. An example is the treatment of a perjurer. Public denunciation (*tashhīr*) is recommended in many other law books, including those of the Ḥanbalīs.[252] However, Sunāmī endeavours to find legal justification from a Ḥanafī source. He states that *Sharḥ adab al-qāḍī* justifies public denunciation of anyone committing perjury.[253] The interesting thing about this reference in the *Sharḥ adab al-qāḍī* is that in this book it is not a question of the punishment that could be applied by a *muḥtasib* but only of punishment generally.[254] Sunāmī has utilised this opinion to declare that a *muḥtasib* is entitled to use this method of punishment. There are many other examples similar to the one just described, which reflects an endeavour to define a starting-point for *muḥtasibs* of the Ḥanafī school.[255]

---

247 Farrā', *Aḥkām*: 269.

248 Amedroz, The *ḥisba* jurisdiction in the *Aḥkām sulṭāniyya* of Mārwardī, *JRAS*.

249 *Ibid*, 81.

250 *Niṣāb*: 61B.

251 *Ibid*: 16A.

252 Māwardī, *Aḥkām*: 239; Farrā', *Aḥkām*: 267.

253 *Niṣāb*: 6A.

254 *Sharḥ adab al-qāḍī*: 96A.

255 *Niṣāb*: 21.

A General Comparison of Niṣāb al-Iḥtisāb with Other Treatises on Ḥisba.

a) **Location**

In order to see more clearly the place of the *Niṣāb* in the history of treatises on *ḥisba*, as we know it, we may profitably turn to Pedro Chalmeta's work on the subject, paying particular attention to regional grouping. After reviewing all the various treatises known to him, this Spanish scholar divides them into three groups.[256]

1. This group covers *oriental* works. It includes the treatises of the following authors: al-Aṭrūsh (d.304/917), al-Shayzarī (d.589/1193), Ibn al-Ukhuwwa (d.729/1329), and Ibn Bassām (14th-15th cent. AD). Generally these manuscripts are much later than the Hispano-Arab manuals; they are also longer and more subdivided.

2. In the *Maghribī* group the authors included are Yaḥya b. ᶜUmar (213–289/828–901)), al-Jarsīfī (fl. 13th or 14th cent. AD), al-ᶜUqbānī al-Tilimsānī (d. 871/1467) and al-Mujaylidī[257] (d.1094/1683).

3. In the *Hispano-Arab* group authors included are Ibn ᶜAbd al-Ra'ūf (fl. 4th/10th cent), al-Saqaṭī (fl. 7th/13th cent.) and Ibn ᶜAbdūn (fl. 5th/11th cent.).

We cannot place *Niṣāb al-iḥtisāb* in any of these regional groups. We therefore need a fourth classification for the *Indo-Muslim* group. Al-Sahāranpūrī (d. 1039/1629) should probably be placed in this fourth group.

b) **A theoretical or a practical work?**

Another classification which could be followed may be based on the author's approach to the subject, whether theoretical or practical:

Theoretical works: Examples are the works of Māwardī (d. 450/1058), Farrā' (380–458/996–1066), Ghazālī (d. 450–505/1058–1111), and Ibn Taymiyya (661–728/1263–1328). These works bear a markedly juristic stamp and their basic principle is to establish the general theory of *ḥisba*. They do, however, include some practical cases.

Practical works: These works were essentially based on the personal experience of a *muḥtasib*, like Shayzarī, or also by scholars who had some knowledge of practical

---

256 Chalmeta, *Zoco*: 311.

257 Chalmeta overlooks this author.

ḥisba cases. Examples of this group are the treatises of Shayzarī, Ibn Bassām, Ibn al-Ukhuwwa (whose work is dependent on Shayzarī's), Yaḥyā b. ᶜUmar and the treatises by Ibn ᶜAbdūn, Ibn ᶜAbd al-Ra'ūf (Hispano-Arabic) and Jarsīfī[258] (Hispano-Arabic according to Lévi-Provençal and Maghribī according to Chalmeta). Once again Sunāmī's treatise cannot be placed in either group. We ought, therefore, to establish a third classification to cover works that combine theory equally with practice.

The *Niṣāb* is far less concerned with the market regulations than many other treatises of *ḥisba*, such as Shayzarī's *Nihāya*, Ibn al-Ukhuwwa's *Maᶜālim*, that of Ibn Bassām, and above all that of al-Saqaṭī. Sunāmī's references to the market place are in the fact of a general nature.

Much of Sunāmī's subject-matter suggests that he dealt with day-to-day cases, such as complaints about leaking spouts dripping down on to property below. Some complainant, it would seem, would come to him and lay the facts of the case before him and ask for his judgment. In other words, he would appear to be acting as a qadi, or perhaps *muftī*, rather than as a *muḥtasib* in the Andalusian and Maghribī sense of that term. Again, in some respects Sunāmī's *Niṣāb* is very similar to works that describe and condemn unorthodox practices (*bidaᶜ*) e.g. al-Ṭurṭūshī's *Ḥawādith*. There are, however certain treatises on *ḥisba* that are not unlike the *Niṣāb* from the point of view of general structure. The concept of the *Tuḥfa* by al-ᶜUqbānī seems very similar to that of the *Niṣāb* in that it is both theoretical and practical. Certainly ᶜUqbānī's legal background is reflected strongly in his work. ᶜUqbānī himself was *qāḍī al-jamāᶜa* for a time in his native city of Tilimsān (Tlemcen). His work is divided into eight chapters of unequal length and interest. The first five are strictly theoretical and very little is added to the classical story of *ḥisba*. On the contrary, the last three chapters are very useful for a study of life in the medieval Muslim West. The subjects of the chapters are :

1. Legality of reform (*taghyīr*).
2. An explanation of whether *taghyīr* is obligatory, recommended or prohibited.
3. Those whose business it is to reform and the conditions applicable required.
4. Methods of *taghyīr.*
5. Severity of *taghyīr.*
6. How to recognise the need for *taghyīr.*
7. Kinds of *taghyīr.*
8. On dhimmis and people living under a pact of protection.

There is a great deal of similarity between this work and *Niṣāb* in more than one respect. Apart from the similarity with regard to the legal background of the authors, there is the alien ambience in which the two works were written, Spain and India

258 See chronological list on p.28–31.

respectively. In both these countries the ambience encountered by Islam was alien to its origin and roots. The problems that Islam faced were completely different, but in their complexity they were very similar. At this point it may be useful to quote some practices which al-ᶜUqbānī considered sufficiently unorthodox to deserve remonstration and which attract the same criticism as that delivered by Sunāmī. These innovations are not necessarily local practices but those recommended by Prophetic Tradition. They include the general social etiquette which should be observed in a mosque, which requires the suppression of begging, talking loudly, cutting one's hair, eating and unsheathing of swords and other weapons;[259] planting trees in the courtyard of a mosque,[260] decorating a mosque; swearing an oath using a name other than God's.

Other matters dealt with are: building over the public road,[261] the previously mentioned problem of overflowing drains,[262] the disposal of litter in a public road,[263] obstruction of passers-by with loaded pack-animals, women's wailing for the dead or going to the public baths without necessity,[264] women's visiting graveyards,[265] the sale of musical instruments,[266] or other prohibited goods such as pictures or statues,[267] the minting or use of forged money[268] and protected people and their violation of general Islamic prescriptions.[269]

The second treatise which could possibly be placed in the same group as *Niṣāb* is that of al-Sahāranpurī.[270] This author is an Indian scholar (d. 1039/1629) who frequently refers to *Niṣāb*.[271]

The text is divided up into the following eight chapters:

1. Introduction, defining good and evil.[272]
2. Prophetic Traditions quoted to prove the esteem of enjoining good and prohibiting evil.[273]

---

259 *BEO*, 42.

260 *Ibid*: 5.

261 *Ibid*: 63.

262 *Ibid*: 64.

263 *Ibid*: 65.

264 *Ibid*: 67.

265 *Ibid*: 77.

266 *Ibid*: 97.

267 *Ibid*: 98.

268 *Ibid*: 126.

269 *Ibid*: 134–180.

270 Levy, *Catalogue*, 276.

271 Iṣmat Allāh b. Muḥammad Aᶜẓam al-Sahāranpurī *Kitāb bayān al-amr bi-l-maᶜrūf wa-l-nahy ᶜan al-munkar*, (India Office Levy, *Catalogue* MS 1697): 1B.

272 *Ibid*: 3A.

3. Anecdotes on the Prophet's Companions and Successors, quoted to prove the esteem of enjoining good and prohibiting evil.
4. Essentials for enjoining good and prohibiting evil.[274]
5. On remonstrating with heretics.[275]
6. Remonstration with sultans and amirs.[276]
7. On governments.[277]
8. Brief stories from caliphal biography.[278]

---

273 *Ibid*: 5B.

274 *Ibid*: 6A.

275 *Ibid*: 17B.

276 *Ibid*: 19A.

277 *Ibid*: 27B.

278 *Ibid*: 31A.

III
English Translation and Annotation of *Niṣāb al-iḥtisāb*

List of the Abbreviations used in the Sources of *Niṣāb*

(The definite article (*al*) has been omitted).

AḥQ	*Aḥkām al-Qur'ān*
AḥS	*Aḥkām sulṭāniyya*
Aj	*Ajnās*
AM	*ʿAwārif al-maʿārif*
AQ	*Adab al-qāḍī*
BA	*Bustān al-ʿārifīn*
Dh	*Al-dhakhīra*
FAL	*Fatāwā Abī al-Layth*
FB	*Fatāwā al-Bayhaqī*
FF	*Fatāwā al-Faḍlī*
FKh	*Fatāwā al-khāniyya*
FN	*Fatāwā al-Nasafiyya*
FS	*Fatāwā ahl Samarqand*
FẒ	*Fatāwā al-Ẓahīriyya*
Gh	*Gharīb al-riwāya*
H	*Hidāya*
Iḥ	*Iḥyā' ʿulūm al-dīn*
Im	*Imlā'*
IMN	*Īḍāḥ*
JṢ	*Jāmiʿ al-ṣaghīr*
JṢKh	*Jāmiʿ al-ṣaghīr al-khānī*
K	*Kaysāniyyāt*
Kash	*Kashshāf ʿan ḥaqā'iq al-tanzīl*
KD	*Kitāb al-diyyāt*
KhF	*Khulāṣat al-fatāwā*
Khul	*Khulāṣa (al-Ghazālī)*
KSh	*Kifāya al-shaʿbiyya*
KSM	*Kitāb al-ṣārim al-maslūl ʿalā shātim al-rasūl*
Mabs	*Mabsūṭ*
Man	*Manāhī*
Maẓ	*Manẓūma*

MM	*Maʿrifat al-ṣaḥāba*
MN	*Multaqaṭ al-Nāṣirī*
MQ	*Mukhtaṣar al-Qudūrī*
Muḥ	*Muḥīṭ*
Mugh	*Mughrib*
Munt	*Muntaqā*
Mut	*Muttafaq*
N	*Nawāzil*
Nd	*Nawādir*
QQ	*Qūt al-qulūb*
R	*Rawḍa*
SA	*Siyar al-atqiyā'*
Saḥ	*Saḥīḥ al-Bukhārī (al-jāmiʿ al-ṣaḥīḥ)*
SAM	*Ṣārim al-maslūl ʿalā shātim al-rasūl*
ShA	*Sharḥ al-awrād*
ShAQ	*Sharḥ adab al-qāḍī*
ShI	*Shirʿat al-Islām*
ShK	*Sharḥ al-Karkhī*
ShMaẓ	*Sharḥ al-manẓūma*
ShSH	*Sharḥ al-shāfiya*
ShSK	*Sharḥ al-siyar al-kabīr*
ShṬ	*Sharḥ al-Taḥawī*
ShṬK	*Sharḥ al-Taḥawī al-kabīr*
Ṣiḥ	*Ṣiḥāḥ*
SK	*Siyar al-kabīr*
SM	*Ṣalāt al-Masʿūdiyya*
SN	*Ṣalāt al-Nasafiyya*
TA	*Tafsīr Abī al-Layth*
Tadh	*Tadhkirat al-awliyā'*
TʿAyn	*Tafsīr ʿayn al-maʿānī*
TB	*Tafsīr al-Bastī*
TGh	*Tanbīh al-ghāfilīn*
TK	*Tafsīr al-kabīr*
TM	*Tajnīs wa-l-mazīd*
UB	*Uṣūl al-Bazdawī*
US	*Uṣūl al-Sarakhsī*
WN	*Wāqiʿāt al-Nāṭifī*
WSS	*Wāqiʿāt al-Ṣadr al-Shahīd*
YM	*Yawāqīt al-mawāqīt*

Classification of the Chapters

Chapters without marks are fully translated

O	Omission.
TS	Part translation, part summary.
S	Summary.
SO	Summary with omission(s).
TO	Translation with omission(s).
TOS	Translation and summary with omission(s).

System of omission

...	Omission of a few words.
... ...	Long omission of between ten and twenty lines of the Arabic text
... ...	Omission of more than a page

Note:

Numbers inserted and underlined in the text refer to the Hyderabad MS no. 2846 (Fiqh Ḥanafī).

Numbers inserted in bold type [] refer to page numbers of my edition of the book 1983.

Introduction

[11] 1B Praise be to God the venerated Reckoner, the Watcher, for His having bestowed the gift of faith and the duty of *ḥisba*. Blessings and peace be upon His beloved and high-born Messenger Muḥammad and his house in abundance that can be neither recorded nor reckoned.

His servant, who is wholly immersed in the overflowing sea of His goodness, namely ᶜUmar b. Muḥammad b. ᶜIwaḍ al-Sunāmī (may Almighty God inspire him with fear of Him in the matter of all that he writes and may God grant him an escape and means of salvation from the griefs of this world and grant him sustenance without reckoning as he writes this book entitled *Niṣāb al-iḥtisāb*), has brought together cases bearing on the worth of the dignity of *ḥisba* and *iḥtisāb* from works that are highly regarded among jurists and well-trusted by religious scholars. This he has done after bringing together [the material it contains], after much worry in setting it down [on paper], after devoting considerable length of time to concluding it and correcting it, and after taking great pains to arrange it so that anyone who may have occasion to put it to the test may be successful in attaining the knowledge he requires through it. This book is divided into many chapters.**[12]**

CHAPTER 1
(TS)
The definition of the terms *iḥtisāb* and *ḥisba*.

Iḥtisāb in Arabic is used in two ways:

The first to indicate calculation (*Mughrib* quoted). Abū Bakr is reported to have said, "I calculate my steps" meaning that I volunteer my action in the path of God. (The Prophet quoted).

The second to indicate the condemnation of an action (*Ṣiḥāḥ* quoted).**[13]**

Legally (*fī al-sharᶜ*) *iḥtisāb* is the enjoinment of good when it becomes commonly abandoned and remonstrating against evil when it becomes commonly practised. (*Al-aḥkam al-sulṭāniyya* quoted)...*2A*

The term has taken a conventional meaning to include the following matters:

1 - Disposing of wine

2 - Destroying musical instruments

3 - Reforming the streets. This section is a large one that includes many issues :

The issue of water spouts

The issue of dirt and mud **[14]**

The issue of preventing people from slaughtering [animals] outside their houses

Preventing pedlars from sitting by doors
Preventing the driving of donkeys and cows in a fast manner (especially those used to carry wood or gypsum)
Preventing people from tethering animals near [others'] doors
Preventing encroachment onto the street by renovated walls
Pricing of goods
Preventing building extensions from occupying street space
Preventing sewage tanks being placed on walls that can only be accessed from the public road
Preventing the erection of canopies
4 - Preventing neighbours from harmful actions like looking [in a lewd manner] or blocking one another's light. The *muḥtasib* is not responsible for matters relevant to possession like illegal possession of land
5 - Ascertaining the legality of scales
6 - Checking the scales' weights *(ṣanjāt)*
7 - Ascertaining the cleanliness of vendors like bakers and cooks
8 - Ascertaining the cleanliness of *faqqāᶜī*
9 - Remonstrating with those who allow their wrapper (*īzār*) to reach below their ankle bone **[15]**
10 - Reprimanding people for their singing or keening
11 - Preventing men and women from imitating one another
12 - Making sure that *tānbūl* vendors clean their water and clothes and that their chalk contains no stones
13 - Burning musical instruments on the day of *aḍḥā* in the *muṣallā*
14 - Deterring people from pigeon tossing
15 - Deterring prostitutes and rebuking them as well as their husbands, those in charge of them (*awliyā'*), and their servants
16 - Instructing the protected people to clean *2B* the utensils which they use to sell liquids like oil and milk
17 - Instructing body-washers to follow the sunna and to avoid any innovative practices when they wash corpses, dig graves, or carry [biers]. The *muḥtasib* should warn them against charging high wages and appoint [as their chief someone] from among the good with regard to their morality and experience in these matters
18 - Inspecting the mosque on the day of Jumᶜa and the ᶜĪd *muṣallā* before the days of ᶜĪd to ensure that no buying or selling takes place within their premises. He should remonstrate with beggars not to walk between the lines, with story tellers not to tell fabricated stories and, with begging women not to walk inside, as well as with lunatics and children
19 - Keeping harmful animals like ferocious dogs away from inhabited areas**[16]**
20 - Preventing *najash* and *taṭfīf* sales

21 - Preventing people from standing in doubtful places, for example men talking to women in the public road

22 - Preventing painters and jewellers from making statues of living creatures and breaking such statues

23 - Preventing Muslims from trading in prohibited items like idols, musical instruments, cymbals, wine, and narcotics (*banj*)

24 - Preventing cooks and bakers from selling food on the first day of Ramadhān

25 - Preventing people from building false graves and preforming pilgrimages to saints or mosques in a way which is similar to pilgrimage to the Kaaba

26 - Preventing women from wearing make up and going out to festivals or visiting graves

27 - Preventing people from illegal usage of cemeteries

28 - Preventing soothsayers, magicians, and fortune-tellers from practising their innovations

29 - Reprimanding the public bath owners for their abominable practices and instructing them to clean their water and not to allow unbearded or naked men to enter. The *muḥtasib* should prevent the cupper from shaving pubic hair or the beard. He should order the construction of a partition between men and women

30 - Preventing the protected people from dressing or riding like the Muslims. Neither should they build their cemeteries in Muslim areas *3A* **[17]**

31 - Preventing Muslims from entering their temples for blessings or requesting help from their mystics

32 - Preventing Muslims from following the customs of the infidels in their birth ceremonies, or during illness. He should also seek to exclude Muslims from their company, and [Muslim] children from the company of their children, be it in urban or rural areas, on land or at sea

33 - Preventing Muslims from learning more of the science of astronomy than is needed in their religion. He should also reprimand those who believe in soothsayers

34 - Preventing innovations on the night of mid-Shaᶜbān, *Laylat al-barā'a*

35 - Preventing the protected people from celebrating the rituals of their faith in the land of Islam

36 - Preventing the playing of chess and backgammon, and confiscating the boards and statues.

37 - Preventing midwives from aborting foetuses after the spirit has entered and they are fully created

38 - Preventing surgeons from stripping men of their genitalia (*jab*) or performing castration

39 - Preventing cuppers from touching women foreign to them (*ajnabiyya*), save in case of necessity. No pregnant woman should be cupped at a time harmful to her

40 - Preventing people from living in mosques or leaving their possessions there

41 - Preventing those possessed by the devil from speaking about the unseen and preventing others from listening to him, believing that he is truthful in his *kufr*. Anyone who believes him is an apostate **[18]**

42 - Preventing calligraphers and Quran teachers from sitting in the mosque

43 - Preventing teachers from accepting gifts at the time of Nayrūz or Mahrajān

44 - It is also an action of *ḥisba* when a runaway slave is reprimanded and returned to his master. However it is incumbent for a reward to be given to the *muḥtasib*. (*Ijmāᶜ* of the Prophet's Companions quoted) **[19]**

Sources: *Mugh*
Ṣiḥ
AḥS

CHAPTER 2

Strictures on those who Trifle with Letters [of the Alphabet], Papers, and Similar, and on those who are Paid Fees for Instruction

It is reprehensible to lay down, sit on, or use a carpet or prayer-mat (*muṣallā*) inscribed with the words 'Sovereignty belongs to God' (*al-mulk li-llāh*) or to excise one of the letters thereof or to stitch *3B* out one of the letters, thus leaving the word incomplete. This kind of thing is no less reprehensible for the simple reason that the letters are still there, and independent letters also command respect because they are the written medium expression for the Quran and Traditions (*akhbār*) of the Prophet. It is related that one of the imams once saw men shooting at a target on which was written 'Abū Jahl, God curse him!' and he forbade them to do so. He went off but later found that they had only erased the name of God and were shooting just the same as before. Whereupon he explained that his prohibition related to the use of the letters.

Sunāmī: by analogy with these men are forbidden to inscribe *al-ᶜIzz wa-l-iqbāl* or similar on staves, basins, washstands and waterjugs, cups, the outer surfaces (lit. coverings) of saddles, and the like. For all such things are in common use, and letters must be safeguarded from such disrespect. If something was written on any of those articles mentioned they should not be used, out of respect for the letters. It is explained in the *Multaqaṭ* that independant letters are to be respected because they form part of the Quran. As regards the prohibition on the name of Abū Jahl, this is much the same sort of thing.**[20]**

It is reprehensible to use papers to wipe oneself with at a banquet (*walīma*). One of our teachers (*mashā'ikh*), al-Ḥākim the imam, would be most strict on this point and condemn it most vehemently.

<u>Sunāmī:</u> by analogy with this men are forbidden to use washstands or pictures made of paper at a banquet on the occasion of the ᶜĪd or the night of the mid-Shaᶜbān because it involves trifling [of the kind referred to]. In the *Multaqaṭ*, Nāsir al-Dīn says that the Shaykh does not mean by the objection using, for wiping purposes, the inferior sort of paper which is unsuitable for writing for this is well known to the ulama of Samarqand and is not censured. Perhaps the reprehension attaches to the good quality paper which is suitable for writing.

The chapter on directives (*waṣāyā*) in the *Multaqaṭ*: discarded books and papers that contain God's name should have it erased and then be thrown into a large stretch of running water or buried in uncontaminated ground. Alternatively, this can be done before erasure. It must not, however, be burned. This opinion is transmitted on the authority of Muḥammad b. Muqātil al-Rāzī. In accordance with this principle, it would be better if the item were washed out in a stretch of running water and then used for making new leaves. There is a ruling in the *Fatāwā al-Khāniyya* relating to the question of a piece of paper on which God's name is written *4A* and in which something is wrapped. Abū Bakr al-Iskāf says that such a practice is reprehensible whether the writing is on the outside or the inside, but that this is not the case with a purse: if God's name or one of His names is inscribed on it, there is no harm in it because a purse is highly esteemed whereas paper is not.

In his *Bustān* Abū al-Layth says that books should not be placed on the [bare] ground, while in the *Muḥīṭ* and the other works it is said that the Quran must not be made in miniature, meaning that one must not write it with a fine pen. This is based on the report that ᶜUmar once saw a small Quran in a man's hand. 'Who wrote this?' he asked.**[21]** 'I did', said the man. Whereupon he had the man whipped with the *dirra*. 'Hold the Quran in esteem', he said. The story is told by Abū al-Layth in the *Bāb al-fawā'id* of his *Bustān*.

<u>Case</u>: It is mentioned in the *Dhakhīra* that to offer payment for teaching the Quran is not permitted because it falls within the category of voluntary religious service (*ḥisba*), and to perform a voluntary religious service (*iḥtisāb*) should entail no fee. The legal decision (*fatwā*) taken in our day to allow an obligatory fee and to permit one to engage a teacher's services arises from the growth of laxity in religious affairs, the loss of teaching posts in the *bayt al-māl*, and the lack of magnanimity among the rich. In bygone days our colleagues found the practice of fee-paying reprehensible because they had a strong sense of religious duty (*ḥisba*) and ample allowances from the *bayt al-māl* and because merchants and men of substance displayed great magnanimity, and so instructors had no need to charge fees. **[22]**

<u>Sources</u>: *MN*
FKh
BA
Dh

CHAPTER 3
(TOS)
Strictures on Effeminates Persons

Men should not behave like women; the Prophet cursed effeminate males and masculine females (quoting the Qadi al-Shaᶜbī, *K. al-istiḥsān*).

The story of Hīt, the infamous catamite banished by the Prophet from Madina, and how he spoke indiscreetly in front of ᶜUmar b. Salama describing the beauty of one women's body upon which the Prophet banned him from freely mixing with women (quoting *Sharḥ al-Karkhī*). Sunāmī concludes that in early Islam effeminate persons were allowed to enter houses, but then permission was withdrawn. They must not be allowed 4B to be invited to partake in wailing for the dead in the company of women in a private house; the reasons for such a prohibition are given. Commentary on a difficult expression in the Hīt story (called Habt in the text with an explanation of the name from *Mughrib*)[279].**[23]** Reiteration of the obligation to expel an effeminate persons found in a private house.**[24]**

Sources: *KSh*
ShK
Mugh

CHAPTER 4
(TS)
On the Difference Between the Official *Muḥtasib* and the Self-Appointed *Muḥtasib*

(1) The *muḥtasib* who is self-appointed (*mutaṭawwiᶜ*) may be excused if he is physically incapable of fulfilling his role, whereas the officially appointed *muḥtasib* (*manṣūb*) is obliged to enforce the law as he can call upon his guards (*aᶜwān*) for assistance and, in the last resort the guards of his appointing authority (sultan). The *mutaṭawwiᶜ*, however, can only rely on men of good conscience (*ahl al-ṣalāḥ*). The reward of the voluntary *muḥtasib* is earned by virtue of what he actually does; to earn his reward he must declare with tongue and mind that such and such is reprehensible (Ibn Masᶜūd quoted). If he can do nothing about a reprehensible act, he may make a threefold declaration of intention of his disapproval.

(2) The official *muḥtasib* received renumeration from the *bayt al-māl* out of *jizya*, *kharāj*, and so forth because he serves the Muslim community; he has the same

---

279 See *Mughrib*: 277.

right to maintenance as *wālīs*, qadis, *ghuzāt*, *muftīs*, religious instructors and students (quoted from *Multaqaṭ*).**[25]**

(3) *Ḥisba* is a duty binding on the unofficial *muḥtasib* when bound by another contract. Thus, if a consignee sees a deposit exposed to the depredations of a thief and does nothing, though able, to restrain him, he is liable for his neglect. But the official *5A muḥtasib* is not so liable because the assignment of liability to a governor or similar official forms no part of his duty. If it were, no one would accept the official post, and that would necessarily be contrary to public interest. Similarly if no one agrees to be a consignee, that would be contrary to private interest.

(4) (Quoting section on criminal offenses of the *Dhakhīra*).

Anyone digging a public well in a public road would be liable in the event of someone falling into it. The act would be criminal because the benefactor has deprived the public of freedom of movement and usurped the authority of the central government (imam) in its right to discretion and administrative function. The central government, on the other hand, would not be liable if it did the same thing because it has the right to govern.**[26]**

Sources: *MN*
Dh

CHAPTER 5
(TS)
On Discretionary Punishment (*Taᶜzīr*)

The basic principle is that grounds for suspicion entails *taᶜzīr*. Examples of where discretionary punishment must be imposed are if the legal authority (imam) sees a man sitting with evil-livers (*fussāq*) at a drinking party or a man walking with thieves. Abū Bakr al-Aᶜmash is said to have held that if a man accused of theft denies the allegation, the imam must give the case the closest scrutiny, and if such scrutiny convinces him that the man is a thief and is in possession of the property [alleged to have been stolen], he must impose *taᶜzīr*. This case is similar to that of the mistaken shedding of blood in self-defence.

Example: If A goes into B, drawing a weapon, and B forms the impression that A intends to murder him, then B is entitled to kill A. The majority of jurists, on the other hand, hold that the imam's sanction in such a case is discretionary punishment of B because he was found in suspicious circumstances. (*Dhakhīra* quoted).

The differences between (h) *ḥadd* ('statutory punishment') and (t) *taᶜzīr* are:

1. (h) is fixed by Revealed Law, while (t) is discretionary.
2. (h) lapses if based on suspicion, whereas (t) is obligatory if there are grounds for suspicion.

3. (h) must not be applied to a minor (*ṣabī*), whereas (t) may be prescribed in such a case.
4. (h) is applicable to a dhimmi if it is fixed [by Revealed Law], but (t) is not, and in such cases the punishment is termed *ʿuqūba* because (h) is prescribed for expurgation (*taṭhīr*) and dhimmis do not believe in expurgation [in this way].**[27]** (Sarakhsī's *Mabṣūṭ* quoted).

Taʿzīr 5B is obligatory; offences entailing it are mentioned.

A case is cited which entails *taʿzīr* because of an offence against property but not civil liability (*ḍamān*) because there is no loss of property.

Another case is cited (from the *Khāniyya*): refusal to acknowledge the considered legal opinion of a *muftī* or dissent from the consensus of ulama entails *taʿzīr*, not religious expiation (*kaffāra*).

As suspicion is the essence of *taʿzīr*, a suspect [offering a plea of not guilty] must be put on oath, and refusal to testify (*nukūl*) entails *taʿzīr*. (Quoting Jaṣṣāṣ's *Sharḥ adab al-qāḍī.*)

Maximum penalties: Abū Ḥanīfa held the maximum number of lashes in *taʿzīr* to be 40. Other opinions are given: 80, 79, 75. The author holds the first opinion to be the best, and declares there is confusion over interpretation.[280]

Nature of the *taʿzīr* sanctions: Prison, slapping, rubbing up the ear, severe scalding, flogging.

Abū Yūsuf: The ruling authority (sultan) is permitted to confiscate property. The consensus of jurists is that *taʿzīr* sanctions must not exceed the limit of those imposed by those of the *ḥadd* (Tradition of the Prophet quoted).**[28]** Abū Ḥanīfa holds that the penalty for slaves in *ḥadd* sanctions is 40 lashes. Differences of opinions are given. The figures given are said to represent the maximum limit; the minimum is at the discretion of the imam.

Blackening of the face is not permitted, for it is unfitting to man's dignity, *6A* but ʿUmar is said to have sanctioned such a penalty for perjury. A possible reason for his decision is given (quoting *Sharḥ al-manẓūma*). Public parading of the culprit among the market folk as a punishment for proven perjury is mentioned in Chapter 49 of Jaṣṣaṣ's *Sharḥ adab al-qāḍī*.

Civil liability in the case of death caused by *taʿzīr*. According to the *Jāmiʿ al-ṣaghīr al-khānī*, no liability falls on the imam in the case of death caused by *taʿzīr*. **[29]** Shāfiʿī's opinion is that there is a difference between *ḥadd* and *taʿzīr*: *taʿzīr* is intended as a means to correction (*ta'dīb*) [it is corrective and comparable to the sort of correction one would administer to a wife or child, and must not, therefore entail

---

280 This paragraph is a literal quotation from Muḥammad b. Aḥmad al-Sarakhsī, *Mabsūṭ* (Cairo, 1331/1912–3): 23:36.

death]. The author's view is that *ta*ᶜ*zīr* is as obligatory as *ḥadd* because it is the penalty for an action which is proscribed. This is not the case with a disciplinary action; such an action is permitted but not obligatory.

Quoting Abū Yūsuf in *Dhakhīra*: if a man dies as a result of 100 lashes inflicted by a governor (*wālī*), no civil liability attaches to the latter since there are many reports of 100 not resulting in death. But if 100 is exceeded, half the blood-money is payable by the *bayt al-māl* because the *wālī* erred. But if the latter is known to have acted deliberately, then there is no question of error, and there is a case here of loss occasioned by *ta*ᶜ*zīr*. Suspension (*i*ᶜ*lā'*) is permitted subject to the condition that entails no injury. But if there is any loss (*talaf*) consequent upon *i*ᶜ*lā'*, civil liability follows and blood money is payable. (Quoted from Jaṣṣāṣ's *Sharḥ adab al-qāḍī*).

The face of a perjurer must not be blackened when he is paraded publicly (*tashhīr*). To do so defeats the object of the punishment. (Quoted from *Jāmi*ᶜ *al-ṣaghīr*).

Sunāmī: accordingly I recommend the uncovering of head and face in cases of public denunciation in the markets (*al-iṭāfa fī al-aswāq*).

*Ta*ᶜ*zīr* is entailed by a man's being seen in a compromising situation with a foreign woman (*ajnabiyya*) but not seen in the act of sexual intercourse. He incurs the maximum penalty (*Dhakhīra*). *6B* The minimum penalty is severe beating on one member of the body; the maximum requires the beating to be distributed. Abū Yūsuf is said to have indicated that only the top of the back and the buttocks may be beaten and that the back is bared for beating.**[30]**

Dhakhīra: a Muslim introducing wine or pork into a Muslim city is to be castigated by whipping (*yu'addab bi-aswāṭ*) and imprisoned until he shows repentance. If only one of the two named commodities is involved, the penalty is *either* beating *or* prison, because *ta*ᶜ*zīr* admits of alternatives.

If a dhimmi commits the same offence in ignorance of the Islamic ban on the said commodities, he must be instructed and suffer no penalty. But if he has acted in full knowledge of the ban, he must suffer *ta*ᶜ*zīr*[281] by imprisonment, beating or both of these two penalties.

Dhimmis are subject to *iḥtisāb* if they assume the appearance of Muslims by using the same types of clothing, mounts, and saddles. They may only ride horses if they are called upon by the imam to render him military assistance. They must be permitted to ride donkeys or mules because a man may not be able to walk. Muslim type saddles must not be used by them, however; only something such as a pack-saddle is permitted them. They may not wear coats (*ridā'*), turbans (ᶜ*amā'im*), and *durrā*ᶜ*as*, such as religious classes do. Footwear must also be different from that of

---

281 Although Sunāmī says earlier (5A) that the term *ta*ᶜ*zīr* is not applicable to dhimmis, this is the noun which he uses here.

the Muslims. The reason behind these prohibitions is that an infidel must be abased and a Muslim honoured.

Al-muḥīṭ: a Muslim woman must not wear the kind of clothes worn by an Indian woman (*libās al-Hindiyya*).

There is a difference of opinion whether only one of these three distinctive signs (corresponding to head, body and feet) applicable to non-Muslims is sufficient. According to Abū Bakr Muḥammad b. al-Faḍl,**[31]** *7A* the rule is one for a Christian, two for a Jew, and three for a Magian.

Sunāmī: The infidels in our country are worse than Magians and must wear all three; otherwise they must be exposed to *taᶜzīr*.

To eat with an infidel is permissible on one or two occasions so as to dispose his heart (*ta'līf al-qalb*) to Islam. Regular eating with infidels is, however, reprehensible. (Quotes Prophet and hadith. Mentions various interpretations of such quotations to be found in the *Dhakhīra*).

Commentary on Jaṣṣāṣ's *Sharḥ adab al-qāḍī*: *taᶜzīr* may consist in a frown. Quotes Karkhī's commentary in which ᶜUmar is shown to have used such a form of *taᶜzīr*.

Taᶜzīr is applicable in cases involving the following offences:

Forging of documents (*ṣukūk*) and signatures (*khuṭūṭ*).

Administering of wine to small children.

Ridiculing the Shariᶜa**[32]**

Deflowering a girl [presumably, by means other than copulation].

Jurists' agreement on this point is unanimous. Whether the bride-price (*mahr*) is to be paid by the offender is a question discussed at length in the *Dhakhīra*.

Cutting a pack-horse's tail and shaving the hair of a slave-girl (Ibn Rustum). The latter is quoting Muḥammad. He adds, however, that nothing more than *ta'dīb* should be imposed because their tails and hair will grow again. In other words, no compensation (*arsh*) should be awarded (*Dhakhīra*).

The killing of a Muslim without due cause, the killer acting under duress and on pain of death and the obligation being imposed by the ruling authority (sultan). In this case retaliation (*qiṣāṣ*) can be demanded of the ruling authority; *7B* the actual killer is liable only to *taᶜzīr* (Abū Ḥanīfa). (Quoted from the *Kifāya*).

Unlawful sexual intercourse under the following circumstances: A compels B to commit unlawful sexual intercourse (*zinā*) and thereby incurs the penalty of *taᶜzīr*, B incurring the *ḥadd*. (Quoting Muḥammad and Zufar.) This was also the original opinion of Abū Ḥanīfa, but he reversed his judgment: The *ḥadd* must not be allowed on the grounds of *shubha*. The offence is punishable by *taᶜzīr* and *ᶜaqr* (dowry for suspected intercourse) (quoting *Kifāya*.)

A man's being found with debauchees in an orgy of debauchery although the man himself is not drinking.

A man's walking with thieves.

A's charging B with theft, B having certain goods upon him, though there is no witness to testify against B. The general consensus is that B incurs *taᶜzīr* because he is found in suspicious circumstances; that A also incurs it for making an accusation of theft against B. (Quotes (*Dhakhīra*).**[33]**

Refusal to accept a recognised legal decision (*fatwā*) in a case such as the following: A is in dispute with B, and, B being presented with the *fatwā* by A, denies the *fatwā* or refuses to abide by it. (Quotes *Muḥīṭ*.)

Dhakhīra: a purged oath and vitiated contact of sale (*bayᶜ*), hire, and lease (*ijāra*) do not entail *taᶜzīr*.

An acceptable mode of *taᶜzīr* is fettering (*taqyīd*) (Quotes *Jāmiᶜ al-ṣaghīr al-Khānī*). Lechers and trouble-makers (*safīh*) may be fettered.

Section on homicide in Khāniyya's *Jināyāt* [lit. 'offences']: If A gives poison to B, and B eats it with fatal results, there is no question of retaliation (*qiṣāṣ*) or of blood money (*diya*). A is to be imprisoned and suffer *taᶜzīr*. But should A have put the poison in B's mouth [as medicine], then A's relatives (*ᶜāqila*) are liable to pay blood money. If A puts poison in a drink which he offers to B, who then drinks it, then no blood money is payable because B drank from choice. *Taᶜzīr* and asking God's forgiveness (*istighfār*) should be inflicted.

Ascetic piety (*zuhd*) which is not genuine (*bārid*) is punishable by *taᶜzīr*. A case is given, supposedly from the time of ᶜUmar, of a man who made an outward show of piety and asceticism. *8A* ᶜUmar had him whipped for hypocrisy.**[34]**

A runaway slave is punishable by *taᶜzīr*.

Dhakhīra: one should imprison a runaway slave until an owner claims him. This imprisonment is *taᶜzīr*. No *taᶜzīr* is applicable in the case of a slave who is merely lost.

How far may one go with *taᶜzīr*? The author quotes Abū Bakr al-Rāzī al-Jaṣṣāṣ on this point. In particular, the question again is raised and discussed: may the punishment be greater than that imposed in cases of incurring the *ḥadd*? The Prophet is quoted as saying that to exceed the *ḥadd* for a non-*ḥadd* offence is an injustice.

Sources: *Dh*
Mabs
FKh
ShAQ
ShMaẓ
JṢKh
Muḥ
KSh
YM
[35] *AQ*

CHAPTER 6
(TS)
On Religious Mendicants

May such innovators practice such religious innovations in places built for that specific purpose? From the *Fatāwā* of Abū al-Layth we have the following judgment: This is permissible as long as the builder of a *ribāt* for Muslims retains possession of the building for as long as he lives. He may not be expelled without good cause (e.g. wine-bibbing, debauchery, etc.)

Sunāmī: if the builder of a *khānqāh* may be expelled for debauchery, how can a man of debauchery and innovation be allowed to remain in one?

Q. May one wear iron objects as the Ḥaydarīs[282] did?

A. No. The Prophet thought that iron was the adornment of an inmate of hell fire. (Quoting *Sharḥ al-Karkhī*). In hadith gold is the ornament of polytheists, silver the ornament of Muslims, iron the ornament of inmates of hellfire. (Quotes *Shirᶜat al-Islām*).[283]

It is more sinful to wear iron than gold. **[36]** (Quotes Abū al-Layth's *Bustān*).[284] *8B* It is the duty of every Muslim to take such offenders to task and reject their false claim that Quṭb al-Dīn Ḥaydar would put on iron. Even if it can be proved that he did so during his vanquishing trances (*ghalabāt*), God's religion and the law of his Messanger are not subject to the laws of people during trances who are not responsible for their actions. They relate of Ḥaydar that he put white-hot iron straight from the blacksmith's bellows on to his neck for a while. If they wish to copy him then let them do what they want to with hot iron as he did until they burn and the community is rid of their evil doings.

Q. May one shave off one's beard like the Jawāliqīs ('men of the sack')?

A. No. (Quoting *Jināyāt al-hidāya* and *Tajnīs wa-l-mazīd*). ᶜUmar cited on beards and moustaches.

Q. May religious mendicants and Ḥaydarīs wear sacks and coarse clothing?

---

282 Ibn Baṭṭūṭa mentions a Ḥaydarī group centred in Khurāsān, south of Mashhad, derived from Qub al-Dīn Ḥaydar, who 'place iron rings in their hands, necks and ears, and even their male members, so that they are unable to indulge in sexual intercourse'. Trimmingham, *Sufi*: 39.

283 A quotation from Shirᶜat al-Islam, 80B. See C. Rieu, Supplement to the catalogue of the Arabic MSS in the British Museum (London, 1894 A.D.). MS no. 178.

284 See Abū al-Layth, *Bustān*: 143.

9A **[37]** A. No. The Prophet forbade extremes in clothing because they make a man distinctive and people must not seek to make themselves ostentatiously different from the rest of the community. The same goes for patched clothing (*muraqqaʿ*). It is of course, permissible to wear patched clothing if the wearer is genuinely poor, but not just for the sake of drawing attention to themselves. It is no defence to argue that such clothing was the garb of prophets and men of piety. (Quotes an anecdote about Jesus).

Q. Is dancing to music (*samāʿ*) permitted?

A. No. It is an enormity (*kabīra*) (quoting the *Dhakhīra*). Those *mashā'ikh* who permit movement restrict it to tremor only, but there is no lawful authority even for tremor.

ʿAwārif: It ill becomes the *mashā'ikh* whose example is followed because it resembles entertainment and loss of control of oneself.

Q. Is chanting permitted?

A. To intone the Quran or a homily is permissable and desirable, but to intone a song is forbidden because to sing or to listen to singing is forbidden. The ulama are unanimously and emphatically agreed on this. Sufi Shaykhs permit such a practice to such persons as have renounced the flesh (*al-hawā*) and clothed themselves in piety and need such a practice as a sick man needs medicine. The symptoms of this condition are that one has abandoned his carnal desires, is drawn to meditate on God (*dhikr Allah*) in his moments of seclusion, neither gives nor takes, is free from praise and blame, etc...**[38]** Granted that men are religiously qualified in this way, they may intone on the following conditions: *9B*

(i) they should have no beardless boy in their company;

(ii) they should be all like-minded and have in their midst no evil-liver, no men of worldly interests and no woman;

(iii) the cantor (*qawwāl*) should be motivated by sincere intentions, seeking neither fee nor food in return for his services;

(iv) they should not meet for the sake of food nor with an eye to monetary rewards;

(v) they should only perform when moved involuntary (*maghlūbīn*);

(vi) they should display no ecstasy (*wajd*) that is not truly genuine...

All this means that nowadays mystical expression in music and dance is not allowed because such expression was renounced by Junayd in his day because of a lack of suitable company (*ikhwān*), a sincere cantor (*qawwāl*) uncontaminated by carnal passion (*hawā*).

Q. If a religious mendicant wishes to kiss the hand of the person from whom he is begging, should that person hold out his hand or withold it?

A. *Muḥīt*: To kiss a hand in hope of worldly reward is reprehensible.**[39]**

Sunāmī: It is best not to extend one's hand to a mendicant ... ...

Q. Some mendicants beat drums and tambourines at the doors of houses – is this permitted?

A. No. Drums must only be beaten for war or to assemble people departing on a journey.

Sunāmī: such a mendicant must be sent away empty-handed and reprimanded for so behaving. A more monstrous type is the sort of mendicant who intones at one's door. He should be given nothing and be prohibited from engaging in this objectionable practice (*munkar*).

(Hadith quoted). Allusion to Abraham's being reproached for withholding food from Magians ... *10A* ...

Q. Some mendicants sit on busy thoroughfares (*qawāriʿ*) displaying garments on which are depicted the graves and towns of men who were the recipients of God's blessing (*mutabarrakia*) and they play *mizmār* (a single-pipe wind instrument) while the stupid and ignorant gather round. What should be done with them?

A. They are forbidden to carry on and if the *muḥtasib* thinks it in the public interest he should tear up the garment. No civil liability is thereby entailed. He is in the same position as one who breaks up musical instruments (*maʿāzif*). **[40]**

Some mendicants are innovators in that they let their hair grow long and let it gather dust, filth and lice. They neither anoint, cut, comb, nor part their hair. It is an innovation because

(i) the Prophet would anoint his head every day (*ghab*);

(ii) it is a practice of a certain type of Indian;

(iii) it breaches a recommended rule of cleanliness.

If a mendicant says [quotation in Persian] 'Poverty is a great misfortune', this is a grave error on his part.

One forbidden practice encountered amongst mendicants is that of wearing wool to indicate that they are religious mendicants. To do this is an enormity (*kabīra*). (Quoted from *Tafsīr al-kashshāf*).[285]

Sources: *FAL*
ShK
ShI
BA
H
TM
Dh
AM

285 Like the other quotations from *Kashshāf*, it has been impossible to trace this quotation. it seems therefore, likely that the author uses another book entitled *Tafsīr al-Kashshāf* which is not Zamakhsharī's, especially given his condemnation of this book qv.Chap 33. 43B.

Muḥ
Kash

[41]

CHAPTER 7
The Powers of the *Muḥtasib* to Assist a Victim of Injustice to Seek Redress against the Perpetrator thereof

The subject of this chapter (*bāb*) is an unusual one. It should be memorised well.
Case 1 (from Karkhī's Commentary): A sees B kill C, who is A's father. B denies that the homicide is unjustifiable, or he says to A privately, 'I have killed your father because he murdered mine' (or, say, 'because he apostatized from Islam'). A is wholly unacquainted with the facts alleged by B, and he is, moreover, C's only heir. He is therefore entitled to take B's life if he so wishes. Should another party D have actually seen B killing C, he is entitled to assist A to take B's life. Similarly, even if D did not actually witness *10B* the killing of C but only heard B's confession (*iqrār*), D may assist A to take B's life. The same applies to anyone who saw the act or heard the confession. The grounds for such action is that once A actually saw B kill C – A's father – the duty of legal retaliation (*qiṣāṣ*) devolved upon him in a *clear* case of the fact (*fī al-ẓāhir*). In B's case, however, his claim that the homicide is justifiable may or may not be true, and justification of an act cannot repose on the probability. It is on this last ground that B's life may lawfully be taken. Furthermore, a confession is as valid evidence as eye-witness report. To assist A is lawful because the assistance is rendered for the purpose of ensuring that the full requirements of justice are fulfilled.[286]

If in place of a confession, the testimony [of two witnesses] is available, and if such testimony is offered on the direction of a judge (qadi), that testimony permits the same course of action to be taken as a confession. On the other hand, if such testimony is not offered in the direction of a judge, A may not take B's life, nor is it lawful for any person hearing the testimony to assist A in homicide because justification is not consequent on a judge's direction.**[42]**
Sunāmī: If any ordinary Muslim may render assistance to A, the *muḥtasib* has all the more reason to render assistance.
Case 2 (from Karkhī's Commentary): A has in his possession a slave or garment, and two witnesses testify that the slave or garment was the property of C, the [deceased] father of B, and that A has thus usurped B's right to such property. If A

286 The sanction permitting a son to kill his father's killer is contained in Quran xvii: 33: 'And if anyone is slain wrongfully, We have given his heir authority (sultan)'. Sarakhsī, *Mabsūṭ*: 10: 181.

denies the allegation and claims the property to be his, B must not dispossess A of the property until the witnesses have been directed to testify by a judge, and that for the reason previously stated, *viz* testimony is no ground for justification prior to a judge's ruling. On the other hand, if B actually saw A deprive C of the property, B is entitled to recover it even by physically defending his right to it, and B may be assisted by any other eye-witness even if A denies the allegation, provided that B has no other recourse by reason of his being in a place where he cannot take his case before a supreme authority (sultan) to obtain his rights. The grounds for such action is that justification rests on his actually having the act of usurpation. A confession is likewise sufficient ground for action against A. If B has no other alternative – but only if – he may kill in defence of his right because A is a perpetrator of injustice (*ẓālim*). The Prophet said, 'He who is killed while defending his property is a martyr'.

The reason for introducing these two cases is now explained.

Sunāmī: the *muḥtasib*'s sphere of competence is less than that of a judge on only one point in three: he has no authority to act on testimony as long as such testimony is not the subject of direction by a judge. But he has the power to act on his own initiative if he is an eye-witness to the grounds for action, *11A* or if he hears a confession of guilt.**[43]**

Sources: *ShK*

CHAPTER 8
The Powers of the *Muḥtasib* with regard to Women

A free woman may not travel in the company of a male who does not fall within the prohibited degrees; she may not travel with her slave or outside her immediate family (*ajnabī*), be he a full male or a eunuch who has been either wholly or partially emasculated.

A free woman must not be allowed to uncover her face or her hand or her foot in such a way that it can be seen by an *ajnabī* because she cannot be sure that some onlooker may be roused to sexual passion. It is permissable to look on the face of an oldish woman (*ʿajūz*) and to shake hands with her since she does not arouse sexual feeling.

Karkhī's Commentary: to look at the face of a free woman outside the family is not forbidden but reprehensible if one has no need to look at it. This is because of the danger of arousing sexual desire.

It is best for a woman not to visit any grave but that of the Prophet. (Hadith quoted.) To visit the tomb of someone the woman has not seen at the time of his death is excusable.

Hadith: ᶜĀ'isha visited the tomb of ᶜAbd al-Raḥmān b. Abū Bakr after he had been brought it for burial, but only did so because she had not seen him prior to his death.[44]

Sarkhasī: ᶜĀ'isha only did so in this case because she wished the visit to make up for her not having seen ᶜAbd al-Raḥmān b. Abū Bakr in life. It is therefore best not to visit graves.

A woman should be censured for going to the public bath (*ḥammām*) without her husband's permission or without being veiled. She may, however, go to the bath without her husband's permission provided she is veiled *11B* and has good reason, e.g. she has been sick or been going through the post-partum period. Some hold – and Sarakhsī inclines to this view – that a woman may go to the bath with her husband's permission but without any special reason provided that she is veiled.[287] Others hold that this is not the case. (Story about ᶜĀ'isha quoted in support of this last view.)

There is no harm in a woman using a saddle when riding if she is veiled and has a good reason for doing so, e.g. she is on the Greater or Lesser Pilgrimage or on the jihad. The womenfolk of the *Muhājirūn* rode horses and went on the jihad, and they were not forbidden to do so by the Prophet. Also the daughters of Khālid b. Walīd rode and went on the jihad to give water to combatants in the field and to tend the wounded.

Action must be taken against women wearing bells on their feet. Little girls are forbidden to wear such ornaments and so there is all the more reason for the practice to be reprehensible in grown women. They attract attention to what should be concealed and are, in addition, frivolous.

If a man and a woman not of the same family are alone together, action must be taken because such a situation is prohibited. If a man has a legal right over a woman, however, he can be with her, sit with her, and take hold of her clothes.

If a woman escapes and takes refuge in a deserted house, there is no harm in a man's going after her provided he has control of himself. If he has not, he must keep away and just keep the woman under observation. To be alone with a woman in such circumstances is justified by necessity (*ḍarūra*).

Some may argue as follows: 'In our territory the *muḥtasib*'s officers (*aᶜwān*) may take prostitutes by the hand and administer corrective punishment, though it is forbidden for a man to touch a woman unrelated to him'. But the fact is that they are committing a sure and certain unlawful act (*ḥarām mutayaqqin*) to prevent one that is only a supposition (*maẓnūn*).

Sunāmī: touching means direct contact with the hand without any barrier to such contact.[45] In cases of ordinary necessity (*ḍarūra dunyawiyya*) a man may touch an unrelated woman if there is some barrier to direct contact and the more so in the case

287 See Sarakhsī, *Sharḥ*: 1:136.

of religious necessity. It is lawful for a man to take the hand of a woman who has fallen into some mud or mire if some garment is a barrier to direct contact.

A man should employ a maidservant inside the house but not an adult male slave because temptation in slaves is greater than that in free men who are unrelated *12A* [to the women within]. This is because slaves are immodest. It is said that a man who employs a male servant in domestic service is a cripple.

For the purposes under discussion a full male and a castrated male (*khaṣī*) are to be equated as also is a male who has been stripped of all genitalia (*majbūb*) but whose seminal fluid has not yet dried up since he can still ejaculate on the application of friction and on that count is open to temptation. According to some Ḥanafī authorities (*mashā'ikhunā*), a *majbūb* whose seminal fluid has dried up may be employed in a house. (Quotes commentators on Quran xxiv:31). But [according to *Sunāmī*] the soundest opinion is that there should be no exceptions.[288]

An adult female slave should not be put on sale without her having her back and belly covered because the back and the belly of a maidservant are (classified as) pudenda.

<u>*Khāniyya*</u>: if a man is told that a woman is being insubordinate [or committing a sin] and wishes to write to her husband in the knowledge that his writing will serve a useful purpose and enable him to restrain her, then he may write. But if he knows that the man can do nothing to restrain her, he should not do so lest the couple be brought into conflict one with the other.

Q. May prostitutes have their head and arms bare when subjected to corrective punishment?

A. Yes, because they do not respect themselves and thus deserve none from others.**[46]** (Situations attributed to ᶜUmar and Abū Bakr al-Aᶜmash and quoted from Jaṣṣaṣ's *Sharḥ adab al-qāḍī* are cited by way of evidence).[289]

---

288 In the eastern part of the Islamic world there are three kinds of castrated eunuch:
(a) Clean-shaven eunuchs who have had both penis and testicles swept off by a single cut of a razor. A tube is set in the urethra, and the wound is cauterized with boiling oil.
(b) The eunuch whose penis has been removed. He retains all the desire for copulation and the procreation without the wherewithal. Sunāmī calls this type of eunuch *majbūb*, one whose seminal fluid has not dried up.
(c) The eunuchs who have been rendered sexless by the removal of the testicles.
N. Penzer, *The Harem* (London 1967): 143.
In accordance with the above definitions, Sunāmī's term 'castrated', in the sense of one whose spermatozoa is inactive, can only be applied to types (a) and (c). Also see Hughes: 310.
Sunāmī also uses the term *'innīn*, a general term for any man who is sexually impotent. *Muḥīt al-muḥīṭ:* 2: 1487.

289 See *Sharḥ adab al-qāḍī*, MS no. 273:68B.

From Shaᶜbī's *Kifāya*: in the waiting period following the dissolution of a marriage by death or irremovable divorce (*ṭalāq bā'in*) a woman should not leave her husband's house and [in the case of a divorcée] even with her husband's permission. From *Fatāwā al-Ẓahīriyya*:[290] *12B* in the waiting period a woman (*muᶜtadda*) should avoid cosmetics of any kind (eye-black (*kuḥl*), henna, dye (*khiḍāb*), oil (*duhn*), etc.) and should use neither jewellery nor scent nor wear anything that has been scented or dyed with safflower or saffron unless such garments are resistant to washing (to remove scent and dye).

Silk and brocade (*qaṣab*) must not be worn.

Q. What action should a *muḥtasib* take against a man and woman if he sees them conversing in a street?

A. ᶜUmar gave a whip-lash to a man and woman whom he caught conversing in the street. The man complained that the woman was his wife, whereupon ᶜUmar asked him why he could not take her home and converse there. Nevertheless, ᶜUmar regretted his action **[47]** and consulted Ubayy b. Kaᶜb. The latter upheld ᶜUmar's judgment.[291] (Hadith quoted.) *13A*

Q. Women are in the habit of visiting certain graves that are regarded as a means of obtaining blessing (*maqābir mutabarraka*). Are they to earn reward or censure?

A. From Shaᶜbī's *Kifāya* (Ch. on Women's Visits to Graves on Thursdays): They will be accursed.[292] (Hadith quoted.) **[48]**

Case (summary of Ṭaḥāwī in his *Sharḥ*): 13B A woman's closest male relative within the prohibited degrees is the person with the greatest right to bury a woman, and after him all nearest male relatives within the prohibited degrees take precedence over persons outside the family (*ajānib*). In the absence of such relatives, it is in order for males outside the family to carry out the duty of burial, and there is no need for women to become involved in the procedure.

Q. If a woman enters another person's house without the permission of the master of the house, what action should be taken against her?

A. If the woman is a close blood relative (*dhāt raḥim muḥarram*) of the master of the house, she may enter it without his permission. The same rule applies if her husband is likewise closely related by blood to the master of the house. This is an unusual case that should be remembered by various scholars.

Case (*Muḥīṭ* quoted): Should a woman steal from the house of her husband's relatives within the prohibited degrees, amputation of the hand does not, according to Abū Ḥanīfa, apply [it is not a *ḥadd* offence].

---

290 See *Kifāya*, MS no. 1698: 297A.

291 *Ibid*: 296B.

292 *Ibid*: 321A.

In all other cases of a woman entering a house, appropriate *ḥisba* action must be taken in accordance with Quran xxiv, 27: 'Do not enter houses apart from your own unless you have asked permission'.

Case (*Tajnīs wa-l-mazīd* quoted): A woman in a state of ritual consecration for the *ḥajj* (*muḥrima*) should loose the veil about her face but her face should not be looked on.**[49]** This case proves that a woman must not be allowed to show her face needlessly to males outside her immediate family (*ajānib*). If she is forbidden to cover her face for the rites of *ḥajj* (*bi-ḥaqq al-nusuk*), this implies that it is to be covered on all other occasions when she is outside the home.

Case from *Nawāzil, K. al-nikāḥ*: Abū Bakr ruled that a woman must not crop her hair even if she has her husband's permission. The practice is forbidden because by cropping her hair she makes herself like a man, and men must not make themselves like women nor women like men. As a man should not cut off his beard so a woman should not cut off her hair.

Q. What if a woman adds someone else's hair to her own?

A. This is not permitted, and any tire-woman (*mashshāṭa*) who engages in such an activity must be censured so that she abandons the practice.

A woman who assumes masculine habits must be excluded from other people's houses. *14A*

Mughrib summarized: The Prophet's curse is upon those women who depilate themselves and others, those who file their own teeth and those of others, those who add extra hair to their own and others' heads and upon those who tattoo themselves or others. Tattooing is defined as ulceration and pricking of the skin which is then packed with indigo and kohl or has charcoal or other blackening substances introduced into it. The Prophet cursed those who engaged in such practices either in an active or passive role.**[50]**

Sources: *ShK*
FKh
ShAQ
KSh
FẒ
ShṬK
Muḥ
TM
N
Mugh

CHAPTER 9
(TS)
On Young Males Persons (*Ghilmān*)

It is reprehensible for a male child to wear bells on his feet. The hands and feet of a boy (*ṣabī*) must not be dyed with henna. It is forbidden for a boy to drink wine or to eat the flesh of an animal which has died [that has not been ritually slaughtered]. The sin consequent upon such actions attaches to those responsible for the administering of the wine and the serving of the meat.

Multaqaṭ: anklets (*khalkhāl*) and bracelets (*siwār*) for male children are reprehensible.

Multaqaṭ: if a young male person measures up to the same standards as men and does not have a pretty look about him, one treats him as a man. But if he does have a pretty look about him, one treats him as a woman, the *ʿawra* in his case extending from the parting of his hair to his feet, that is to say one may not look at him with a sexual intent (*ʿan shahwa*). There is no harm in greeting him and looking at him provided there is no sexual intent, and for this reason he must not be instructed to wear a veil (*niqāb*). Narratives, Traditions etc. are cited on the subject of looking at young males persons with sexual intent. In *Kifāya al-shaʿbiyya*, a story is related about a scholar who died. He was seen by someone in a dream. His face was black. When asked why his face was blackened, he replied that he had glanced at a good-looking youth with lust. This caused his face to be blackened in Hell.[293] It is also related that a devout man was seen after his death in a dream. He said that all his sins save one were forgiven by Allah, when he had asked for forgiveness. He was embarrassed to ask Allah for this sin's forgiveness, and this sin caused him to be severely punished. When asked as to the nature of this sin, he replied that he had looked at a youth with lust. It is also narrated that ʿAbd Allāh b. ʿUmar went into his house when he saw a good-looking youth approaching him. He only emerged when told that he had passed. He commented that **[51]** the Prophet said looking *14B* at them is *ḥarām*, talking to them is *ḥarām*, and it is *ḥarām* to be in their company.

Khāniyya: The father of a son who has a pretty look about him and is still beardless may forbid him to go out for the purposes of study (*ṭalab al-ʿilm*). By analogy the *muḥtasib* should not allow men to unnecessarily frequent the company of male persons who are pretty and are still beardless. Muḥammad b. al-Ḥasan was good-looking and during his classes Abū Ḥanīfa would have him sit behind him or behind a pillar in the mosque so that he might not see him for fear of committing a visual crime (*khiyānat al-ʿayn*), and yet Abū Ḥanīfa was a man of consummate piety.

---

293 See *Kifāya*, MS No. 1698: 275A.

Abū al-Layth's *Bustān*: to keep the company of youths, boys, and shameless men is reprehensible because it takes away one's dignity.
Taḥāwī's *Sharḥ al-kabīr*: it is reprehensible for men and boys to wear silk and gold (Prophet quoted). If it is argued that the prohibition may be taken as not applicable to boys. The answer is that it is. Tradition from Jābir quoted – silk should be left to girls.

Anyone administering wine to his son should be subjected to corrective punishment and not retributive punishment (*ḥadd*) (quoted from Multaqaṭ). If a reprobate administers wine to his son or tells him to take wine and his relations then come and scatter dirhams and sweetmeats, they have acted as unbelievers.**[52]**

Sources: *MN*
KSh
FKh
BA
ShṬK
Muḥ

CHAPTER 10
On Eating, Drinking and Medical Treatment

It is reprehensible for a man to eat the crumb of bread and then leave the crusts if he is going to waste them, but not if he is going to give them to someone else to eat because he is then in the position of someone who chooses to eat one loaf rather than another.

To wipe one's knife and fingers with a loaf without afterwards eating it is reprehensible. Some religious authorities (*mashāyikh*) disapprove of the practice even if it is eaten, while others see no harm in it.

To wash your hands *15A* with bran provided it no longer contains flour is not reprehensible, but to use flour for the same purpose is. To eat in a recumbent position is reprehensible if such a position is adopted out of haughtiness. Otherwise it is not.

To eat clay (*ṭīn*) is reprehensible.
Al-Ḥalwānī: it is reprehensible if the substance is harmful, but if only a little is taken or if it is taken infrequently, no harm is done.
Sunāmī: by analogy it is permissible to eat lime with the kind of leaves that are eaten in India because only a little is taken and it is beneficial. It is permissible because the purpose for which the leaves are eaten cannot be achieved without the lime.**[53]**

It is reprehensible to put the salt-cellar on the bread, but not salt, of course. It is reprehensible to hang bread from a canopy (*khuwān*)[294] or to put it under a big bowl (*qaṣᶜa*), though some say that it is not.

To eat or drink from polytheists' vessels before washing them is reprehensible – but not forbidden – owing to the possibility of pollution.

Sunāmī: one thing we have to contend with is the purchase of clarified butter, vinegar, *leban*, milk and other liquids and semi-liquids (*mā'iᶜāt*) from Hindus because of the likelihood of pollution in their vessels since their women pay no attention to dung.[295] They [the Hindus] eat the flesh of such animals as they kill – in other words, ritually unclean meat. But, if one is obliged to deal with them, the *muḥtasib* must ensure that they have no contact with dung or ritually unclean meat. If this proves difficult, he must at least ask them to give their vessels to a Muslim for washing and to wash their hands under the direct supervision of a Muslim. If this is impossible, there is nothing one can do except to be ever vigilant. It says in the Quran (v, 4–5): 'They will question you on what is permitted for them. Say "The good things are permitted you ... the food of those who were given the Book is permitted to you" ' without any distinction being made between a slaughtered beast or otherwise'.

All food supplied by Zoroastrians (*Majūs*) is acceptable apart from the flesh of a slaughtered beast, for that is forbidden.

To take away food from your host's table is completely forbidden unless your host permits it.

To use wine or anything else that is prescribed for medicinal purposes is completely forbidden unless a cure can be absolutely **[54]** guaranteed by its use. There is no disagreement about its impermissibility [because in the case of something that is forbidden there must be no possible doubt about its efficacy]. If a cure [from something that is forbidden] can be absolutely guaranteed, but there is at the same time an alternative medicament capable of producing the same result, it is held by some that it is still not permissible to use anything that is *ḥarām* because of Ibn Masᶜūd's observation, *15B* 'God will not effect cures for you from things which He has forbidden you'. On the other hand, it is held by others that a medicament [that is normally *ḥarām*] is permissible by analogy with the use of wine to quench [desperate] thirst. The *responsum* indicated by Tradition is that unless a thing is no longer *ḥaram* as a result of necessity, it should not be used for healing purposes. The *muḥtasib* should therefore send a legal representative to the physicians to ensure that

---

294 The practice of hanging bread from a canopy is also common in some Arab countries like Iraq. It is normally done to cool the hot bread and to distinguish bakeries from other shops.

295 The veneration of dung by Hindus is a well-known practice in India. Ibn Baṭṭūṭa also reported this practice. Ibn Baṭṭūṭa, *Riḥla*: 435–7.

they do not prescribe for a sick person anything involving the use of forbidden substances except in the circumstances described.

Cuppers, phlebotomist and leechers should be warned against treating a pregnant woman before the child shows movement or is near the time of delivery because treatment could be dangerous at these times. Once the child has moved and as long as the delivery is not near, there is no harm in such treatment.

One should not wait for other dishes once bread has been served, but, rather, begin to eat before the other dishes arrive out of respect for the bread. The Prophet said, 'Honour bread; it is one of the blessings of heaven and earth'.

Sunāmī: this rule is especially applicable in one's own house. In someone else's house one waits for the host's permission to start.

In Abū Ḥanīfa's view, horse-meat is disapproved of. Anyone who eats it should be told not to do so and be reproved, but not beaten or imprisoned because there are differences of opinion on the subject.

It is reprehensible to slaughter a pregnant ewe if she is about to lamb.**[55]** (quoted form *Multaqaṭ* 'On Slaughtering Animals').

Tradition from Abū al-Layth's *Bustān*: meat must not be cut with knives as is done by non-Arabs, but bitten.[296] The Tradition does not convey a *nahy al-taḥrīm* but a *nahy al-shafaqa*. It concerns imitation of non-Arabs and involves *karāha*.**[56]**

Sources: *MN*
BA

CHAPTER 11
(S)
On Playing Games

To play chess, backgammon or 'fourteen' (*arbaᶜat ashar*) is reprehensible, and in this context reprehensible means forbidden.

Jāmiᶜ al-saghīr (on chess): gambling (*qimār*) is forbidden by *ijmāᶜ*. All else [in the way of games] is amusement and is also forbidden by Quran (xxiii, 115) as well as Prophetic Tradition, which allows only the exercising of horses, archery practice, and diverting oneself with the family. *16A Maysar* is taken by 'Aṭā' to denote all kinds of *qimār* (games of chance), even the children's game of knuckle-bones.

Argument in favour of chess refuted (Tradition from ᶜAlī quoted): the pieces represent animate beings; it diverts attention from prayer, and leads to idle talk. It is no argument to say that chess helps instruct in the art of war... **[57]**. Story of a Persian's attitude to chess. Question of whether chess is lawful if the purpose is to train the mind and sharpen one's wits. The answer to those who argue that Shāfiᶜī is

296 A quotation from Abū al-Layth, *Bustān*: 65.

quoted as declaring that there is no harm in playing chess is that Ghazālī in his *Khulāṣa* gives a contradictory report of Shāfiᶜī. It may well be therefore that the first opinion was the earlier of two contrary opinions. *16B* **[58]**

Sources: *JṢKh*
Dh
TM
Khul

CHAPTER 12
(TS)
On Judges (*Quḍāt*) and their Enforcement Officers (*Aᶜwān*)

A qadi should not accept a private invitation (*daᶜwa khāṣṣā*) as, for example, from someone returning from a journey. He should accept gifts from no-one but a near relative (*dhū raḥim muḥarram*) or those to whom he was wont to give presents before appointment to the office of judge and who are not parties to a lawsuit of which he is judge. The authority (*wālī*) who has appointed a judge may give him presents because it is clear that such a person's gifts are not intended to influence his judgments in his favour. Moreover, a judge cannot be more powerful than the man who appoints him.

Jaṣṣāṣ's Sharḥ adab al-qāḍī: authorities differ on the question of whether acceptance to the appointment to the office of judge is optional. The correct view is that such acceptance is a divine permission (*rukhṣa*) and refusal is preferred by God because it reflects greater piety (*ᶜazīma*).

Ẓahīriyya: a judge may not ask for the loan of fungible or non-fungible objects. A judge must not engage in sale himself, but delegate such business to someone else.

Muḥammad: there is no harm in a judge's transacting a sale outside his court.

The correct view is that a judge may engage in a sale neither in the court nor out of it because he will be treated leniently and the effect will be the same as an acceptance of a bribe. A judge should not assist either party to a case which he is hearing nor pronounce a *fatwā*. A judge's usher (*bawwāb*) may not accept anything in return for allowing someone to enter.**[59]**

Multaqaṭ: Chapter 'On Manumission': a man drew up an instrument, supplying forged testimony of well-known persons. The slave to whom the document related fled. The misdemeanour of the writer entails *taᶜzīr* but not civil liability.

Multaqaṭ: a judge was asked about the case of a man who had killed a weaver, what shall we do with him? The judge answered mockingly. He was then summoned before the Caliph Ma'mūn and said that he had jested. Ma'mūn had him beaten for mocking God's ordinances and he died under the lash.

Al-Faqīh: *ta'zīr* would have been sufficient in this case.

It is forbidden to add clauses such as are commonly added on oaths not sworn by the name of God to contracts of the bride-price (*khuṭūṭ al-muhūr*). Anyone swearing oaths of this kind commits a sin (*ithm*), and a notary who includes such is a party to his transgression. A notary must not be a party to such acts (supporting Tradition from ʿUmar).

A judge should not ask for a larger fee for the performance of a notarial duty or for a written judgement (*sijill*) than anyone else. There is a practice *17A* among judges in our country today which is flagrantly wrong, namely that of taking a fee in respect of marriages, after which the legal guardians of the two parties to the marriage are permitted to proceed with the execution of the marriage. Unless they receive a satisfactory consideration judges withhold permission. Such a practice is forbidden to both parties.**[60]** If anyone making such a payment has no option but to do so, he is not culpable, but if he has, he is committing a sin, and his action is tantamount to bribery. The party receiving payment always commits a sin, but not always the party who pays, if he does so under duress. Otherwise he is.

Hidāya and other works: The practice of appointing one man as a paid partitioner (*qassām*) of deceased persons' estates is forbidden. The *muḥtasib* must instruct the qadi who compels people to accept such a practice to desist from unlawful activity.**[61]**

Sources: *ShAQ*
FZ̧
MN
KSh
H

CHAPTER 13
(TS)
Regulations Governing the Administration of Cemeteries

Multaqaṭ: an old cemetery no longer bearing signs of being such may not be used for building or grazing or riding of animals (*dābba*), much less for foraging.

Multaqaṭ 'On Wills': a body may be buried in an old grave where there are no longer traces of old bones or anything else. If a grave is dug and found to contain the bones of a deceased person, the bones must not be disturbed. A Prophetic Tradition forbids walking on graves and more so burials above previous burials.

Fatāwa al-Khāniyya 'Section on the Lawful and Unlawful': if A digs a grave on B's land to bury C, a corpse belonging to A, but the grave was used by D, there is no question of exhumation, but D is liable for the amount required to dig another grave for the burial of C.

Abū Yūsuf: if a body is buried on another's land without his – the owner's – permission, the owner may have the body disinterred and the land levelled above and sown.

Muḥammad in the *Dhakhīra*: 'On the Waqf': if anyone else assigns his land for use as a Muslim cemetery, he may do so, but he may not recant after completion (*tamām*). By this term is meant that one human being, or more, is buried there with his **[62]** permission.

Whether it should be stipulated that the land be entrusted to a keeper (*mutawallī*) is a controversial matter, *17B* but in a matter of burial, poor and rich enjoy the same status.

Whether the cemeteries of Zoroastrians (*Majūs*) may be transformed into Muslim cemeteries is a question to which there are two sides. If all traces of the use of the cemetery by Zoroastrians have been effaced, there is no harm in such transformation. But if such traces still exist and if any bones remain, they are to be removed. The site of the Messenger of God's mosque was a polytheists' cemetery that was dug up and used as a mosque.

Ṭaḥāwī at the end of the Section *'Ṣalāt'*: Abū Ḥanīfa disapproved of graves being walked upon or sat upon as well as the relieving of the calls of nature in cemeteries with the deposition of urine, excrement, and so on.

Sleeping on graves or performing the *ṣalāt* in the vicinity of them is also reprehensible.

Answer to the question whether one may lay one's head on a grave is to be found in Abū Qulāba's story of his experience of so doing and seeing the occupant in a dream. He said, 'I arrived in Baṣra from Sham during the night. I washed myself near the moat and prayed two *rakʿa* and then laid my head on a grave and went to sleep. I saw in a dream the grave's occupant, who said that he had been disturbed by me sleeping on his grave'. Abū Qulāba's conclusion was that the practice disturbs the dead.**[63]**

Sources: *MN*
FKh
Dh
ShṬK

CHAPTER 14
(TS)
On Reporting Unlawful Practices (*Munkarāt*)

A man may report another to the ruling authority (sultan) for engaging in unlawful practices.

Al-khāniyya: Only if one knows that the ruling authority has the power to put an end to unlawful practices, should one make a report. There is no point in creating pointless animosity. (Prophetic Tradition quoted).**[64]**
Sources: *FKh*

CHAPTER 15
On the Mosque (*Masjid*)

It is not permissible for a man to sell in the communal mosque (*al-jāmiʿ*) an amulet containing words from the Torah, the Gospel, or the Quran and to receive *18A* money for it while declaring that he is making a present of it. If he is making a present of it, he cannot take money for it, and the rule is of general application, and not restricted to the mosque. Appropriate action must therefore, be taken in the mosque and elsewhere.

To wipe one's feet on dust that has been scattered on the floor of the mosque or on reed mats (*bawārī*) is not permissible. There is no harm in using a pile of dust or a mat (*ḥaṣīr*) that has holes in it.[297]

It is reprehensible for teachers (*muʿallim*) and copyists (*warrāq*) to work in the mosque if they are being paid for so doing unless they have no alternative.
Khāniyya and Muḥammad b. Salama: on the grounds of necessity (*ḍarūra*), there is no harm in a man's plying his trade as a tailor and sewing in a mosque while at the same time safeguarding it against intrusion of children and pack-animals.

Objection must be made to those who perform supererogatory prayers in the oratory (*muṣallā*) before the ʿĪd prayer and those who perform the funeral prayer (*ṣalāt al-janāza*) in the mosque in which the communal prayer (*jamāʿa*) is being performed because that is reprehensible.

No one must be allowed to climb on the roof of the Kaaba or of any mosque.**[65]** Such a practice is reprehensible.[298]

No well may be sunk in a mosque, but a pre-existing well such as Zamzam may be left as it is.

---

297 Here Sunāmī is referring to *tayamum*, which is a substitute for ablution (*wuḍūʾ*). *Tayamum* consists of two beats with the hand on a clean piece of ground or dust, rubbing the face after the first beat and the arms after the second. Anything which was originally from the earth may be used instead, including sand, kohl, and stones. Marghinānī, *Hidāya*: 1:25.

298 Sunāmī's statement prohibiting climbing on the roof of the Kaaba or any mosque is probably out of respect for these holy places. A similar idea can be found in the *Hidāya* concerning Mount Abū Qubays in Makka. Marghinānī, *Hidāya*: 1:95.

It is reprehensible for a tailor to sew garments in a mosque because ᶜUthmān saw a man doing just that and, disapproving of it, had him expelled from the mosque.

It is reprehensible to perform the prayer facing any human because it gives the impression that one is magnifying that person.

One must not expectorate either under or on top of mats. (Tradition quoted.) Mats belong to mosques and are appurtenances of them. One should, therefore, deposit mucus discharges on one's sleeve or some other part of one's clothing. If one has absolutely no alternative, it is better to deposit mucus on top of the mats because mats are not really an integral part of the mosque.

Trees may be planted in the mosque if they are for the public good by virtue of the shade they cast and provided they neither cause obstruction nor intersect the rows (*ṣufūf*) for prayer. They may not, however, be planted for such personal benefit as may accrue from their leaves or their fruit. Moreover, they must neither intersect the rows nor be so located that the mosque resembles a synagogue (*bīᶜa*).

It is reprehensible to allow a beggar in a mosque to disturb the congregation by stepping over them. One should not give him alms if he is behaving in such a way, for to do so is to aid and abet him in his sin.

Multaqaṭ: it is reprehensible to give alms to the poor of the Great Mosque *18B* because to do so is to encourage them to step on people. Our authorities (*mashāyikh*) are very strict on this point. (Khalaf b. Ayyūb and Abū Bakr Ismāᶜīl al-Zāhid quoted.)

Multaqaṭ: should the nest of a swallow or bat be causing defilement in the mosque, it may be thrown out together with any young it may contain.**[66]**

Shaᶜbi's *Kifāya*: the judge (qadi) was asked about the case of giving alms to beggars in the mosque. He categorically prohibited such an action if it is performed during the sermon (*khuṭba*). During the sermon even the most important acts of worship or praise of God are to be prevented. The beggar may be given alms if only he begs before the *khuṭba* and does not cross the worshippers' lines or disturb their prayer. Otherwise to give him charity is *ḥaram* and the sin that he commits is shared by any who donates money to him. The Prophet is reported to have said, 'On the Day of Judgment a voice will call upon God's enemies to stand up, only the disruptive beggars will rise'. The reason for this strictness is that the mosques are built for God's worship and not for making money. God said [mosques are only for God] (lxxii:18). He who begs is actually complaining about God before God's friends and this would cause God's anger. *19A* Sunāmī's view is that on the basis of Tradition and common sense, alms should never be given to beggars in the Great Mosque.**[67]** Alsmgiving and the right of a beggar are generally recognized providing there is no question of stepping on people in a mosque. In the *Khāniyya*, Abū Naṣr al-ᶜIyāḍ declared that he prays for God's forgiveness for anyone who drives beggars out of mosques in recognition of his service in so doing, and from this Sunāmī concludes that the *muḥtasib* may expel beggars from the Great Mosque. According to *Tajnīs wa-l-mazīd*, it is allowed to give alms to the beggar so long as he does not pass across the prayer lines and is not insistent in begging. The principle of giving to a beggar is acceptable since there were beggars in mosques during the time of the Prophet. ᶜAlī is reported to have given his ring to one of them while praying and God praised ᶜAlī for this incident in the following verse [they give charity while in prostration] (v:55).

Sunāmī's view is that the *muḥtasib*'s enforcement officers (*aᶜwān*) should not drive the poor away by shouting at them during the *khuṭba* but by signalling to them. (Tradition quoted.) In *Aḥkām al-Qur'ān*, Abū Bakr al-Jaṣṣāṣ notes that according to the Prophet's Traditions, the mosque should be kept free from children, lunatics, raised voices, selling, buying and the execution of *ḥadd* penalties.**[68]** Sunāmī declares that when he was concerned with *ḥisba* he used to apply this rule. He would give orders for the mosque to be cleared of children and lunatics on the occasion of Friday prayer. *19B* He also forbade the sale of water, fans, toothsticks (*siwāk*), and other goods which it had previously been the custom to sell.

The *Khāniyya* allows a person trading in a religious retreat (*muᶜtakif*) to buy and sell – by which is meant food and other things which are indispensable. Ordinary trading, however, is reprehensible. (Tradition quoted.)

Ẓahīriyya: to perform the lesser ablution in a mosque unless there is a place provided for the purpose is reprehensible as is also the practice of taking a short cut through the mosque unless there is a good reason.

There is no harm in sitting in a mosque for a purpose other than the performance of ritual prayer, but civil liability attaches to the act if any damage results therefrom. To sit in a mosque for three days or even less to mourn a catastrophe is reprehensible. A man may, however, sit for three days elsewhere, but it is preferable not to do so. (*Khāniyya* and *Muḥīṭ*).

To perform the ritual prayer on top of the Kaaba or to climb to its top surface is reprehensible unless there is a need to repair it.

Moreover, it is reprehensible to climb on the roof of any mosque. If the weather is very hot, **[69]** it is reprehensible for people to perform the Friday prayer on a roof unless the mosque is too small to take all the worshippers. One may climb on the roof out of necessity (*ḍarūra*), but heat does not constitute necessity. It only makes the prayer a greater hardship and entails a greater recompense [in the hereafter]. (*Muḥīṭ et al.*)

Muḥīṭ 'On Pious Endowments' (*waqf*): the question of a mosque that has become too small for its users and cannot contain them unless they extend it. A neighbour asks them to assign the mosque to him so that it may be integrated into his residence and he offers to give them a space superior to it. The inhabitants of the quarter are prepared to allow this. Muḥammad declares that they must not.

The *Muntaqā* allows a man who builds a mosque to build a room on top of it so long as he remains the owner. But if he assigns the use of it to the community, he no longer has the right. To donate one's land for [the construction of] a mosque and stipulate that some benefit shall accrue to the donor is not permitted according to consensus (*ijmāᶜ*).

Muḥīṭ Sect. 22 of 'On *Waqf*': Shams al-Islām al-Awzajandī states that one may not convert a ruined and disused *20A* mosque into a burial ground.

To spread one's own prayer-mat (*muṣallā*) in a mosque is not forbidden. If one man spreads his mat and another comes along when there is room elsewhere he should not jostle the first because it will impede him. If there is no room, he will inevitably jostle him, and this shows that jostling is not forbidden. So should the newcomer jostle the first man, it is permissible. It is, however, reprehensible in the same way as it is when a man digs a grave in lawful land where there is ample space and another man buries a corpse there. This is lawful, but reprehensible.

To decorate a mosque with gypsum and gold leaf for worldly show is reprehensible, but if it is to glorify the mosque then it is not, because ᶜUthmān allowed it in the case of the Prophet's mosque.**[70]** (Tradition and the Prophet quoted)... ...

To perform *ṣalāt al-janāza* in a mosque is reprehensible.

Sunāmī: some people are accustomed to deposit, in a mosque, the body of someone who has died in the night and is not yet ready for them to bury. This is reprehensible.

Sharḥ al-Karkhī: the Prophet said, 'Keep your children away from mosques because there is a danger of ritual uncleanness'. This principle is applicable in the case of a dead body.

Tajnīs wa-l-mazīd: to rinse the mouth in the mosque is as reprehensible as to perform the lesser ablution there. Nor should one pursue an adversary (*mulāzama*) in a mosque because a mosque is built for concentration on God.

One should not sleep in a mosque nor indulge in idle, tumultuous or contentious talk in a mosque. *Tajnīs wa-l-mazīd* considers trade in a mosque reprehensible when practised by secluded persons (*muᶜtakif*). Stepping on people is reprehensible and is a practice which must be forbidden. *20B*

One should not sit listening to professional story-tellers (*quṣṣaṣ*) on Fridays. It is reprehensible before the communal prayer. Traditions are quoted to support his view. (*Qūt al-qulūb* quoted). Story-telling is *bidᶜa*. Story-tellers used to be expelled from the Great Mosque in early Islam. The Prophet said, 'On the Day of Judgment the person who crosses over the rows will be made like a bridge for people to cross.' Story-tellers should not be listened to before prayer, according to the *khabar* of the Prophet. If the speaker is a scholar who teaches religion, then it is a different matter. In *Qūt al-qulūb*, [it is stated that] the story-tellers should be expelled from mosques according to the practice of Ibn ᶜUmar. Ibn ᶜUmar once found a story teller occupying his chair. When Ibn ᶜUmar asked him to leave the story teller refused on the grounds that he came first. Ibn ᶜUmar reported him to the police chief (*ṣahib al-shurṭa*) who expelled the man from the mosque. Ibn ᶜUmar would not have had the man expelled if what he was doing had been right, especially since he had himself narrated the Tradition of the Prophet that states that no one should cause his brother to leave his seat so that he can take it. It can also be concluded that calling the police in a case like this is lawful. ᶜĀ'isha was once disturbed by a story-teller who was sitting next to her room.**[71]** When she complained to ᶜUmar about him, he hit the story-teller so hard that the stick was broken. This tradition (*athar*) leads to the following conclusions: *21A* ... ...

(i) story-telling is an innovation;

(ii) it is permissible to complain to the *muḥtasib* about any story-teller who is in breach of the rules relating to their presence in the mosque;

(iii) a story-teller may be beaten with a stick;

(iv) a story-teller may be driven out; indeed it is prescribed by the sunna.

Quotation from Abū al-Layth, *K. al-tanbīh* lists the points of behaviour to be observed in a mosque. These are:

1- Any one who enters the mosque should bid *salām* to those present in the mosque so long as they are not busy studying or praying. If no one is in the mosque, a person should bid *salām* to himself.

2- A person who enters the mosque should pray two *rakᶜas*.

3- No buying or selling should be practised in the mosque.

4- No sword to be drawn.

5- No lost property should be publicly advertised.

6- Voices should not be raised except to mention the name of God.

7- No worldly matters should be discussed in the mosque.**[72]**

8- Worshippers' lines should not be crossed.

9- There should be no arguments about where to sit.

10- The space that one takes should be reasonable and cause no jostling.

11- A praying person should not be obstructed by someone walking in front of him.

12- There should be no spitting.

13- There should be no finger clicking.

14- Children, lunatics, and all forms of dirt should be avoided including that which is caused by the performance of *ḥadd*.

15- The praise of God should be often... ... ...

Question of whether it is permitted to disturb a man who may be engaged in devotional acts *21B* but not actually performing ritual prayer. The answer is that if a man wishes to perform his ritual prayer and the mosque is crowded, the man engaged in his **[74]** devotions may be asked to make room. The Prophet never stopped *ahl al-ṣuffa* from sleeping or talking in the mosque provided that their talk was seemly. Case of a beduin who urinated in the mosque: the Prophet prevented others from interupting him, but immediately afterwards had the area swilled with water.**[75]**

<u>Sources</u>: *FKh*
MN
TM
KhF
AḥQ
TᶜAyn
FẒ
Muḥ
Munt
ShK
KSh
QQ
TGh
Dh

CHAPTER 16
(TS)
On Persons Attending Mourning Ceremonies in Mosques or Cemeteries on the Second and Third Days Following a Death

An enumeration of various practices connected herewith and held to be forbidden or reprehensible.

Such practices include the following:

1. Failure to observe prostration upon recitation (*tilāwa*) or during the ritual prayer is reprehensible. (Quoted from *Sharḥ al-Ṭaḥāwī al-kabīr.*)
2. To sit in the mosque to mourn a loss (*muṣība*) is reprehensible though Abū
22A al-Layth approves of it in *Tajnīs wa-l-mazīd*. A similar practice in the home is not, however, reprehensible, though it is better not to observe it. The matter will be dealt with on the chapter 'On Funerals' (Chapter 42).**[76]**
3. To spread carpets on days of mourning is one of the most shameful practices. This will also be dealt with in the chapter 'On Funerals' (Chapter 42).
4. To stand for any person beginning to read the Quran is forbidden unless it be for one's father or teacher (*ustādh*). (Quoted from *Khāniyya*).
5. To adapt the Quran's arrangement for the purposes of song (*ghinā'*) and even to listen to such an adaptation are forbidden. (Quoted from *Muḥīṭ.*)
6. To use braziers (*majāmīr*) fashioned in the forms of living beings such as falcons, etc. is reprehensible. No angel would ever attend a gathering where such things were in use.

At this point there follows a discussion of what kind of representational art is allowed, where and under what circumstances. (Quoted from *Muḥīṭ* and *Jāmiᶜ al-ṣaghīr*). The discussion mainly bears on carpets portraying figures. Then comes a discussion of braziers, whether portraying figures or not.**[77]**

7. To collect copies of the Quran from people because the most distinguished person in a congregation (*ṣadr al-majlis*) has finished his reading is to prevent people from reading the Holy Book in order to flatter some human's sense of dignity.
8. For women to go out and visit (cemeteries, occasions of mourning, etc.) is contrary to Islamic Law (Shariᶜa). The matter will be dealt with in the chapter entitled 'The powers of the *muḥtasib* with regard to women' (Chapter 8).
9. Singing and dancing (*al-samāᶜ wa-l-raqṣ*) by a grave is forbidden. The matter will be dealt with in the chapter entitled 'On Funerals' (Chapter 42).
10. The practice of blatant falsehood *22B* inheres in people declaring that they are visiting a grave for the sake of God when in fact they attend merely to flatter the dignity of the next-of-kin (*walī*) of the deceased. To judge the sincerity of their intentions one must take into account the following considerations:
    (a) When a rich but impious man dies, the attendance at his grave-side is greater than when a poor but pious man is being interred;
    (b) Next-of-kin of a deceased person may take umbrage if no one is present at the grave-side;
    (c) When someone attends a funeral, the relatives apologise to him (for inconveniencing him) and account it a favour to them. If God were their main concern, they would not act in this way.
11. People drink sherbet at grave-sides. This is contrary to the implication of a saying of the Prophet.
12. To cut foliage from trees to fashion them into the shape of **[78]** bushes for the purpose of adorning the grave area is forbidden because it is forbidden to cut fresh vegetation needlessly. There follows a discussion as to whether the ban applies only to the cutting of grass, etc. in the evening. (Quoted from *Khulāṣat al-fatāwā*.)[299]
13. To recite the Quran in public before or after the closure of the grave is reprehensible because people are too preoccupied to listen. Discussion of the various views about the recital of the Quran at grave-sides. (Authorities quoted.) *23A*

---

299 See *Khulāṣat al-fatāwā*, end of chapter 25; O. Loth, *A Catalogue of the Arabic Manuscripts in the Library of the India Office* (London, 1877) MS no. 205.

14. To recite the Quran aloud in the mosques, as some do, is reprehensible. The practice of what the Persians call *sīpāra khwāndan* is reprehensible according to Prophetic Tradition. (Quoted from *Muḥīt*.)

15. To wear scent on the third day after death is to imitate a female practice.**[79]** The reason women wear it is that they are forbidden to wear mourning clothes beyond three days. If they were to put it on on the fourth day the limit of mourning would be exceeded.
Tradition quoted.
Sunāmī: To use rose water on the third day after death is to be avoided solely because it is a woman's custom.

16. To engage a poet to eulogize a man for what he has not done is falsehood and, as lying, is forbidden.

17. It is reprehensible for a proclaimer (*muʿarrif*) to stand in the line where the sandals are and after the end of the burial to recite a verse from *Sūrat al-Ikhlāṣ* (cxii) three times and one from the *Fātiḥa* once while he is standing and the congregation is sitting. This is an innovation and not a practice handed on from early Muslims (*salaf*). Anyone who claims that the case is otherwise must explain how it can be when it involves disrespect for the Quran. For it looks as though the reciter, while reciting, is deferring to the most important persons and most distinguished members of the congregation in the mosque. Does he not face them whether that is the direction of the qibla or not? How can he put his hands in the appropriate posture for the act of worship (*ṣalāt*) and wait for the order to be given *23B* by the distinguished members of the congregation and others in their company? At the word of a command, he performs a *rakʿa* in the direction of him who has given the order by way of rendering a service that is well known to persons such as those who are dazzled by rank. Then from the next-of-kin of the deceased (*awilyā' al-mayyit*) he receives a fee for his recitation as though he was a hireling of theirs.**[80]**

18. It is reprehensible to drape the grave with silk garments when such have been the normal apparel of the deceased during his lifetime. This is a testimony to the fact that the man was a profligate in life, and to mention a man's iniquity after his death is forbidden.

19. It is a reprehensible practice to drape the grave of a dead man who lived a pious life with a cloth bearing the *Sūrat al-Ikhlāṣ* inscribed upon it. To put the Quran on the ground is an act of disrespect towards it. Such a garment will be in common use and to put God's book into common use entails God's punishment. Abū al-Layth in the *Bustān* declares that the book should not be put on graves.

20. It is reprehensible to bring copies of the Quran to cemeteries and to distribute them among those present and not to recite, but to wait for the arrival of the

most distinguished person. If the Quran is opened and those present begin to recite, and then the most distinguished participant arrives, he will be furious with them and think it an insult and an injury to his dignity and rank. What else is this but the soul which incites to evil (Quran xvii). Only unbelievers interrupt recitation of the Quran.**[81]**

21. If a deceased person's grave is a long way from one's home, *24A* it is reprehensible for one to leave home before the Dawn Prayer after the appearance of daybreak so that one may arrive in time to join the mourners. Quotation from Chapter 15, on leading prayer, of the book of *Khulāṣa*: 'If an imam who qualifies to conduct prayer lives in one area and goes to another area of the town to lead the prayers of its people during the month of Ramadhan, he should leave his home before the time of the *ᶜishā* prayer'.

    A man should set out for the place he is going to before the time for Evening Prayer has arrived. To go afterwards is reprehensible, and his case is similar to that of man who travels after the time for the Friday Prayer has arrived.

22. For one to leave his seat at the place of the ritual prayer to attend ceremonies on the second and third days of mourning is reprehensible. It is recommended that one should sit until sunrise, then hasten to make one's visitation (*ziyāra*) if such a visitation is the intention. If it is not, then it is shameful. To sit in the place of the ritual prayer from after the Dawn Prayer until sunrise is not only recommended (*mustaḥabb*) (*Tajnīs wa-l-mazīd*), but it is necessary according to the sunna. (Quoted from *Qūt al-qulūb*).

23. It is reprehensible to shroud the grave (*tasjiya*) of a deceased person with a cloth on the third day of the customary days for visitation, or indeed on any day. To shroud the grave is, in the case of men, quite contrary to religious law as it is also in the case of women once the bricks have been put in place. ᶜAlī is related to have removed a shroud from a grave, saying that it was the grave of a devout man.**[82]**

Sources: *ShṬK*
TM
FKh
Muḥ
JṢKh
KhF
BA
QQ
ShA

CHAPTER 17
(TS)
On Preachers (*Khuṭabāʾ*)

Prophetic Tradition quoted by Anas and Ibn ᶜAbbās to prove the punishment in the grave that erring preachers will suffer on the Day of Judgment.

Abū al-Ḥasan in *Sharḥ al-Karkhī* advises that sermons should not be protracted. The length of the Prophet's two sermons for Friday are equal to one long Sura of *Mufaṣṣal*.[300] *24B*

Qūt al-qulūb advises the pious not to sit in the first row during the Friday Prayer as they might note some untoward deed on the part of the imam which they would have to point out or prohibit (e.g. the of wearing silk or brocade).

Sunāmī: in our time there are two kinds of objectionable practice observable in preachers. The first is that they include in their sermons materials which ought to be prohibited. Secondly, they wear *taylasāns* of silk.**[83]** In the *Muḥīṭ* it is related on the authority of Māturīdī that if any man has declared the sultan of our day to be just, he has made himself an unbeliever. However, there are some who disagree that unbelief is entailed.

Sunāmī: preachers must avoid the use of such words lest their faith be called into question.

Dāwūd al-Ẓāhirī was questioned about preachers who deliver sermons from pulpits and about the titles given to the sultan when described as *al-sulṭān al-ᶜādil, al-sulṭān al-ᶜālim al-aᶜẓam, shāhinshāh al-aᶜẓam, mālik riqāb al-umam, sulṭān arḍ Allāh, mālik bilād Allāh, nāṣir ᶜibād Allāh, muᶜīn khalīfat Allāh.* His reply was that all this kind of thing is forbidden. Some of these are expressions of unbelief, while others are lies. Abū Manṣūr al-Māturīdī al-Samarqandī considers that the man who wrongly describes a ruler as just without any qualification when some of his acts are unjust is an unbeliever. [His reasons are given.] As regards the style *shāhinshāh 25A al-aᶜẓam* ('most great king of kings'), this is one of the characteristic appellations of God and not to be used for any other human being. As for *mālik riqāb al-umam* ('master of the necks of all peoples'), this implies that he is master of *jinn* and angels as well as men and other living creatures. Moreover, *mālik arḍ Allāh* ('master of God's earth') is mendacious and a title applicable only to the Prophet. He added (*al-Māturīdi*), 'Using any of these names as a formal title when addressing a king or a sultan without really meaning them, might not **[84]** be a sin. This is based on the fact that the metaphoric usage of names is accepted, for example, calling black, white, or a blind man a person of vision.

---

300 *Mufaṣṣal*: the latter part of the Quran beginning with Sura xlvii. It is called *mufaṣṣal* because of the many chapters it contains. *Mughrib*: 97.

Nowadays it is impossible to deal with rulers without becoming involved in the sort of outrages we have been describing. It is better to stop delivering sermons and devote oneself to piety. The glory of the next world is preferable to the baubles of this. **[85]**

Sources: *ShK*
QQ
Muḥ

CHAPTER 18
On People who Take Oaths on Things Other than God

Case (*Kifāya* – Chapter of *Imān* quoted): it is not allowed to take an oath on anything other than the name of God. If a person makes an oath by someone's life, he could be committing a major sin or even an act of infidelity according to some scholars. If a person makes such an oath, he is not to honour it since it has no value more than being a sin. Ibn ᶜAbbās is reported to have said that he prefers to make a false oath in God's name than to take an oath on something other than God's name. Both Ibn ᶜUmar and Ibn Masᶜūd maintain that any oath on things other than God's name is a form of polytheism (*shirk*).

Accordingly in a court of law it is not allowed to ask a witness to make an oath by divorce, *25B* freeing a slave, or performing *ḥajj*.[301]

Sunāmī: all oaths of this form are not allowed and he who takes them is committing a major sin as well as the one who demands it. However, the book of *Hidaya* states an exception. It states that a court judge may use the divorce or slave freeing formulas of oath in order to safeguard other people's rights.[302]

From *Muḥīṭ* and the *Jāmiᶜ al-ṣaghīr al-khānī*: ᶜAlī al-Rāzī stated that he would have given a *fatwā* that all these oaths are polytheism had he not known that many common people used them without fully realising their meanings.**[86]**

Sources: *H*
KSh
Muḥ
JṢKh

---

301 The meaning of Sunāmī's statement that ᶜa *ḥakīm* must not ask a defendant to swear by divorce or the emancipation of a slave' is defined in Hamilton's *Hidaya*: 'A defendant must not swear by divorce or emancipation by saying, if the claim preferred against me be just, my wife is divorced, or my slave is emancipated'. Hamilton, *Hidāya*: 405.

302 Quoted from Marghinānī, *Hidāya*: 4:159.

CHAPTER 19
(OTS)
On Persons who Use Language Impying Unbelief [86–88]

This topic involves three groups of people: the *muḥtasib*, the *muftī*, and the ordinary individual. The *muḥtasib* should reprehend any action in whatever form that could lead to blasphemy. He is expected to do so even if the action has occurred in error providing that it does not lead to *kufr*. The deterrent measure that the *muḥtasib* should employ depends on his personal discretion. Alternatively he should consult the ulama. It should be borne in mind that the punishment that he can employ may not reach the amount of the legally specified punishment (*ḥadd*).

The *muftī* should give the ordinary individual the benefit of the doubt. Thus, if there are two possible meanings of a certain statement and only one of them implies unbelief; the accused should be acquitted. However, if it transpired that the person's intention had been blasphemous, then the acquittal *fatwā* will be valueless. Legally he would be ordered to repent and renew his marriage with his wife.

In short, a person would be blasphemous (*kāfir*) if he pronounced blasphemy deliberately. Even if he thought that the word was not a statement of *kufr*, although uttered willingly, the majority of ulama still consider him to be a *kāfir* since ignorance does not form an excuse. However, if he simply uttered the word in error he is not a *kāfir*... *26A* **[87]** Reference from Ajnās citing Muḥammad [b. al-Ḥasan al-Shaybānī]'s statement that if a person meant to say 'I ate' and instead said 'I do not believe', he will not be blasphemous... ...**[88]** *26B* Abū Ḥanīfa is cited as having considered that to accept other people's *kufr* is *kufr* in itself...**[89]**

Sources: *Aj*
SK
ShSK

CHAPTER 20
(SO)
On Parents and Children [90]

Our duty towards our children and parents is a duty which remains constant and for the mutual good of the parties concerned. Quran quoted (xix: 42–47; xxvi: 86) *27A* ... ... A mother may lawfully restrain her son from participating in the jihad provided her restraint is merely verbal. If he will not be so restrained, she must not obstruct him in any other way.**[91]**

Sources: *ShI*
FKh
MN

CHAPTER 21
(TS)
On Legal Disputes between Neighbours

If a man demolishes his house and his neighbours suffer damage as a result, they may compel him to rebuild if he is able to do so because in law they have a remedy against damage suffered (*wilāyat dafᶜ al-ḍarar*). This is the opinion given here but the prevalent opinion is that a man cannot be compelled to rebuild that whereof he is the owner.

If a man wishes to build high [increase the height of a building that is his] and it so happens that it then prevents his neighbour from seeing because the building blocks off the light, he may be restrained because light is one of man's essential needs (*ḥawā'ij aṣliyya*). But his neighbour has no such remedy if the building only blocks off the sun and the wind because these are only conveniences (*ḥawā'ij zā'ida*). *27B*

The legal principle in such cases is that if a man in the matter of his own property (*milk*) acts in such a manner as to cause manifest damage to his neighbour, he must be restrained from so doing. Otherwise, he may not.

Another legal principle, relating to this case, to upper and lower storeys is that if the person above is clearly causing damage to the storey below or is in doubt as to whether he is doing so or not, he may not act without the permission of the one below.**[92]** If he is certain that he is not causing any damage, there is a difference of opinion as to the correct course of action, but that which is preferred is that he may act at his discretion.

Another legal principle is that anyone who acts with his property in such a way as to deprive his neighbour of a convenience (*nafᶜ*) may act at his own discretion and may not be restrained from so acting even if his neighbour's wrath is incurred. Thus a man wishing to uproot a tree giving shade to a neighbour may not, as owner, be restrained from so doing. This is similar to the second case mentioned in this chapter.

Another basic principle is that the enjoyment of another person's property is only permissible so long as the owner of that property does not withhold such benefit.

Air is the property of [the person who owns] the land or building over which it happens to be. An heir or purchaser of such property has the same basic right as the original owner. Thus, should a man purchase or inherit as estate (*ḍaᶜya*) where an adjacent tree's branches overhang his property, the heir or purchaser has the right to require his neighbour to clear the air space over his own property.
<u>Sunāmī</u>: by analogy, if a wall intrudes into a neighbour's air space in such a way as to divert any air from that neighbour's house, then that neighbour is entitled to require that the air space be cleared and the wall demolished, even though there is no danger of its falling down. Also by analogy, it is not permissible to build over

graves, houses, or mosques. In the case of graves, these are considered to be the property of those interred therein. (Some further details are given.)

Q. If the owner of a tree will not cut its branches and thus free the air space, has the neighbour a right to cut off overhanging branches from an owner's trees?

A. (By Muḥammad). A neighbour needs no permission to cut off such branches. It is, however, held that two courses are open. First, if one's neighbour can clear the air space by tying back the branches, he need not cut them. But if he takes no such action the town-governor (*ḥākim*) should instruct him to do so. Secondly, if there is no alternative to cutting off the branches, an aggrieved neighbour should ask the owner of the tree if he may cut it *28A* himself. If the owner grants permission, he may go ahead. But, if not, the matter should be referred to the town-governor so that he may grant permission to cut. There follows a discussion of liability if A (the owner of a property) causes damage to the tree of B ((his neighbour) by cutting at some unauthorized point or by excessive pruning. A may not cut from his own side of the tree but must refer the matter to the qadi so that he may instruct B to cut. If B will not act, the qadi should send a duly authorized person (*amīn*). Any expense involved in this operation should be borne by A.**[93]**

<u>House Doors in Streets</u>. If a man buys an apartment (*bayt*) adjacent to his house (*dār*) and backing on to a street with a door opening on to a different street, and he then wishes to gain access to his apartment by creating a new door opening on to the street on which there was no door previously, he may not do so, and the residents in the street may take action to prevent him from so doing. Some jurists, however, hold that he is entitled to create a new door.[303]

If he wishes to create a new door in his apartment leading from the apartment to the house and enabling him to have access to the street, the residents may not prevent him from so doing. However, one may not rent the apartment to someone and keep the house for oneself so that the tenant may gain access to the apartment via the house. There is no difficulty if one rents both the house and the apartment because the tenant is in the position of the landlord in the second case, the reason being that there is only one seeking access whereas in the first case there were two. This would give the right to prohibit such a situation. If several heirs share a cul-de-sac and it is apportioned among them, each may create a new door opening on to it, and no resident can prevent him from so doing. [Let us now consider the case of] a man who owns a house with a door opening onto a through road, the house in past time having the door opening on to a cul-de-sac. If he comes to sell it and the purchaser wants to create a new door not opening on to the through road, he is entitled to do so if the residents acknowledge his claim that a previous door existed because the purchaser has the same rights as the vendor. But if the residents deny his claim, one of them may swear on oath [to that effect] and he will then have no right to a new door unless he can prove his claim. If one of them refuses the oath, one after the other may be

---

303 See figure 1, p: 153.

called upon to swear until the point is reached where all refuse [even though called upon]. If all do in fact refuse the oath, then his title is established and the new door is permitted.

If the residents of a street wish to create an alley (*darb*), they may not block off the top of a street to do so because even if such a street *28B* appears to belong to the residents, the public also have a certain right in it. Thus, in the case of overcrowding in the [main] thoroughfare, people may enter a side road to relieve congestion. The residents may not, therefore, sell it or divide it among them.

Abū Hanīfa: the residents of a cul-de-sac **[94]** may store wood in it, tether their animals in it, and perform the lesser ablution (*wuḍū'*) in it without having any liability for mishaps to passers-by arising thereon.

Every resident of a street may enjoy the use of the frontage of his own house (*fanā' al-dār*), though not that of someone else, for the purpose of depositing snow and earth (*ṭīn*), stacking firewood, tethering animals, sitting outside, setting up shop or a baker's oven (*tannūr*). The only condition is that the safety of others must be assured. Some declare that to set up shop or a baker's oven is permissible in a public place, but where private dwellings are concerned the permission of all residents is required.

The residents of a street may not dig a well into which water is to be poured even if there is general agreement.

Fatāwā al-Fāḍlī: The residents of a street may tether riding animals on the frontage of their houses, but they may not construct a trough. If such a trough is constructed, any resident may destroy it because it is common property. Joint usufruct of an appartment (*bayt*) is permissible and tethering is usufruct. None of the tenants in such a case, however, add to the construction.

To dump earth [for building purposes] in a cul-de-sac is not prohibited provided that enough room is left for people to pass, that it is quickly removed, and that tubs are employed for the purpose, all in a single undertaking.

According to the *qiyās*, a house in a populous area may be demolished, but according to *K. al-istiḥsān* it may not. Al-Karkhī's *fatwā* is based on the latter view, while that of al-Ṣadr al-Shahīd Ḥusām al-Dīn is based on the *qiyās*.

Cases of nuisance obviously prejudicial to other people's **[95]** rights and interests must be prohibited. Examples are:

1. Since a neighbour's wall can be damaged by the turning of a miller's mill in the adjacent building, one may be forbidden to install a mill on his premises.
2. Smoke from a bathhouse (*ḥammām*) may create a nuisance, and so the amount of smoke issuing from it may not exceed that issuing from a neighbour's house.

3. To use a disused dwelling as a stable may cause damage to a party-wall because of the kicking of the animals against it. Some hold *29A* that one is not liable for the natural actions of the animals, while others take a contrary view.[304]
4. A man may sell the branches of a mulberry tree belonging to him. The purchaser may not climb the tree if it overlooks a neighbour's private quarters. Al-Ṣadr al-Shahīd in *Wāqīʿāt*, however, holds that this is permissible if due notice is given so that steps can be taken to protect one's privacy.
5. A window may be installed in such a way that it opens on to a neighbour's women's quarters. This is not permissible.
6. A baker must not be permitted to set up business among premises used by cloth-merchants. This was the decision of Abū al-Qāsim, whose decision causes Sunāmī for the same reason to forbid a gypsum manufacturer installing an oven (*maṭbakh*) in the middle of Tuhana market where it would cause damage.

In the case of the party-wall where one man's house is only one or two cubits higher than that of the other, building of the wall should be undertaken by both parties. But if one man's house is much higher (4 cubits and over in excess of the height of his neighbour's house), the man in the lower house must repair the wall in such a way as to bring it up to the level of the adjacent house.[305]**[96]**

There must be no objection to dhimmis who live among Muslims having a cemetery because they have a right to dispose of their own property as they see fit.

The owner of a small building that is lower than that of his neighbour may, if water is dripping on to his property, raise the height of his building, but he must ensure that the water drains away from his neighbour's side. *29B* If the lower building collapsed, may the owner of the higher building force the rebuilding of the lower one in order to maintain the drainage system of his building? According to *Faṭāwā al-Nasafiyya*, he cannot. However he has the right to reconstruct the lower building at his own expense and prevent its owner from using it until he is recompensed for what he has spent.**[97]**

Sources: *FF*
WSS
MN

---

304 No responsibility was put on the owner because the owner is not responsible for his animals' actions unless accompanied by negligence. Marghinānī, *Hidāya*: 197–203.

305 See figure 2, p. 154.

CHAPTER 22
(OS)
On the High Esteem in which the Office of *Muḥtasib* is Held[306]

The esteem of the office of *muḥtasib* is derived from the high value given to the action of ordering good and prohibiting evil, and the warning of those who do not practice this action.**[98]**
Quotation from Quran lix: 71.
Traditions of ᶜAlī, the Prophet *30A*, ᶜUmar b. ᶜAbd al-ᶜAzīz, and Yawshaᶜ b. Nūn. *30B-31A* **[99]**
Sunamī: One of the causes that can lead people away from the action of ordering good and prohibiting evil is their attachment to this world.

Further quotation from the Prophet and pious people like Sufyān al-Thawrī**[100]**...

Sunāmī raises the point that some might argue that although what has been cited proves the esteem of *iḥtīsāb*, some of the Quranic verses may be understood to clearly indicate otherwise, that is, that a person should only be concerned with his own affairs. Sura v:105 states: [O you who believe, be concerned about yourself since he who goes astray cannot harm you.] **[101]**
Sunāmī: a threefold refutation is possible:
First: This verse makes the stipulation that you may not remonstrate against others so long as you are guided.
Second: *31B* It is concerned with the unbelievers who are not to be subject to *ḥisba* because they pay the *jizya* instead. This meaning is clear from the fact that they are described as those who went astray. This is an attribute of the *kuffār* alone since a Muslim is still guided even if he commits a sin. Added to this is the fact that the sequence of verses in the text deals with the *kuffār*...

There is no contradiction between the two meanings if we take Abū Bakr's interpretation. He said, 'Some of you misunderstand this verse. I heard the Prophet of God saying, "If sins become widespread and no one bothers, then everyone will be punished"'... *32A* ...
Quotation from *Shirᶜat al-Islām*: The greatest duty imposed on those who deal with the public is that they should order good and only be angry for God's sake[307]... ... *32B–33A* **[102–106]**
Sources: *R*
ShI
FẒ

306 Most of the traditions and anecdotes referred to in this chapter seem to be quoted from Abū al-Layth, *Tanbīh*: 32–35.

307 A quotation from *Shirᶜat al-Islām*: 170A. Rieu, *Supplement* MS no. 178.

CHAPTER 23
(SO)
On Those who Expose Their Private Parts and Those who Look upon Others' Private Parts

In *Kifāya al-Shaᶜbiyya* it is held that to look upon the genitals of another is allowed for the purpose of *ḥisba* or for a medical reason. Accordingly it is allowed to look at the private parts of a couple while they are in the act of illegal sexual intercourse (*zinā*) for the purpose of *ḥisba*. It is not allowed to look at them if the reason is lust. From *Hidāya*: anyone who exposes his kneecap should be gently rebuked since there is a difference of opinion whether it is *ᶜawra* or not. But if he exposes his thigh, then he should be harshly reprimanded but not physically punished since this too is a subject of disagreement among the scholars of hadith. If a person exposes his genitals then he will have to be disciplined since, according to *Hidāya*, no legal doubt exists about its being *ᶜawra*.[308]

Discussion of the meaning of verses 30–1 in Sura xxiv (Say to the believing men/women that they should lower some of their gaze and guard their pudenda).**[107]** The article 'some' (*min*) is given three definitions, (Imam Nāṣir al-Dīn al-Bastī cited): The first possibility is that the meaning is redundant, the second is that it means that they should lower their gaze from only what is not allowed, while the last meaning is that they should cast down their eyes to avoid some of what is not allowed. *33B* There next follows a discussion of the meaning of 'to guard their pudenda'. The article *min* is not used before the word 'pudenda' because the action of guarding here refers only to what is prohibited. Every time the word pudenda (*furūj*) (lit. orifice) is used in the Quran it refers to *zina* except here, when it means modesty. The word *furūj* is used because it represents the entrance to the body cavity that should be guarded.**[108]**... Further elaboration on the meaning of the two verses taken from various Quranic interpreters including Ibn ᶜAbbās, ᶜĀ'isha, Ibn Masᶜūd, al-Ḥasan, Ibn Sirīn *34A*, and Saᶜīd b. al-Musayyab... ... *34B–36A* **[109–114]**

Sources: *KSh*
H
Chapter of *istiḥsān* of an unidentified book by Abū al-Layth.

---

308 See Marghinānī, *Hidāya* : 4:85.

[115]

CHAPTER 24
On Persons Who Exhibit False Tombs and Liken Cemeteries to the Kaaba

36B It was narrated in the tradition (*akhbār*) that some people went dressed like pilgrims towards Jerusalem. They were stopped by ᶜUmar, who in his reprimand said to them that they should not liken Jerusalem to the Kaaba. The reason for ᶜUmar's action was that they were an innovators and all innovations should be removed in the Muslim land (*dār al-Islām*). From the chapter of *Tarāwīḥ* in the *Kifāya al-Shaᶜbiyya*.[309]

Sources: *KSh*

[116]

CHAPTER 25
On Pictures in Houses

Iḥtisāb should be made upon anyone who decorates his house with a pattern that contains images [of living beings]. Such an image in a house prevents angels from entering that house. Jibril said, 'We do not enter a house that contains a dog or images.'

It is permissible, according to Ibn Sīrīn, to decorate a house with patterns that do not contain images (*ṣuwar*). It is reported that the meaning of the images mentioned in the Quranic verse xxxiv:12: 'They worked for him as he desired arches, images...' is images of non-living objects.

From *Multaqaṭ al-Nāṣirī*: if a person demolishes a house that is decorated with images of men or birds, then his legal responsibility will be restricted to the value of the house and the materials used.

Sources: *MN*
Im

[117]

CHAPTER 26
On Dirhams, *Dīnārs* and Other Coinage (*Athmān*)

Abū Yūsuf holds that even dirhams that are good coin must not be struck secretly outside the mint (*dār al-ḍarb*). Dirhams bearing Quranic inscriptions must neither be touched by unclean persons nor be trodden on because they are as sacred as the

309 A quotation from *Kifāya*, MS no. 1699, folio 111B.

Quran itself. They can be put in a purse and touched in the same way as the covering of a Quran, but the purse must not be put under the foot just as a Quran in a covering may not.

There is no harm in a man's putting a book or Quran under his head for safekeeping. Our view is that to safeguard property while one is asleep is a necessity, and, in using the head for the purpose, there is no intent to demean. The foot, *37A* however, is ordinarily associated with the intent to demean, and so action should be taken to stop money-changers' placing purses of inscribed dirhams under their feet.

In the *Qūt al-qulūb* it is held that transactions in dirhams that are forged or worn or of a silver content that is unknown are reprehensible as is any transaction in which a value is unascertainable, or in which **[118]** silver is mixed with other metal that cannot be distinguished from silver. Older authorities [Thawrī, Fuḍayl b. ᶜIyāḍ, Wahb b. al-Ward al-Makkī, Ibn al-Mubārak] took a very serious view of such matters, and transactions in coin of the kind described were proscribed. For each counterfeit coin spent sins are committed that amount to the weight of each atom of that counterfeit coin, each atom being the equivalent of a dust particle seen in the sun's rays. One of the Muslim warriors said, "On a battlefield my horse three times failed to attack an infidel (*ᶜilj*). As I was wondering why my horse failed me, I fell asleep and saw my horse telling me in a dream, 'You were not successful in your attack because you fed me fodder which was purchased with forged money'." The warrior went back to the seller of the fodder and retrieved the forged money from him.

ᶜAbd al-Wahhāb: Bishr, al-Muᶜāfā, and al-Thawrī all agreed that transactions in counterfeit or 'kohled' money are forbidden. Aḥmad condemns commercial transactions in both types of coin. Some scholars think it better to steal 100 dirhams than to spend just one counterfeit dirham because the latter may remain *37B* in circulation **[119]** for a century or more after one's death. A person who knowingly spends forged money is more sinful than a person who spends it unintentionally. The former is guilty because he is acting deliberately while the latter is only committing an error. An error which infringes the rights of others cannot be negated.

Anyone finding a counterfeit coin (*zuyūf*) must never spend it but throw it away. For, to throw such a coin away is better than to give the same amount of good coin in alms.

Transactions in *sattūq* are not reprehensible provided that the parties concerned are all aware that they are intended as token money. Sunāmī, however, holds that the ruler ought to do away with this kind of token lest it be used unwittingly by those who do not understand its significance. According to Bishr, Abū Yūsuf had commented that it was a sin to use bad coin (*nabahrajā*), *sattūqa*, forged or 'kohled' coins (*mukaḥḥala*) or commercial (*tijāriyya*) tokens. It is sinful because it prejudices the interests of the masses, and anything that affects the public interest is reprehensible. Even if the two parties agree to deal with this kind of token, it will still be reprehensible since it will harm other people once their forged coins are in public use. They will become a tool used by the evil to fool the innocent. Any similar reprehensible practice should be stopped and the offender should be punished.

Sunāmī: it is a very common practice for sultans to mint and put into circulation money on which they set a value greater than its actual worth. When they are no longer in power, the money in circulation is then valued at its true worth, and many people suffer financial losses. Perpetrators of this kind of offence will be punished on the Day of Judgment. Al-Ḥajjāj, in justification of himself, observed that he had never debased the coinage.**[120]**

Sources: *MN*
QQ
Dh
Im

CHAPTER 27
On *Ahl al-Dhimma*

The *Multaqaṭ* does not permit a *mushrik* to play a lute (*barbaṭ*). Muḥammad comments that he forbids the *mushrik* everything that he forbids the Muslim with the exception of wine and pork.

Fatāwā Nasafiyya: *38A* a Muslim garden or house purchased by a community of Jews in a large town (*miṣr*) may be turned into a cemetery because those Jews are the owners and in this respect have the same rights as Muslims. However, any such place may not be turned into a church (*kanīsa*) or synagogue because such conversion would publicize the error of their ways and be an affront to Islam and its adherents.

Khāniyya: the unbeliever (*kāfir*) may not touch a copy of the Quran.

Ẓahīriyya: provided an unbeliever performs a full ablution (*ightasala*), he may touch the Quran.

Dhakhīra: in *Siyar al-kabīr*, Muḥammad quotes the Prophet as declaring that in Islam there is neither castration nor churches.

However, this statement is to be interpreted as applying to the building of churches in large towns (*amṣār*). **[121]** Apparently it does not apply to villages.

Sunāmī and Abū Ḥanīfa: It depends on the size of the population. If the Muslim population of a village is large, it puts it in the same category as a large town. Accordingly, in such villages wine and pork may not be displayed for sale nor may there be any transactions involving unlawful gain (*ribā*). Likewise churches, synagogues, and places of fire-worship (*buyūt al-nīrān*) must be forbidden.

The custom of displaying the cross on a holy day (ᶜĪd) must be prohibited. Crosses must be kept within the confines of old-established churches and not be displayed around large towns. If taken outside a town under cover, the cross may be displayed.

Church bells may not be rung apart from in old-established churches *38B* where the sound of bells must not be able to be heard outside the church. Dhimmis must also be prevented from marrying persons within prohibited degrees, and from doing anything in public that is unlawful in Islam since it is an affront to Muslims and the setting of falsehood against the truth.

Sunāmī: during Ramadan dhimmis may not chew betel (*tanbūl*) in public by day.

If an old-established synagogue or church falls into ruins in a large town and is to be rebuilt, **[122]** it may not be larger than the original even if compensation is paid. Also the same rule applies to the resiting of a place of worship within a large town.

The jurists have several views on the purchase of a house in Muslim districts by dhimmis. Some allow it, others forbid it, while yet others hold that it is permissible provided that it does not interfere with the community centred on the local mosque.

A dhimmi may only build a place of worship (*bayt ᶜibāda*) for his own personal use. The creation of a hermitage (*ṣawmaᶜa*) in such a place of worship must be prohibited because it is tantamount to using the place as a church.

If an old-established church is in a large town that was once a village gained by peaceful treaty (*ṣulḥan*), the inhabitants may retain their churches. This measure is taken to avoid any similarity between the rituals of Islam and those of disbelief.

But if the place was taken by force (*ᶜanwatan*) and the inhabitants were allowed in their churches because it was a village and then it became a large town in which Islamic sanctions now apply, the Friday Prayer is held, and the festivals are celebrated, they may not retain their churches.

Neither a Muslim nor an unbeliever should openly bring wine or pork into a town (*miṣr*) in which the Friday prayer is celebrated and the *ḥudūd* are applied. If a dhimmi does so in ignorance, the imam should return his property to him and expel him with the warning that, if he returns, he will punish him. The imam should adopt this course of action because wine is lawful in a dhimmi's religion. The expression 'in ignorance' means that the person in question does not know that he should not be doing what he is doing, for which reason the imam should not pour away his wine or slay his pigs because, for dhimmis, they are [lawful] property. However, if he thinks it appropriate to punish him by flogging or imprisonment, he may inflict such punishment. *39A* **[123]**

If a Muslim spoils a dhimmi's wine, he is liable for damages unless he is an imam who was under the impression that he was so acting in order to inflict punishment.

All towns and villages inhabited by dhimmis must observe the terms of the treaty they have with Islam, and their inhabitants may commit no acts of notorious depravity such as unlawful sexual intercourse or anything forbidden by their law.

Drunkenness must be prohibited because no reasoning person can countenance it as being in any way lawful.

The open sale of such musical instruments as *mazāmīr* and the *ṭanbūr* is forbidden, as also is singing in public. Discussion of the question whether musical instruments may be broken.

To put the matter in a nutshell, the status of dhimmis is exactly the same as that of Muslims, except in matters relating to pork, prohibited degrees of marriage, and worship of a deity that is not God. A contract given to a group of enemy subjects will not be valid if it permits them to build churches, synagogues, or to consume wine or swine. This kind of agreement is annulled because it violates the fundamental law of Islam. There would be a similar violation if they were given permission to deal in usury (*ribā*) or employ prostitutes.

Multaqaṭ: Muslims (*al-nās*) may return a greeting made by dhimmis, but in reply they must go no further than the words of the greeting offered. If necessary, there is no harm in a Muslim's offering a greeting, but it is reprehensible for a Muslim to shake hands with dhimmis. **[124]**

It is our view that action should be taken against a Muslim entering into a partnership with a dhimmi. A *mufāwaḍa* partnership is not permissible because it is illegal between a Muslim and an unbeliever. An *ʿinān* partnership is reprehensible between a Muslim and a dhimmi (*Sharḥ al-Taḥāwī*).**[125]**

Sources: *MN*
FN
FKh
FẒ
Dh
SK
ShṬK

CHAPTER 28
On Travellers

There is no harm in carrying a Quran or any work on Shariʿa in a sack loaded on a beast of burden with the owner of the sack sitting upon it provided there is a garment placed between the rider and the sack. *39B* This will be like sleeping on the roof of a house where a copy of the Quran is kept. Even if there is no garment placed between the rider and the Quran, it is also acceptable since there is no disrespect intended for the Quran, based on the same principle involved in a sitting and sleeping on a sack where a Quran is kept.

A woman may travel with a man who is related to her within the prohibited degrees provided there is no danger of sexual attraction. A man unrelated to a free woman may not be alone with her or travel with her. Some allow a woman who is a slave-girl to travel with a man, while others do not. Some of those who permit travelling with a slave girl do not allow the man to assist her in mounting and dismounting since this might lead to sexual attraction.**[126]**

A Muslim may not show a dhimmi who asks for directions the way *to* a synagogue, but there is no harm in showing him the way home *from* a synagogue.

A Muslim travelling in the company of wrongdoers should not neglect his religious obligations because he is with them.

[Illustrative anecdote] His example may influence the behaviour of his companions.

Bustān al-ʿārifīn: it is reprehensible for a traveller to satisfy the calls of nature on a road or on a river bank or under fruit bearing trees or a tree that gives shade.[310] *40A*
The Prophet is said to have declared such a person accursed.**[127]**

Sources: *KSh*
BA

CHAPTER 29
(TSO)
On the Burning of Goods and Merchandise

An example of this is the burning of musical instruments in the open-air oratory (*muṣalla*) in which the *ʿĪd al-aḍḥā* is being celebrated. Some argue that this practice is abominable because it occupies the *muṣalla* with something that is not part of its function. The reply to this objection is that the *muṣalla* does not possess the full restricted status of a mosque because it is meant to give the public flexibility.

If the *muḥtasib* burns the property of street vendors, he will have to compensate them unless he does it to protect the public interest.

To burn the house of a winemaker is allowed if the *muḥtasib* ascertains that this action is the only means of reprimanding him. Discussion on the reason for burning the musical instruments only at *ʿĪd al-aḍḥā*. The reason given is that burning is an elimination of a heretical practice which is similar to the rituals that the pilgrims perform. The Muslims who do not perform *ḥajj* emulate the pilgrims' actions of praying and slaughtering sheep by burning musical instruments.

From *al-Khāniyya* on a person who practices beastiality with an animal: If the culprit owns the animal, he should slaughter it and then have it burnt. If he does not own it, he should buy it from its owner before doing the same. If the animal is normally eaten, it should only be slaughtered.

It might be asked why musical instruments are burnt during *ʿĪd al-aḍḥā*. The answer consists of a few points:

---

310 A quotation from Abū al-Layth's *Bustān*: 133.

Some claim that playing the tambourine (*duff*) and using it to accompany singing is allowed. They base this allowance on a hadith which relates that Abū Bakr visited the Prophet and found two young girls playing tambourines. When Abū Bakr scolded them, the Prophet said, 'Leave them, Abū Bakr, it is a day of celebration (ᶜĪd)'. However, this hadith is abandoned (*matrūk*)[311] by the Quran: x:97 ...

40B–41A

Secondly, since the ᶜĪd day is a joyful day, rightous people would be even more happy when they burn the instruments of evil.

Thirdly, all pilgrims should observe five rituals which are imitated by non-pilgrims:

1 Going from Mina to the holy mosque (*al-Masjid al-Ḥarām*).
2 *Ṭawāf*. This is imitated by going to the ᶜĪd prayer ground (*muṣalla al-ᶜĪd*)
3 Hair and nail-cutting and other deeds that accord with the sunna. This is imitated by burning musical instruments because both remove heresy.
4 Throwing the stones. This is imitated by the public's throwing stones at the instruments as they are being burnt.
5 Animal sacrifice (*qurbān*). Non-pilgrim Muslims sacrifice an *uḍḥiya...*

[128–130]

... The Prophet said, 'I was about to ask someone to lead the prayer while I followed those who do not join the congregational prayer and burnt their houses.' This hadith proves that it is permissible to burn the house of the man who does not join the congregational prayer. Despite the fact that the Prophet did not say that he actually burnt anything but merely intended to do so, his action should be followed, since he would not even attempt a sin. If burning can be applied to ignoring a definite sunna, we can conclude that it can be applied to neglected duties (*wājib*) and even to burning the instruments of sin... *41B* **[131]**

Sources: *FKh*
ShAQ
Mabs
Dh

CHAPTER 30
On the Difference between a Censor (*Muḥtasib*) and a Rigorist (*Mutaᶜanit*)

[In the situation of] a stream in a cul-de-sac. A plants a tree on the edge on his own frontage. B, an owner-occupier in the same street, proposes to uproot the tree, though there are other similar trees in the street and he has only objected to that of A.

311 It is curious that the author used the word 'abandoned' (*matrūk*) and not *mansūkh*. This may indicate that he has no ground for this abandonment but his own opinion.

B is a rigorist because he has only singled out one tree for uprooting. The jurist Abū al-Qāsim al-Ṣaffār stated that 'on hearing a complaint about the public roads, consideration should be given only to those which have been made by a person who does not commit such a violation. The reason for this is that if the complainant cares about the public interest, he should begin with himself, otherwise it can be concluded that his intention is to be a rigorist and nothing more.'

This is similar to a *muḥtasib* who demolishes a building extension that obstructs the public road. He will only be a acting as a *muḥtasib* if he applies the same action to all the houses in the street that have such an obstructing extension.

One may not demolish part of a property that projects into the main street unless all projections in the same street are likewise demolished.**[132]**

Sources: None

CHAPTER 31
(S)
On Those who Inscribe Talismans and Those who Solicit them

It is forbidden for a woman to have a talisman made for herself in an attempt to regain an estranged husband's affection. Charms in Hebrew and Syriac are reprehensible as amulets. The Prophet forbade the hanging of charms on camels' necks.

Sunāmī: this Tradition is sufficient basis for prohibiting Muslims (*al-nās*) from putting amulets, necklaces, and suchlike *42A* around their children's necks in the supposition that they will ward off the evil eye (*ᶜayn*) and the assaults of the Devil. This is tantamount to polytheism; only God can protect. A thread put around one's finger to jog one's memory (*ratīma*) does not come into the same category.

Amulets, charms (*tawla*), etc. are polytheistic. (Prophetic Traditions quoted from *Mughrib*[312]). Quranic phylacteries (*maᶜādhāt*) are permissible as containing Quranic quotations and the names of God.**[133–4]**

Sources: *FKh*
JSKh
TᶜAyn
Saḥ
ShK
Mugh

---

312 See *Mughrib*: 59:60.

CHAPTER 32
(S)
On Those who Accept Money for their Duties as *Muḥtasibs* and on Salaries to be paid to *Muḥtasibs*

Payment from dhimmis is permissible since it forms part of the poll-tax (*jizya*). As regards Muslims, the only payment permitted is that for the *muḥtasib*'s enforcement officers (*aʿwān*) who are not a charge on the public treasury (*bayt al-māl*). Some religious authorities regard enforcement officers as unbelievers, but Sunāmī does not agree, providing that they do not view their act of injustice as permissible (*ḥalāl*). *42B*

A *muḥtasib* receiving money other than his official salary is suspect and must be investigated lest there be any question of bribery (*rishwa*). The same rules apply to a *muḥtasib* as apply to a judge. According to *Sharḥ adab al-qāḍī* of Jaṣṣāṣ, bribes might be offered for one of four purposes. These are:

(1) to avoid maltreatment;**[135]**
(2) to secure good relations between oneself and the ruling authority;
(3) to secure appointment as a judge by the ruling authority;
(4) to bribe a judge to give judgment in one's favour.

In the first case the giver of the bribe is acting lawfully in that he is acting in self-defence, but the recipient is acting unlawfully in using menaces to extort money. In all the other three cases the bribe is unreservedly illegal... **[136]**

Sunāmī: this is also our opinion with regard to any payment received by the assistants of the chief *muḥtasib* (*muḥtasib al-mamālik*). Any payment for the assistants for a favoured treatment by *malik al-ḥisba* is a prohibited form of bribery similar to what is given to those who mediate between judges seeking appointments and the sultan.

Gifts made to the Prophet and in the Prophet's time were friendly gestures and not bribes. ᶜUmar b. ᶜAbd al-ᶜAzīz *43A* recognized that times had changed and was forced to distinguish between bribes and honest gifts.

Sunāmī: gifts to judges and *muḥtasibs* are to be regarded as bribery if they originate from someone requiring a favour from them in their official capacity. But if there is no vested interest on the part of the giver and they are intended as tokens of friendship and goodwill, they are lawful.**[137]**

Sources: *AḥQ*
ShAQ

CHAPTER 33
(S)
On Teachers and Teaching

No one should debate a question of scholastic theology unless he knows what he is talking about. Some forbid involvement in scholastic theology (*ʿilm al-kalām*) altogether. Debate and polemics lead to heretical innovations, doctrinal rifts, etc. In any case, ignoramuses only engage in such debates for the wrong reasons; they are not really concerned with the truth. However, learning concerned with knowledge of God, His unity, and knowledge of Prophethood should not be forbidden.

The Imam Abū al-Yusr Ṣadr al-Islām draws attention to works on the unity of God (*tawḥīd*) which are in fact philosophical treatises written by philosophers such as al-Kindī and al-Isfarā'īnī. The content is pure sophistry, and such works are filled with polytheism and error. *43B* Moreover, the writings of such Muʿtazilīs as ʿAbd al-Jabbār, al-Jubbā'ī, al-Kaʿbī, and al-Naẓẓām must be eschewed; they sow the seeds of doubt. Likewise the writings of anthropomorphists like Muḥammad b. al-Hayṣam must be eschewed.**[138]** The works are the worst known to the heretics (*ahl al-bidaʿ*).

Al-Ashʿarī wrote a number of works in defence of the Muʿtazilīs but he later recanted and, when God was pleased to bring him back to the fold, he refuted their teachings. He did commit some errors, but his books are permitted reading as long as one is aware of the points on which he erred. Sunāmī had a copy of al-Zamakhsharī's *Kashshāf*, but when he read that he was forbidden to possess Muʿtazilī works, he got rid of it but not by selling it because that would have been tantamount to selling wine or pork.

Any pedagogue who pronounces Jews to be much better than Muslims because they pay their children's teachers their full due is an unbeliever.

No man must proclaim himself the most learned of men. Knowledge in the highest degree belongs only to God. (Prophetic Tradition relating to Moses quoted.)**[139]**

Sources: *MN*
FKh
Dh
Ṣaḥ

CHAPTER 34
(S)
On Magicians, *Zindīqs*, Sorcerers, and the Like

44A A man who has a doll made for the purpose of dividing a man and his wife is an apostate and liable to the death penalty if he believes in the efficacy of the doll because he is an unbeliever.

A sorcerer's repentance for his so being is acceptable if it precedes his apprehension; otherwise, it is not. The same applies to a *zindīq*.

Discussion of the Prophet's view on sorcerers and soothsayers.

Discussion of practices intended to treat a man's impotence caused by a magic spell (*akhdha*), especially:

(a) urination on the edges of a heated axe (*ḥall*) and **[140]**

(b) the decoration of spring flowers for pouring over the subject's body (*nashra*).**[141]**

Sources: *Muḥ*
YM

CHAPTER 35
(S)
Authority over Goods 44B and Immovable Property

Land adjacent to a small and overcrowded mosque may be compulsorily purchased at market value (*qīma*).

A Zoroastrian cemetery to which no value attaches ranks as wasteland if it dates from the pre-Islamic period. If it dates from the post-Islamic period, it can be claimed as *luqṭā*.

The billeting of soldiers on campaign on civilian houses is permitted. **[142]**

Sources: *MN*

CHAPTER 36
(ST)
The Prohibition of *Banj* Whether Owned by Muslim or Dhimmi and the Punishment Applicable to Those who Eat or Drink it

Banj may be used for medicinal purposes unless it impairs one's mental faculties. Sunāmī recounts an incident within his own experience with the conclusion that Abū Ḥanīfa declared *banj* forbidden. He said:

I heard from my shaykh and teacher the eminent scholar Kamāl al-Dīn al-Sunāmī that a young man from Bukhāra asked Ḥamīd al-Dīn al-Ḍarīr while he was on the pulpit about the permissibility of *banj*. When the young man had no reply, he put his question on two consecutive weeks. This made Ḥamīd al-Dīn angry and he said to him in Persian, 'Sit down now and I will give you an answer by next week.' As soon as Ḥamid al-Dīn finished his lecture, he and Ṣadr Jihān Bukhāra, the great scholar, called together all the ulama qualified for giving *fatāwā*. He then asked them to open the library and study the books to see if there was any narration (*riwāya*) that prohibited *banj* according to their school. They found one narration from Abū Ḥanīfa that *banj* is prohibited (*ḥarām*). The ulama reached the consensus that *banj* is prohibited on the ground of public interest (*maṣlaḥ*a), bearing in mind that the reprobates flock to it as they do to intoxicants. When he next preached, **[143]** Ḥamīd al-Dīn asked for the young man who had asked the question. When the man stood up, he told him that they had found a *riwāya* from Abū Ḥanīfa that it [*banj*] is forbidden. *45A* Therefore they had made a consensus (*ijmāᶜ*) that it is so, owing to the *maṣlaḥa*. Accordingly the divorce pronouncement of a person under the influence of *banj* is not valid.

Sunāmī: in reference to this incident reported about Ḥamid al-Dīn, some maintain that the *Hidāya* and other legal sources state that *banj* is permissible (*mubāḥ*) and this is only a single narration (*khabar al-wāḥid*) which is not binding. We consider that a single narration (*khabar al-wāḥid*) if narrated by a scholar is compulsory. On this matter the narration of a consensus (*ijmāᶜ*) is similar to that of hadith. With regard to the *Hidaya*'s narration, we do not deny it, but its existence does not alter the possibility that there is another narration. [In fact] the book of *Taᶜlīq*[313] [states] that *banj* is *ḥarām* and if there is a consensus among the ulama to adopt one scholar's view then no one can subsequently disagree with it.

Sunāmī: pronouncement of divorce is invalid only if he did not know that *banj* was *banj*. If he knew that *banj* was *banj* and proceeded to take it, his divorce is valid.

Abū Ḥanīfa is reported to have declared intoxication (*sukr*) from *banj* to be forbidden and punishable by a *ḥadd* penalty. (*Muḥīṭ*, Shāfiᶜī, and the Prophet quoted). Sunāmī discusses a view to be found in the *Hidāya* and elsewhere that *banj* is permissible and, in so doing, gives his view of pronouncements by single authorities (*khabar al-wāḥid*).

Sunāmī: the evidence for the prohibition of *banj* is plain because medical authorities classify it as poison, and all poisons are forbidden as being injurious to health. If *banj* is harmful, why do intelligent people take it without being harmed? **[144]** Perhaps they take something to neutralise its effect, such as oil or butter. Be that as it may, intelligence has nothing to do with the matter; consensus (*ijmāᶜ*) is what

---

313 *Al-Taᶜlīq fī Uṣūl al-Fiqh* by ᶜAlī b. Muḥammad al-Shāfiᶜī al-Kayāharsī (d. 504).

matters. It is commonplace to describe as *banjī* anyone who is given to making a lot of slips in word or deed. Even animals, devoid of reason as they are, give *banj* a wide berth.

It is quite lawful (*mashrū*) for a *muḥtasib* to destroy *banj*, and no liability for compensation is entailed. *45B* ᶜAbd al-ᶜAzīz al-Tirmidhī stated that he put the question of whether the action of a man divorcing his wife while under the influence of *banj* should be considered valid? Abu Ḥanifa and Sufyān al-Thawrī both said that the validity of his action depends on his free will in consuming the drug. (From *Dhakhīra.*)

Both *Khulāṣa* and *Fatāwā al-Bayhaqī* states that to consume *banj* for a medicinal reason is acceptable provided it does not lead to loss of reason. Traditions narrated by Jābir are cited to the effect that he who consumes *banj* is a distraction to the Muslim community and no intercession will be granted for someone who consumes it. Jābir and Ibn ᶜAbbās are quoted to interpret the meaning of the cursed tree referred to in Quran xvii: 60 as *banj*. **[145]**

Sources: *Muḥ*
H
Dh
KhF
FB
ShSH

CHAPTER 37
(TO)
On Those who Use Gold and Silver

Gold and silver vessels for eating and drinking are reprehensible. However it is not reprehensible to pour substances like oil or food from such a vessel before using them for annointing or eating. The ban applies to men and women, although the latter may wear ornaments of gold and silver.

In the case of silver inlay, this is permissible provided that the silver is on the outside and not on the part being used. The same goes for a chair as for a vessel: one may have inlay of silver or gold provided that it is not the actual seat that is inlaid.

One may gild ceilings, oil cruets, censers, Qurans, stirrups, saddles, bridles, and similar objects. Abū Ḥanīfa's view is that precious metals may not be in contact with the body. It is held that the prohibitions on the use of gold and silver are a reaction to the practice of the pompous and earthly potentates.

There is no harm in using gold and silver for the purpose of plating objects made of base metals because the precious metals are no longer pure.

Breastplates of gold and silver may be worn in war. In Abū Ḥanīfa's opinion, however, they were considered as reprehensible as silk.[314] Swords ornamented in gold or silver may not be used even in war... They said,[315] "the reason why gold and silver may be used in breastplates is because they deflect arrows." In the case of swords, however, such ornamentation is of no advantage. *46A* Sitting on a bed made of gold is said to follow the same rule as for silk, but, according to Ḥulawānī, it is merely abominable by consensus.

From *Al-Nawādir*: Abū Ḥanīfa stated that to sit on a golden chair is prohibited for men. ... **[146]**

A ring should not be worn unless it is necessary for the wearer as in the case of a judge or a ruler. Some, however, think that only a ruler should wear a ring. It is, however, permitted by the general body of the ulama. It must be of silver – rings of iron, copper, lead, and so on are forbidden to men and women alike. Women may wear gold rings, but not men, according to the majority of ulama. Some of the latter think that there is no harm in it.

The use of jasper as a signet stone is forbidden, but some allow it. **[147]**

If a man wears a signet ring he should have the stone facing inwards towards his palm, though a woman may display it as an ornament. Such a ring may be worn on any finger, but the little finger of the left hand is best. The ring may not bear the image of any human, bird, or insect. (Quoted from *Multaqaṭ*.) **[148]**

Sources: *Nd*
MN

CHAPTER 38
(S)
On Clothing

To wear silk and brocade is forbidden. Any garment of silk is forbidden, and this prohibition applies to a garment of silk warp with a weft not of silk.

All red garments are forbidden, even if made of cotton or worn underneath other clothes. All red clothing is forbidden because red is the Devil's uniform. (Tradition quoted.) Silk padding in clothes is, however, permitted.

Clothes that are dirty may not be worn for the prayer, and they should not be worn at all unless there are no alternative clothes available.

It is reprehensible to wear clothing dyed with safflower or saffron unless a garment be of cotton that is naturally red. (Tradition quoted.) *46B*

---

314 The *Hidāya* does not prohibit the wearing of a garment containing silk providing that the weft is not silk. Marghinānī, *Hidāya*: 4:81.

315 *Qālū* is a reference to Ḥanafī jurists in general. *Qālā* (dual) refers to Abū Yūsuf and Muḥammad al-Shaybānī. Marghinānī, *Hidāya*: 4:79, 81.

Men should not wear clothes inscribed with gold or silver letters, but women may do so.

On most occasions people should wear clothes which are of average style and quality, but on some occasions rich clothes may be worn to show that God has bestowed His bounty on you. Such clothing may not always be worn **[149]** since this would be an affront to the needy.

For the same reason several garments should not be worn at the same time in winter unless it is so cold that they are necessary.

Anecdote quoted about clothing, ᶜAlī's view being given.

To wear a band around the waist or to throw an *ᶜasalī* over one's shoulders or to wear a Mazdean *qalansuwwa* is prohibited. Any of these actions implies unbelief (*kufr*), whether they are implied in jest or in earnest. The only exception is when they are worn in war to mislead the enemy, (quoted from *Multaqaṭ*), but there is a contrary view upheld by the argument that clothing of this kind is anti-Islamic. (Quoted from *Kifāya*.)

A silk trouser cord is forbidden.

Sunāmī: By analogy the use of a silk hair-band is reprehensible.

To swear an oath never to wear anything but woollen clothing is not an act of worship; it is merely for show.

Sunāmī: by analogy it is not permitted to wear sackcloth (*jawāliq*) **[150]** since it is seeking recognition of personal piety and setting oneself apart from the others for worldly gains as in the case of woollen garments.

47A The Prophet condemned the wearing of wool for worldly purposes. (Tradition quoted.)

Persons wearing clothes ornamented with forms of living creatures should be be subject to action by the *muḥtasib* because such portrayals are similar to idols, and no one should pray wearing such a garment. (Tradition quoted.)

Dhimmis should not wear clothes similar to those worn by men of religious learning and piety, and action must be taken to stop them. **[151]**

Anecdote about ᶜUmar's reactions when he went to welcome a victorious army and found silk clothing being worn. From this anecdote ten conclusions are drawn (seven relate to the wearing of silk).

Abū Ḥanīfa's views on the quantity of silk that may be used in the decoration or identification (*ᶜalam*) of a garment. *47B* **[152]**

Sources: *Munt*
Kash
MN
KSh
FKh
ShK

CHAPTER 39
(SO)
On Things which One May not Behold

Multaqaṭ: According to Khalaf b. Ayyūb, a person who goes out to watch an amir's procession is not a creditable witness (*ʿadl*). One view dissents, allowing it providing that he went out just to amuse himself.
Quotation from Abū al-Layth, *Bustān*: No one may peer into someone else's house without that person's permission. Different interpretations are discussed, and the question arises whether the responsibility for privacy devolves upon the householder, who should see to it that his house is properly curtained.[316] *48A* ... ... **[153]**

Sources: *MN*
FKh
BA

CHAPTER 40
(TS)
Occupations

It is reprehensible to sell a *mukaʿab* embroidered in silver thread if it is known that a man is to be the wearer.
Sunāmī: by analogy it is reprehensible to sell men *qalansuwwa*s of silk brocade (*nasīj*) or *qabā*'s and so on if of silk. Partial or total emasculation of a man is forbidden even if he is a slave. Anyone dealing in emasculation must suffer discretionary punishment. Abū Ḥanīfa disliked all trading in or the employment of eunuchs. The Prophet forbade castration.

A midwife must be prevented from aborting a child once it is evident that a child has formed[317]. Prior to such an event, there is no harm in applying treatment for

316 See Abū al-Layth, *Bustān*: 94–5.

317 According to the Prophet, animation takes place in 120 days, that is four months after conception. Abortion is allowed (after animation) for certain causes, as for instance when the woman is known to experience hardship in delivery and doctors are decided that her pregnancy, if allowed to continue, will be injurious to her health. As to abortion before animation, jurists are disagreed here. Some, like al-Ghazālī, rejected it. Others, including some Ḥanafīs, are of the opinion that it is permissible, although there are some among the latter who deem it as disfavoured, if carried out with no sufficient reason. One of the excuses in this respect for authorizing abortion before animation is the drying up of the mother's milk at a time when the husband is unable to hire a wet nurse to suckle the baby and save its life. *Islam and Family Planning*. Translation from Arabic

abortion. It is tantamount to *ᶜazl* (*coitus interruptus*) in this respect. Some hold that abortive practices are forbidden at any time because the child is alive from the moment that the sperm is deposited in the womb, and do not consider abortion comparable to *coitus interruptus* **[154]** because sperm alone does not form a living being. ᶜAlī considered *coitus interruptus* reprehensible.

The length of time taken for a child to be formed and come alive is, according to the Prophet, 120 days.

Sunāmī: this hadith does not apply generally; the Prophet was dealing with a specific case. Doctors dislike generalizations. The length of time for delivery varies with different women; so also will the time taken for formation. *48B*

Other occupations subject to action on the part of the *muḥtasib* are those practised by persons engaged in one of the following: keening; singing; professional cantors (*qawwāl*); magic; wine keeping; manufacture of flutes from wood, hide, or pottery; drawing of pictures; shaving of men's beards **[155]** or women's heads so that they resemble men; the braiding with human hair of a woman's hair to give her a finer crop of hair for a wedding – this was prohibited by the Prophet; training a falcon with live birds – dead birds must be used; producing Qurans that are small by using a fine pen. (Authorities quoted to prove that those who do not master trading should be expelled from the market.)

Waist belts and *qalansuwwa*s may be sold to Christians and Zoroastrians respectively, for these are for them symbols of humiliation. Shoemakers must not produce slippers of the style worn by Zoroastrians and evil-livers (*fussāq*). Similarly, a tailor must not produce garments of a style worn by evil-livers.

A Muslim may work in a church because there is nothing intrinsically sinful about the nature of the work, but he may not be employed to ring church bells for five dirhams a day when he would only be paid one dirham in any other occupation. He must look elsewhere for his livelihood.

The *muḥtasib* must instruct blacksmiths to have a screen between his smithy and the street to prevent sparks from flying all over the street.**[156]** Red-hot splinters of iron may kill, blind, burn clothing, cause the death of a riding animal, and so on. Should any of these things happen, the blacksmith is liable for damages. His family will be liable for payment of compensation arising out of death or the loss of an eye. *49A*

Milk may not be watered down. In this connection a long anecdote about ᶜUmar is told in Persian. From the story numerous conclusions may be drawn, *viz*:

1. A *muḥtasib* may make tours of the market.
2. He may make enquiries about the traders and so on without notifying them of the fact. **[157]**

---

of the proceedings of the International Islamic Conference in Rabat (Morocco), December 1971, (Beirut 1974): 2:98.

3. There were market rogues in ᶜUmar's time – so how much more so in aftertimes?
4. The *muḥtasib* may threaten traders with the oath.
5. A child may forbid his parents to lie.
6. If a child realizes that he cannot restrain his parents by admonition, he may inform the *muḥtasib* of the fact.
7. If the *muḥtasib* is apprised of the adulteration of milk *49B* or any other substance, he may punish the offender.
8. If a woman is party to an offence, then she is subject to the same punishment as a man.
9. If a child speaks truthfully, contrary to what is expected of him and contrary to inclination, this is proof of innate goodness. **[158]**
10. The choice of a marriage partner should not depend either on exalted rank or on occupation. The proof of this lies in ᶜUmar's action in the anecdote: although his son was the son of the Caliph and of Qurashite origin, ᶜUmar commanded his son to marry a market girl, who was a milk vendor.
11. This story shows ᶜUmar's acumen.
12. Obedience of a child to his parents (ᶜUmar's son) is preferable to his following his own reason.

Hoarding and the practice of traders going out to meet people bringing produce to the markets (*talaqqī arrukbān*) at such places where such action would be prejudicial to the interests of the public are reprehensible because hoarding is forbidden and the expression 'going out to meet caravans' is to be interpreted as meeting any vendor of produce in circumstances prejudicial to the public interest. (Quoted from *Sharḥ al-Taḥāwī al-kabīr.*)

It is reprehensible to sell arms to the enemy, to dissidents, and the troops of dissidents.

Taking birds by night is permissible. Any ban there may be on the practice arises out of compassion since God has permitted hunting without restriction.

Anyone witnessing a document in the slave market involving sex (*muwāḍaᶜa*) is accursed. (Quoted from *Multaqaṭ.*) Also accursed is anyone who testifies to the oral affirmation of such a contract, knowing **[159]** the reason for agreeing to bear witness. Ignorance of the reason for the contract, however, makes the testimony lawful.

The testimony of one who sells a singing girl because of her ability to sing is not to be regarded as a credible witness.

Wheat and barley are to be ground by hand, not by animals. (Quoted from *Shīrᶜat al-Islām.*) *50A*

A merchant should not swear oaths in order to push the sale of his goods. (Examples are given from *Bustān.*)

A number of Persian expressions which may imply man's independence of God are quoted form *Dhakhīra* as being unacceptable, and so prohibited.

A vendor should declare any faults or defects in the object he is offering for sale, but failure to do so would not make him an unacceptable witness in law. Some, however, would dispute this.

According to a Tradition in *Bukhārī*, the Prophet prohibited pictures of living creatures, but allowed the painting of trees, leaves, dead animals, and so on. **[160]**

Action must be taken against Muslims taking certain materials into enemy territory.

Muḥammad: the rule only applies to horses and mules, weapons and captives. Trading with the enemy is best avoided since it is a form of cooperation. *50B* There is no harm in trading in food and clothing and similar substances. Thumāma became a Muslim at a time of supply embargo which was imposed by the Prophet upon the people of Makka. When the Prophet was requested by the people of Makka to allow Thumāma to carry food to them from Madina, he gave such permission even though he was at war with them. The permission was given for reasons of mutual interest since the two parties needed each other. The only exception to this rule is of objects that can be used in war like weapons (*silāḥ*) and riding animals (*kurāᶜ*).**[161]** Sarakhsī defines *kurāᶜ* as pack animals of any kind, while *silāḥ* is to be taken as anything whatever that can be turned to use in warfare. Cotton and clothing do not come into such a category. Iron, however, does since it is the material from which weapons are made. Brocade and raw silk also fall into the same category since they can be turned to use in war. The same does not apply to light silk clothing.

If the enemy is likely to use padded cotton jerkins, in combat, then they are proscribed. *51A* Vultures that are alive or dead but with wings still attached may not be taken into enemy territory because the purpose for which they will be used is to supply feathers for use as fletchings on arrows and bolts. The same applies to eagles if their feathers are also to be made into fletchings.[318]

A Muslim may visit enemy territory under safe-conduct for the purpose of trading and at the same time take with him his weapons and his horse provided that he does not sell them. If suspected of wishing to do so, he must swear an oath that he will not sell until he returns, unless he is in dire need (*ḍarūra*). The same conditions apply to ships and their contents.

Dhimmis must not be allowed to take into enemy territory horses, pack-horses, and weapons because it may be assumed that they will serve the interests of their co-religionaries. They may take donkeys, mules, ships, cows, and calves, but they are

---

318 In describing the characteristics of arrows, Latham and Paterson say, 'There are different types of fletchings (*rīsh*). The best and most serviceable are vulture feathers, after which come those of the eagle'. J.D. Latham and W.F. Paterson, *Saracen Archery* (London, 1970): 26.

to swear that they do not intend to sell them until after leaving that territory unless they be in dire need.

An enemy alien, resident in Muslim territory (*musta'min*), must under no circumstances be allowed to transport anything to his home territory unless he be employed by a Muslim or a dhimmi as a muleteer.

Mules, donkeys, oxen, and camels may be taken into enemy territory since no trade is possible without them. **[162]**... ... This is a matter of *istiḥsān*; the position of *qiyās*, however, is diametrically opposed to that of *istiḥsān* in the matter. (Quoted from *Dhakhīra*.)**[163]**

Sources: *ShṬK*
MN
FKh
SA
KSh
ShI
BA
Dh
Saḥ
ShSK

CHAPTER 41
(S)
On Slaves (*mamālīk*)

It is reprehensible for one to put a neckerchief (*rāya*) *51B* around a slave's neck, but not reprehensible to shackle him. The reason for the difference is that the purpose of the neckerchief is to expose a slave to unwarranted public humiliation (*ishhār*, *muthla*), whereas shackling is retribution that is merited in the same way as beating administered by way of deserved discipline. (Tradition quoted in support of the view, which Sunāmī also uses to prove that one may have an unbeliever in one's service, be he slave or hireling.)

No man who daily and hourly abuses his slaves and his household is to be regarded as a credible witness, etc. (Quoted from *Multaqaṭ*.)

From Tanbīh: Abū al-Layth al-Samarqanī stated that ᶜĀmir al-Shaᶜbī said, 'One of the Prophet's Companions requested some water from a household. When the maid was late in bringing it to him, the lady of the house cursed the maid. The Prophet's Companion said to the lady, "You will be punished by *ḥadd* on the Day of Judgment unless you can present four witnesses who can testify that what you said is true."

The lady then freed the slave girl. The Prophet's Companion said, "May this action cause Allah to forgive you.'[319] **[164]**

It is forbidden to preserve curls in a slave-boy for corrupt purposes. (Quoted from *Dhakhīra*.)

It is reprehensible to fit a slave or slave-girl with an iron collar that will not allow him or her to move their head. It is an act of cruelty and a punishment meted out to the inmates of Hell. However, *Jāmi^c al-ṣaghīr* gives an opinion that permits the practice because of the frequency of the runaway Hindu slave as opposed to the infrequency of such in the early Muslim community.

A slave may not be maltreated by his master. *52A* If he is, he has the right to plead his case, if corroborated by evidence, before the qadi.**[165]**

Sources: *ShK*
JṢKh
Dh
MN
TGh

CHAPTER 42
(TOS)
On Funerals

Washers must not charge for washing the corpse, but payment may be made for carrying the dead, grave-digging, and burial. The reason for the distinction is that the first is a meritorious act which God will reward (*ḥisba*). If a man is somewhere where there is no one to wash and carry him apart from these persons, they are entitled to no payment. But if there are others available, they are so entitled.

To raise one's voice (*raf^c al-ṣawt*) at a funeral is reprehensible. However, there are differing interpretations of *raf^c al-ṣawt*. One is that it denotes wailing, rending of clothing, and scratching of faces, all of which are reprehensible. Another is that it refers to the practice whereby a man stands up before a congregation that has come together for the ritual prayer and prays aloud for the deceased. This practice is also reprehensible since such prayers should take the form of silent supplication to God. For this reason the common laments prevalent in our town are reprehensible since they incorporate a lot of exaggeration and public supplication. Yet another interpretation is that since it relates to the pre-Islamic practice of exceeding all reasonable bounds in eulogising the dead it is not reprehensible; it is in fact sanctioned by Prophetic precedent (Tradition quoted), but the eulogy must represent the strict truth. **[166]**

---

319 See Abū al-Layth, *Tanbīh*: 127.

The dead should be interred in the burial grounds of the community in which they have died, but it is permissible to transport a body over a distance not exceeding two miles. There is a difference of opinion on the distance.

Living thorns and grass should not be removed *52B* from around a grave because these are living creatures giving up praise to God, and, as long as they continue to live, they are a comfort to the dead.

A garment or a quilt (*maḍraba*) may be laid under a body in the grave.

To engage a Quran-reader to read at the graveside is an innovation (*bidᶜa*).

A testamentary instruction to a man to build around his father's grave is acceptable as long as the purpose is preservation of the site and not ornamentation. One view is that a man's testamentary instruction for his grave to be covered with mud or covered with a dome or for a paid Quran-reader to read at his grave side is null and void.

Dhimmis have the right to use land which they own as a burial ground. This is because it is their lawful property.

If a pregnant woman dies and is buried, she may not be exhumed because she is seen in a dream to have given birth.

The question of keening is dealt with elsewhere.

People suffering a bereavement in the family may remain in their home for three days while others come to express their condolences, but it is better not to follow such a practice. To sit at the door of one's house, however, is forbidden since this is a pre-Islamic practice forbidden by the Prophet. **[167]** (Quoted from *Khāniyya* and *Muḥīṭ*.) The practice prevalent in Persian territories (*bilād al-ᶜajam*) of laying carpets out and standing in the middle of the road is one of the worst practices.[320]

A grave should not be squared in accordance with the custom practised by those who ignorantly imitate mystical ideas. Our rite prescribes that a mound be raised shelving at both sides (*tasnīm*).

A body may be transported over one or two miles. Any distance beyond that is reprehensible.

The news of a person's death may be announced to his relatives and friends, but it may not be publicly proclaimed in the markets. Some later jurists commend such proclamation in the markets on the grounds that it inspires people to say the ritual prayer for the deceased, but others do not allow it.

A person washing a corpse should be in a state of ritual purity.

No one should raise his voice in praise of a deceased person while he is being carried on his bier. One view is that no one should ask God's forgiveness for the deceased while walking in the funeral procession.

---

320 This practice of laying out carpets and standing on the roads and pavements can be seen in modern Arabic countries such as Iraq or Saudi Arabia, where it is known as *majlis ᶜazā'*.

A man must not rise *53A* if he catches sight of a bier. The practice was permitted in early Islam, but then it was revoked.

The niche (*laḥd*) in the grave must not be bricked if the corpse is to be in contact with the bricks. If the bricks are to be concealed (*muwarāt*), it is acceptable.

A body may only be exhumed from the ground in which it has been laid if it has been misappropriated or is the subject of pre-emption (*shufᶜa*).

A grave may be uncovered if it is discovered after it has been covered in that some item fell into it at the time of burial.

Anyone who has died or been killed should be buried in the cemeteries of those among whom he died. To carry the body one or two miles before burial is permissible. Similarly, anyone dying outside his own country is best left there, but there is no harm in transferring his body **[168]** to another country as happened in the case of Jacob who, after a time, was taken from Egypt to Syria. Also Saᶜd b. Abū Waqqāṣ was carried four parasangs back to Madina.

Once one has been buried, one must not be disinterred after a short time or long unless there be a good reason to do so. A corpse may be carried one or two miles, but it is reprehensible to carry it from one area to another.

The case of a woman who wanted to disinter her son and take him to his home town is cited: she was not allowed to do so.

One should not be buried with weapons, skins, furs, padding, slippers, and *qalansuwwa.* (Tradition quoted from *Muḥīṭ*)

A woman should be shrouded in five garments, a man in three (Tradition from ᶜUmar). It is most appropriate for a woman to be covered from breasts to thighs. (Quoted from *Hidaya.*).[321]

Cosmetics may be used apart from saffron and *wars* in the case of men. **[169]** *53B* Men may not have a shroud of silk (*ibrīsam*) or material dyed with safflower. This does not apply to women.

If a man dies a pauper, the community must provide a shroud, and if they are not able to do so, they must beg a garment for him since he cannot do that for himself.

The mourners must not all precede the bier; some may precede [and the rest follow]. One may ride in a funeral procession but at a distance, the reason being that humility is required. Torches may not be used.

To purchase a shroud is a voluntary meritorious act.

One must not pray over an unbeliever or stand at his graveside. (Quran quoted in support.) The exception to this last rule is when an unbeliever dies leaving only Muslim relatives. Then they should wash him as they would a defiled garment and then cast him on dunghills. (Tradition referring to ᶜAbd Allāh b. Abū Salūl quoted.) **[170]**

---

321 See Marghinānī, *Hidāya*: 4:268.

Sources: *MN*
Dh
FKh
Muḥ
H
ShṬK
AḥQ

CHAPTER 43
On the Disposal of Wine and the Slaughtering of Swine

A *muḥtasib* will be under no legal liability if he disposes of wine that belongs to a Muslim. This is owing to the fact that he is doing good (*muḥsin*) and there is no [adverse] responsibility for such a good action [Quran quoted (there is no complaint against those who do right) ix:91].

If the wine belongs to a protected person (dhimmi) and the one who disposes of it is not a *muḥtasib*, there are two possible outcomes, *viz*:
- If he disposes of it after buying it, there is no [adverse] responsibility for him, whether he is a *muḥtasib* or not, because once it is sold the vendor has given him full authority to do whatever he wants with it. It would be similar to the case of an owner giving someone else permission *54A* to kill one of his animals. The Muslim in this case is under no legal obligation to pay the price of the spilled wine because this is not expected.
- If he disposed of it without buying it he is responsible, since wine to them is like vinegar to Muslims. It represents an object that has a value and this entails responsibility for him who damages it. Shāfiᶜī, however, believed that even in these circumstances wine has no value in a Muslim land. The solution to the problem is that already stated. If a *muḥtasib* destroyed wine that belonged to a protected person (dhimmi), then the *muḥtasib* cannot be held liable because he is using his personal judgment (*mujtahid fīh*). Full details of this matter can be found in Chapter 27 on *Ahl al-dhimma*.

From *Dhakhīra*: No one has the right to bring wine or swine into a Muslim town, that is one in which *Jumuᶜa* prayer is held and legal punishments (*ḥudūd*) are executed. This rule applies to Muslims and non-Muslims.**[171]** If a Muslim is caught in this action and refutes the accusation, then his claim should be examined. If in defending himself he says he is only in transit to another area, or that he intends to convert the wine into vinegar, or even if he claimed that it does not belong to him, his status should be looked into. If he is known as a religious person, he should be released and told to convert the wine into vinegar. This is because his appearance should be trusted until proved otherwise.

If he is a person who might be expected to consume the wine or eat the swine, then either should be destroyed. **[172]**
Sources: *Dh*

CHAPTER 44
(S)
On Proprietors of Plantations and Gardens

According to Ibn ᶜUmar human excrement should not be used to improve cultivatable land. Saᶜd, however, does not prohibit the practice, and Muḥammad allows its use on condition that it be mixed with a much larger quantity of soil. Abū Ḥanīfa is said to have expressed both opinions. Reasons and conditions for permissibility are given. (*Qūt al-qulūb* quotes a Tradition in this respect.) *54B*
Sources: *QQ*

[173]

CHAPTER 45
(TS)
On Dyeing the Hair and Body

To dye the beard red is sanctioned by the practice of the Prophet. Black may only be used in war to frighten the enemy; it may not be used by men as a cosmetic to make them attractive to women. Males, old or young, must not dye the hands and feet, but women may do so. It is also permissible for a girl's ears to be pierced; a boy's ears may not be pierced.

Any name (*ism*) not found in the Quran or known through the practice of the Prophet or known to have been common among early Muslims should not be used. It is best to avoid innovatory practices in this respect.

To trim the beard is permissible. *55A*

Fatāwā al-Khāniyya: Abū Ḥanīfa said, 'I had my hair shaved once and I was corrected by the barber on **[174]** three matters. When I sat not facing the qibla, he told me to do so. When I gave my left side to start cutting, he said give me the right side. Finally when I was about to go, he told me to bury my hair first.' Sunāmī concludes from this story, in addition to the manner of hair-cutting that:
- Abū Ḥanīfa's hair was shaved.
- Advice should be taken even if it comes from a person of a lower social status.

Multaqaṭ al-Nāṣirī: Shāfiᶜī prayed after he had his head shaved while his clothes were covered with trimmed hair. When he was asked about this, he replied, 'We have to lower ourselves when following the Iraqi school.' Some conclusions from the story:

- Shāfiᶜi's head was shaved.
- He would follow our *madhhab* in what he needed rather than his own.
- Trimmed hair does not prevent the follower of the Ḥanafī school from praying. **[175]**
- Shāfi'ī may not have meant by 'lower himself' a degrading remark about the Ḥanafī school but merely that he considered that following an easy choice is a form of lowering his view. **[176]**

Sources: *FKh*
MN

CHAPTER 46
(S)
On Innovations

It is reprehensible to recite the Quran in front of people who are not giving their attention to it because that is disrespectful to the Quran. For this reason some authorities find it reprehensible to dispense charity to beggars reciting the Quran in the markets.

Various innovations relating to the recitation of the Quran and the occasions thereof are discussed as well as the question whether the Quran may be sung or not – likewise the call to prayer. **[177]** Some authorities disallow sculpted decor on the qibla wall and the wall of the *miḥrāb* because it serves as a distraction to worshippers. *55B* Other authorities do allow the ceiling to be decorated.

Vendors of *fuqāᶜ* should not, when opening *fuqāᶜ*, invoke God's blessing of the Prophet. The same goes for those whose job it is to clear the streets for an approaching procession. (Quoted from *Multaqaṭ*.)

Some hold that a watchman (*ḥāris*) is acting sinfully if he recites the *shahāda* while on duty because that is not part of the work for which he is employed. (Quoted from *al-Jāmiᶜ al-ṣaghīr al-Khānī*.) Sunāmī opines that this is not so; for, if he did not recite the *shahāda* aloud, he would need something else in its place to keep him awake, and there is danger of his singing, which is prohibited.

The *muḥtasīb* should enforce Islamic ritual such as the call to prayer, the ritual prayer, and the sunna. **[178]** Any person ceasing to perform these duties must be punished. The practice of celibacy is proscribed in Islam (Traditions quoted); *56A* for Muslims celibacy is the jihad.

To pronounce the *takbīr* either in the markets or in the mosques on *tashrīq* days is prohibited. **[179]**

Sources: *ShSK*
MN
JS
Dh
ShK

CHAPTER 47
(SO) [180-184]
On the Times when *Iḥtisāb* Ceases to be a Duty through Incapacity to Perform it

Inability to carry out the duty of *iḥtisāb* is sufficient reason to allow the duty to lapse, though it is highly meritorious to perform the duty in difficult circumstances. Different traditions and an anecdote about Abū Muḥjin al-Thaqafī *56B*, *57A* and *57B* are quoted from *Kifāya*[322] to prove that the duty of *iḥtisāb* may be allowed to lapse if it is liable to cause hardship.

The question whether one may stop performing the ritual prayer if one sees a crime being perpetrated against oneself (e.g. theft), is discussed. It is held that if someone else is seen to be the victim of a crime or to be suffering from some untoward situation (e.g. a blind man walks into a hole *58A* (*Kifāya* quoted) or a man is drowning), one may interrupt the prayer ... ...

Sources: *TA*
TB
FZ̤
KSh
Saḥ

CHAPTER 48
(SO) [185-189]
On Excessive Deference to Others

Action must be taken against any person who prostrates himself, bows or kisses the ground before any but God. To perform any such act is considered by some to constitute unbelief. To bow down before a ruler (sultan) or anyone else is reprehensible, since it is tantamount to a 'Magian' practice. (Multaqaṭ quoted.) The question whether one may kiss someone's hands apart from those of the just ruler (*sulṭān ʿādil*) and the religious scholar (*ʿālim*) is discussed.

---

322 A quotation from *Kifāya*, MS no. 1699, 183 A–B.

Sunāmī observes that the imams of his day kissed not only the hands of rulers, but also their feet, and, even worse, the hooves of horses presented to them by rulers *58B* ... ... *59A* ... ...

Sources *MN*
KSh
FKh
WN
Muḥ
Tadh

CHAPTER 49
On the Difference between an Official *Muḥtasib* and the Voluntary *Muḥtasīb* (i.e. Censor)

First

According to Abū Saᶜīd al-Khudrī, the Prophet said, "if you see an evil, you should alter it with your hand; if you do not, then you should alter it by your tongue; if you cannot then deny it in your heart, which is the weakest action of faith. Using the hand for remonstration is for the rulers, while the tongue is for the scholars, and the heart is for the common people." *59B*

Second

The voluntary *muḥtasib* is only obliged to advise people if he thinks that they will listen to him. Accordingly if a voluntary *muḥtasib* sees dirt on a Muslim's clothes which is larger than the size of a dirham, he should tell him if he believes that he will become occupied with cleaning it. If he believes that if he tells him that he will not listen to him, then he need not tell him. The appointed *muḥtasib* is compelled to remonstrate against people because he has the power to do so.

Third

A voluntary *muḥtasib* is civilly responsible if he causes damage providing he had a reasonable excuse. Accordingly, if a person knocked down a house to stop a fire from spreading to his home; he is only responsible for the damage he caused. This is similar to a person compelled by fear of death to eat from another person's food without permission. **[190]** If a *muḥtasib* is appointed, then he will bear no responsibility because his actions are done in the public interest.

Fourth

If a voluntary *muḥtasib* believes that his remonstrations will be heeded, then he is obliged to exercise *ḥisba*, but if the voluntary *muḥtasib* knew that the offender would not listen to him or would fight with him, then he need not remonstrate with him. However, if he chose to carry on with his action he will be considered as a *mujāhid* acting in the way of Allah. If he knew that he could not bear the suffering resulting from his exercise of *ḥisba*, then it is better that he avoids being hurt.

Fifth

Both forms of *muḥtasib* may remove a public hazard although for a volunteer it is advisable that he first ask permission of the appointed *muḥtasib.*

Sixth

An appointed *muḥtasib* is not responsible if he damages musical instruments but the voluntary *muḥtasib* is. The advice here is that he should ask the owner to donate it to him and then break it, as Ibn **[191]** al-Mubārak is reported to have done with people playing the *ṭanbūr. 60A*

Seventh

The voluntary *muḥtasib* needs to intend that his action is for God alone. The appointed *muḥtasib* does not need to make this intention since he is doing his job and *riyā'* is therefore not expected. Abū Bakr al-ᶜAyyaḍ once met a group of youths drinking alcohol. When he approached them they brandished knives and swords in his face, which caused him to retreat. But when he made his intention pure for Allah, he managed to cause them to flee. **[192]**

Sources: *KSh*

CHAPTER 50
(S)
An Explanation of Why the Institution of *Iḥtisāb* is Attributed to the Caliph ᶜUmar

First

ᶜUmar said, "There are three things I love about this world of ours: ordering good, prohibiting evil, and the application of God's legal punishment (*ḥadd*). (Quoted from *Yawāqīt al-Mawāqīt* by Nasafī.)

Second

It has been narrated in the *Akhbār* according to *al-Kifāya al-Shaᶜbiyya* that the flag of justice on the Day of Judgment will be carried by ᶜUmar. Some people may wonder how ᶜUmar could be so just when he is reported to have whipped his son Abū Shaḥma until he died. The whipping is claimed to have continued even after the death of his son which violates the respect due to the dead. The answer to this claim can be found in the Fatāwā al-Ẓahīriyya in the chapter on how to divide the apostate's property. It states that this story is an incorrect fabrication by the liar Muḥammad b. Tamīm al-Dārī. The truth is that he survived the whipping and recovered to die from natural causes.

Third

The removal of evil cannot be exercised unless the fear of people caused by the Devil is removed from their hearts. Since ᶜUmar caused the Devil to run away, it is only expected that *iḥtisab* is attributed to him. **[193]**

Fourth and Fifth

ᶜUmar's orders used to be obeyed. When there was an earthquake, his order stopped it. *60B* He was also able to dry up water and cause it to flow again. A story is told about ᶜUmar commanding the Nile to flow again when it had dried up. The previous remedy had been to drown a young woman, fully dressed in clothes and jewellery. ᶜUmar instead wrote a letter ordering the Nile to flow by God's permission. Quoted from *al-Kifāya al-Shaᶜbiyya* in the chapter of stories. **[194]**

Sources: *YM*
KSh
FẒ
MM

CHAPTER 51
(S) [194-195]
On Action Taken in the Matter of Musical Instruments and Wine Vessels

First comes a discussion of points raised earlier as to whether compensation is payable to owners of musical instruments and wine containers in the event of these being broken for pious reasons. Also the question of listening to music and the playing of certain musical instruments is discussed. *61A* The matter of backgammon and chess is raised. **[196]**

Sources: *K*
MN
FN
FKh
SM

CHAPTER 52
(SO)
On the Conduct Required in the Practice of Ḥisba

The *muḥtasib* should fulfil the following personal requirements:
- He should enjoin discreetly. This is the most effective way of preforming *ḥisba.* Abū al-Dardā' stated that 'to remonstrate upon brethren in secret is a compliment but to do so in public is an injury'. Public remonstration can be resorted to as an alternative for him who does not respond to a discreet admonishment.
- He should only be acting for the sake of God and the reverence of the faith and not out of personal anger, otherwise God will not help him.

Sunāmī: I read (*balaghanī*)[323] that ᶜIkrima narrated that a man passed a tree which was being venerated and worshipped it instead of God. *61B* The man was about to cut down the tree when the devil, Iblīs, in human form stopped him and offered him a dirham a day if he did not. The man collected the money under his bed for a few days. Then one day he woke up to find that there was no money. **[197]** He picked up his axe and went to cut down the tree. Again he encountered the devil who said to him, 'if you attempt to cut down the tree, I will kill you. Before I had no power over you because your action was for the sake of God, but now you are here for the money. Thus, the man was rendered incapable of action.'
- He should be a learned person since without this requirement he might do exactly the opposite of what is expected of him and this would make him look like a hypocrite. (Quran ix:67 quoted.)
- He should be kind and gentle like Moses when he remonstrated with Pharaoh. (Quran xx:44 quoted.)
- He should be wise and patient if he suffers on account of his actions like Luqmān. (Quran xxxi:17 quoted.)
- He, himself should practice what he says like Shuᶜayb. (Quran xi:88, ii:44 quoted.) The following tradition of the Prophet is also cited. The Prophet said, *62A* "When I ascended to heaven I saw some men with their lips being clipped with clippers. When I asked Jibrīl who they were, he said, 'These are the pulpit speakers of your people who would order good but neglect themselves'."
- His intention should be only to do good like Shuᶜayb. (Quran xi:88 quoted) **[198]**
- He should be aware that his success is in God's hands alone. He should therefore depend only on Him like Shuᶜayb. (Quran xi:88 quoted.)

---

323 The word *balaghanī* seems to mean to the author, 'I read somewhere'. The anecdotes he reports here appear to be quoted verbatim from *Tanbīh al-ghāfilīn*, but Sunāmī does not make reference to it. Abū al-Layth, *Tanbīh*: 33.

If the *muḥtasib* himself commits a sin, should he still order others not to do it? The answer to this can be found in the following hadith of the Prophet: 'Order good even if you do not do it and reprehend evil even if you fall into it.'
Sunāmī: such an action will be rewarded by God. Yet if he does not repent, he will be severely punished by God. (Hadith quoted.)
Sunāmī: the Sufis require another condition for the practice of *iḥtisāb*. This condition is that it should not be performed for a personal reason. Abū Bakr al-Shiblī is reported to have seen a ship loaded with wine jars that was being imported for the caliph from Egypt. He jumped into the ship and began to destroy all these jars and no one dared to say a word. Finally only one jar remained. Abū Bakr was escorted to Muᶜtaṣim, the caliph. The caliph said to him, 'I know you want me to kill you in order that you would be a martyr and that I am not going to do.' He then enquired from him about the reason that had made him leave the last jar untouched. The answer which Shiblī gave was that it was the only one that he felt he would be breaking for his own personal satisfaction.[324]
- The *muḥtasib* should fear no one but God. **[199]** *62B* A story about the bravery of Abū Ghiyāth al-Zāhid while facing Prince Naṣr b. Aḥmad is cited.
From *Shirᶜat al-Islām*: The conditions for enjoining good are three.
- The *muḥtasib*'s intention should be only for the sake of God.
- He should know the justifying reason (*ḥujja*) for his action.
- He should be patient in the face of any mischief that he may encounter.

He should also have three personal attributes:**[200]**
- Gentleness (*rifq*), since harshness can only lead to corruption (*fasād*). (Quran iii:159 quoted.)
- Mild temper (*ḥilm*), when facing other's harsh words, and
- Knowledge (*fiqh*), so that his action will not be evil itself.

From *Adab al- qāḍī*: The judge may say a general *salām* to the opponents. On this point the *mashāikh* disagreed as to whether *salām* is compulsory or not. *63A*

Sunāmī states that he is inclined to take the view that the qadi should not bid *salām* to preserve respect. He states that other scholars state that the qadi should say *salām* because it is a *sunna*. When the judge sits, he should neither bid the opponents *salām* nor should they bid him *salām*.
Sunāmī: by analogy to the judge the *muḥtasib* should not bid people in the market *salām* in order to preserve respect... ... **[201–202]**

Following that Sunāmī cites a story relevant to the conduct of *muḥtasib*s. ᶜUmar once viewed a man listening to a woman singer while drinking alcohol. When he climbed over the fence to rebuke the man, the man said, "O, prince of believers, let

324 See *Sharḥ adab al-qāḍī*: 37B.

me defend myself. If I disobeyed God once, you have disobeyed him three times." When 'Umar asked, "How?" the man said, "You have violated God's order when He said, Do not spy (xlix:12). Also you did not enter the house from the main door, violating the verse that says it is not right to enter houses from their backs (ii:189). Finally, you entered without permission. In doing this you violated the verse that states, 'Do not enter other people's houses without asking for permission' (xxiv:27)." ʿUmar acknowledged his error and apologized. Sunāmī concludes from this story that the *muḥtasib* may not spy or climb over fences of people hiding themselves. Another question that is raised is whether a *muḥtasib* should walk round the markets or whether he should summon the traders to his house for examination. The answer given is that he should go round the markets himself because to summon them to his house would interfere with their lawful business and inflict hardship in the absence of proof of any misdemeanour on their part. The position of the *muḥtasib* in this respect is different from that of a qadi because in the case of the qadi there is a clear case to be answered.**[203]**

Then the chapter concludes with anecdotes about ʿUmar, al-Ḥasan, and the Prophet ... *63B-64B* ... ... **[204]**

Sources: *ShI*
AQ
KSh
QQ

CHAPTER 53
(TS)
On Taking Action against Innovations (*Bidaʿ*) in Private Houses and the *Muḥtasib*'s Raiding the Premises of Wrongdoers Without their Permission

To write notes during *Nayrūz* and to stick them on doors is reprehensible because it is disrespectful to the name of God and the Prophet. Authorities are cited to demonstrate that privacy need not be respected if householders are *known* to be engaging in unlawful practices, e.g. playing unacceptable musical instruments. *Adab al-qāḍī* is also cited in support of the view that if the sounds of unlawful practices are heard coming from a house, it may lawfully be entered. The author of the *Iḍāḥ* stated that Abū Yūsuf was flexible in giving permission to the *muḥtasib* to attack a house from whence there issued the sounds of corruption. Hishām narrated that Muḥammad [b. al-Ḥasan]'s view was also the same on this...

ʿUmar's entry into a house in which wine was said to be kept and into another house in which a woman was keening are taken as the precedents for lawful entry into the homes of wrongdoers.

The manner in which a house may be raided is described by reference to a case in which A owes B some money and is hiding in his home in order to avoid B. If the qadi is certain that the situation is as described, he should send two of his agents (*umanā'*) accompanied by a company of **[205]** officers (*aʿwān*) and some women. The enforcement officers stand at the door, around the house, and on the roof to prevent the wanted man from escaping. The women then enter without seeking permission and without standing on ceremony and instruct the man's womenfolk to go into a corner. The judge's enforcement officers enter and search the house room by room and any hiding places until they find the culprit and bring him out. If they cannot find him, they tell their women to examine the women, for he may be hiding among them.

Any person who does not attend the community [prayer] should be remonstrated with. *65A* A Prophetic Tradition is quoted to show that anyone who abandons the community [prayer] should have his house burnt. **[206]**

Sources: *AQ*
Muḥ
IMN

CHAPTER 54
(TS)
What is to be Prohibited on Public Roads and What is not to be Prohibited

No one has the right to take legal action over drains in a street or do away with them. (*Multaqaṭ* quoted.) An opposite view will be stated later in the book. Children must not be allowed to play with walnuts and the like in the street, whether gambling or not, because they cause obstruction, but their nuts may not be broken. Anecdote about Abū Ḥanīfa in this respect.

Children if they are playing in the street should be prevented whether or not the game is a game of chance. Otherwise they may play, for ʿUmar and ʿAlī both bought their children walnuts on the occasion of the ʿĪd, and the children would play with the walnuts and eat them.

Removal of clay or earth from a public road. On days when there is mud and mire around, removal is permitted because it cleans the road. On the other hand, if the street is not muddy and removal is against the public interest, it is prohibited since private interest cannot override what is prejudicial to the public. **[207]**

It is not permissible either to leave a beast of burden on the street or to sprinkle the street with water. If a bleacher (or "fuller") leaves his donkey in the street and it causes someone a mishap, then he is liable only if the victim was unaware of the possible accident.

If anyone sprinkles water on a road and a donkey slips on it, the person who did the sprinkling is liable for damages. This also applies if someone else suffers a mishap providing he had no alternative route. There is nothing wrong with sprinkling the road to keep dust down, but it is not permissible to exceed reasonable bounds.

The case of a house that is one of a row and to which an upper room has been added prior to the purchase of a neighbouring house whose new occupant may have grounds for objecting to the structure. The rights of the new owner are upheld.

A dunghill in a public thoroughfare should not constitute a nuisance to neighbours and passers-by in consequence of its becoming a public tip. Any member of the public *65B* may object to the nuisance and have it abated. But if the road is a cul-de-sac, only the residents are entitled to take such action.

The legality of constructing a canopy that projects into the public highway or bridging the latter by some construction that runs across it from one house to another is discussed. **[208]** The differences of opinion among jurists are discussed as well as the difference between cul-de-sacs, private roads, etc. **[209]**

The case of spouts and gutters and injuries resulting therefrom. The *K. al-Diyyāt* is quoted as differentiating between the case of one who is injured on someone's premises and one who is injured *66A* in the street. In the first case, no liability attaches to the owner of the gutter or drainpipe, whereas in the second case it does. If there is doubt about the location, *qiyās* would permit the conclusion that there is no liability, but preference (*istiḥsān*) (according to the *Khāniyya*) divides the liability equally between the owner and the injured.

The case of the man in a cul-de-sac who wishes to put in another door to his house that is higher or lower than that already existing. A *fatwā* declares that he may do so.

A public mosque may be built by the inhabitants of a quarter if the road is large enough provided that it does not adversely affect the road.

Action should be taken to stop persons walking through cemeteries unless the footpath is an old one. Anyone may find a path through a cemetery and use it provided he knows within him that he is not unclean (*muḥdith*).

Vendors of goods may not take up a pitch in a road if it is going to be a nuisance to the public, nor should people make purchases from them. If there is no nuisance, then all is well.

According to Abū Yūsuf, to plaster the wall of a house is not permitted if it encroaches on a road. By analogy the wall could be demolished but not if we apply [the principle of] preference (*istiḥsān*). Naṣr b. Muḥammad al-Marwazī, the disciple of Abū Ḥanīfa, would hack old plaster off his wall before he replastered it, if it was located on the public road. Aḥmad Ibn Ḥanbal abandoned one of his students because he plastered his wall so that it encroached on the street. **[210]**

Returning to the subject of canopies, drains, etc., no one may dig a drain in a road that causes blockage at the top of it. (Quoted from *Multaqaṭ al-Nāṣirī.*) A *fatwā* bearing on a *muḥtasib*'s dealings with a cotton merchant who dumped cotton on the road. Having warned the merchant to discontinue the practice under pain of having his cotton burned, was the *muḥtasib* entitled to carry out his threat without incurring liability for the loss? Not unless there was a serious misdemeanour and it was clear that burning was in the public interest. (Quoted from *Fatāwā al-Nasafiyya.*) The same principle is applicable to the breaking or bursting of wine containers, or the burning of the house of a wine merchant, who was noted for being such.

If a well is sunk in a public place with the authority of the imam and an accident occurs, no liability for injury follows, as it would, if the well were not so authorized.

The owner of an animal *66B* is not liable for damage and injury caused by it if it is in a place reserved for animals by the authorities.

A wall that has collapsed onto the highway must be removed by the owner on the instructions of the *muḥtasib*. The owner is liable for any injury caused by such a wall. **[211]**

Returning to the subject of sprinkling of the roads.

<u>Sunāmī:</u> the matter is to be left to the discretion of the *muḥtasib*, the reason being that water-carriers and sellers of beverages are in the habit of emptying their waste onto roads.

The owner of a house in a cul-de-sac may put earth or stones on which to step on [when passing] in and out of his house. But if such things are left by a door in a public thoroughfare, the owner will be liable for any injury caused to passers-by. (Quoted from *Fatāwā al-khāniyya.*)

Beasts of burden may not be left in the markets except when authorized by authorities. An anecdote about ᶜUmar b. al-Khaṭṭāb is recounted from *ᶜAwārif al-Maᶜārif.* According to it, he ordered the removal of a spout hanging out from the house of ᶜAbbās, the Prophet's uncle. The house was in the street between Ṣafā and Marwa. **[212]** ᶜAbbās objected to ᶜUmar's action on the ground that the Prophet himself had constructed that spout. ᶜUmar apologized and let ᶜAbbās climb on his shoulder to replace the spout.

The following conclusions are drawn from this anecdote:

1 - All spouts should be removed from the public road. *67A*

2 - The *wālī* has the right of removal without witness or a lawsuit.

3 - The permission of the owner is not needed. His admission of guilt is also not necessary for such an action.

4 - All similar actions that can cause harm to the public road can be removed on the same basis.

5 - Ordering good and prohibiting evil can be applied on anyone despite his position or wealth just as ᶜUmar did to the rich and noble ᶜAbbās.

6 - Accepting the narration of ᶜAbbās by ᶜUmar about the Prophet's action indicates that the individual narration (*khabar al-wāḥid*) is acceptable.

7 - The narration is accepted even if the narrator has a vested interest in what he narrates so long as he is a fair person (*ᶜadl*).

8 - All the Prophet's actions are taken as law for Muslims even if it was something that happened before the prophethood because ᶜUmar did not enquire whether the Prophet had built the spout before or after his prophethood. **[213]**

9 - It is possible that ᶜUmar wanted ᶜAbbās to replace the spout so that he would be responsible for that action. This indicates that the individual narration is not a reliable source of knowledge.

10 - Fulfilment of a duty is more important than being polite. ᶜAbbās's obedience to the duty of restoring the Prophet's action is more important than the disrespect caused to ᶜUmar by stepping on his shoulders.

11 and 12 - An example can be taken in dealing with a brother from ᶜAbbās, who was not angry with ᶜUmar, and from ᶜUmar, who helped ᶜAbbās.

13 - It is recorded that the Prophet's Companions used to repair their houses themselves.

14 - If an injunction is taken to re-establish an old structure in the road, it should be put back exactly as it was before.

15 - It is permissible to put one's foot on another person's shoulder if necessary. It is therefore acceptable to employ a slave or an animal. *67B*

16 - To help relatives in the house is a sunna. Similar to this are other household and domestic chores.

17 - The Prophet was humble in that he served his uncle himself. **[214]**

18 - It is preferable to remove a protruding spout rather than to break it. The reason for this is that the removal of an obstruction is preferable to its destruction.

19 - Individual interest should be sacrificed for that of the public.

20 - This incident shows us the high qualities of ᶜUmar, straightforwardness in religion, humbleness and following the truth when he finds it.

21 - A judge, like a *muḥtasib*, should admit a mistake.

22 - The assistants of the *muḥtasib* should not be held responsible for their actions if they have been ordered to do something.

23 - No legal responsibility falls on the *muḥtasib* if he errs; rather he should apologize. **[215]**

24 - The *wālī* or *muḥtasib* may appoint someone to act on his behalf. *68A*

25 - Obeying the judge is similar to obeying the *muḥtasib* in this case; it is obligatory unless he is ordering something *ḥarām*.

26 - If a Rāfiḍī claims that ᶜUmar only removed the spout because he hated the house of the Prophet, then we answer him by asking why ᶜUmar humbly put it back.

27 - A person may object about the *muḥtasib*'s action in an indirect way, as ᶜAbbās did when telling ᶜUmar that he had removed what the Prophet had personally

built. He did not put it directly, saying, 'You should not have done this.' To speak directly is acceptable when there is a case of clear injustice, which is not the case here. **[216]**
28 - A solitary person's narration (*khabar al-wāḥid*) about the Prophet is a definite proof against the narrator only. That is the reason why ᶜUmar asked ᶜAbbās to act according to his knowledge.
29 and 30 - The narration of a person who is learned is preferred to *qiyās*, but if the *qiyās* is correct (*ṣaḥīḥ*) and a solitary person's narration is general (*mujmal*), then the narration will be interpreted to accommodate the meaning of *qiyās*. *68B*
31 - The *muḥtasib* is not expected to repair what he has damaged if he undertook an action in error, but he should permit the owner to carry out repairs.
32 - An owner of an old spout will incur no sin so long as it caused no nuisance when it was first built. **[217]**
33 - The Sufis of Baṣra claim that it is better for the Sufi to be physically weak. This statement is refuted by the fact that services of this kind require physical strength. (ᶜUmar needed to be strong to be able to assist ᶜAbbās).
34 - Uncertainty about the donated benefits in general transactions should not affect such an obligation. This is similar to ᶜUmar's uncertainty about the duration of ᶜAbbās's usage of his shoulder.
35 - This incident shows ᶜUmar's modesty.
36 - It can be concluded that the height of houses at that time was equal to the height of two men.
37 - ᶜUmar called his shoulders (*ᶜātiq*) which is the same root as the word that means 'freeing a slave' although it does not carry the legal implication. This point can be used in seeking to understand the legal implication of a word and its derivation.
38 - This incident indicates that the houses of Makka used to belong to their occupiers and this solves a disagreement among scholars (*khilāf*).
39 - To construct a building is not prohibited so long as it is done in accordance with human needs, otherwise the Prophet would not have done such an action.
40 - The building profession is not a humiliating trade, otherwise the Prophet would not have undertaken it. **[218]**
41 - This incident can support a statement in the *Dhakhīra* that was unreferenced. This statement is that any building alteration in a cul-de-sac is treated as old, but if it is done in a connected street, it will be considered as new.
42 - It may be wondered why ᶜUmar degraded himself *69A* when he was a great judge and judges should be revered. To answer this we have to realise that this could be the custom of his time which is not like our custom. Also ᶜUmar has his own personal reverence which he did not need to increase with further reverential actions. Ordinary judges need to cause others to respect them and must be careful not to degrade themselves.
43 - A *wālī* can look left and right when he is patrolling the streets...

44 - If the rain ruined a roof because of the removal of a spout, the *muḥtasib* will not be liable. However, in other cases he may be liable for example, [in permitting] delay in the cauterisation of the amputated hand of a thief. **[219]**
45 - A person may benefit from what he builds in the road. No rebuke is recorded from ᶜUmar to ᶜAbbās for benefiting from the public road by putting his spout to it.
46 - A technical trick like the spout is allowed to make life simple. A court settlement could take place based on denial. Moreover, bribery can be paid by an orphan's guardian and the manager of *waqf*, in order to protect their interests.
47 - A house which is made of wood and mud is not an indication of hope of a long life, since the Prophet repaired a house of this kind...
48 - *69B* It is not abominable for Makka to be inhabited by it's people.
49 and 50 - A person may stand in the street to repair his house. **[220]**
51 - Building a spout is not an indication of hope for a long life (*ṭūl al-amal*) because this action is a sunna. However, if a person intends to live to a certain time to benefit from the spout, then that would be hope of a long life which is prohibited.

Sources: *MN*
KSh
KD
FKh
FN
Dh
AM
ShK

[221]

CHAPTER 55
(TS)
On Ritual Prayer

Advice is given on what must and must not be done if a Muslim's wife does not pray and if a man does not attend the communal prayer. The imam must not stand in a recess in such a way that he cannot be seen – the Kufan *miḥrābs* used to be so shaped as to present this kind of difficulty. If an imam prostrates himself in the *miḥrāb* but stands up outside, it is acceptable because he can be seen.

The ritual prayer must not be performed hastily and carelessly, and any person who does this should be reminded (of his obligations). *70A* The Prophet said to an Arab man who prayed in haste, 'Pray again since you have not prayed.' A story **[222]** about Abū ᶜAbdullah al-Khawārizmī is quoted from *al-Kifāya al-Shaᶜbiyya*. He saw a man praying in an abrupt manner. After he finished he invited him home and offered him sweet food, then asked him if he was ill. When the man replied in the negative, al-Khawārizmī commented, 'I thought you were ill when I saw you praying in such an abrupt manner.' The man admitted his guilt and repented. *Al-Kifāya al-shaᶜbiyya* is quoted again to the effect that a person who neglects a single prayer will be considered as a *fāsiq*, whose testimony is not accepted in court. Nor would he will be eligible for public office. His status will be similar to that of a man who has committed a major sin like *zīna* or homicide.

Abū Ḥanīfa said that he who does not pray for three consecutive days deserves killing.

Sunāmī: a question about a *muḥtasib* who discovers that certain employees are not praying, using as an excuse that their time is not their own. Various opinions can be found regarding this case. One holds that he may pray only the obligatory prayers. Some of our scholars hold this opinion and according to the *fatāwā* of the people of Samarqand, he may pray sunna too. They all agree, however, that he does not pray a voluntary prayer (*nafl*). Abū ᶜAlī al-Daqqāq stated in *Gharīb al-riwāya* that an employer should not prevent an employee from praying *Jumuᶜa*. If he lives far from the mosque, he may deduct from his wages an amount to compensate for the time he spends in travelling. The *muḥtasib* may remonstrate with people if they do something abominable (*makrūh*), the details of which can be found in the books of *fiqh* and cannot be covered in this manual (*mukhtaṣar*). A person who enters a mosque in which prayer has been called may not leave without praying unless for a reason, [for example] with the intention of coming back or to help another group to organise themselves. **[223]** If he has already prayed, he may leave unless the *iqāma* has been called. The exceptions to this rule are for *Fajr*, *ᶜAṣr* and *Maghrib* prayers.

Abū al-Layth stated in his *Bustān* that a person should not pray while sleepy. *70B* A hadith narrated by Anas is quoted about a man who was advised by the Prophet to pray while awake and to sleep when he feels sleepy, and not to lean on a rope that he had tied to support himself. Another hadith is narrated in which the Prophet said, 'By Him who has my soul in His hand, I was going to order another man to conduct the prayer (instead of me). I would then have followed the men (who do not attend prayer) and burnt their houses.'

Specific parts of the Quran must not be recited at specific times lest the people regard the practice as obligatory or a practice of the Prophet (examples of suras for certain times are cited). **[224]**

Sources: *ShṬK*
KSh
FS
Gh
BA

CHAPTER 56
(S) [225-6]
On Riding Animals

This chapter treats a miscellany of points relating to riding animals and beasts of burden. Some bear on cruelty, others on *jāhiliyya* practices connected with sheep and camels, others on *71A* birds and dogs (the question of rabies is raised).

Sources: *SN*
TGh
TM
TʿAyn
Saḥ

[227]

CHAPTER 57
The Drawing of Bad Omens, Soothsaying and Astrology are to be the Subject of Action by the *Muḥtasib* but not the Drawing of Good Omens

A tradition is cited to support the condemnation of certain practices by the Prophet. Both the Quran and the Prophet condemn the use of divining arrows (*azlām*). They were used by pagans to help them (a) to make decisions whether to travel or not, and (b) to decide how the flesh of slaughtered camels was to be apportioned. Opinions cited on the etymology of *istiqsām*. *71B*

The author quotes a detailed and interesting description of the manner in which *azlām* were used, after which comes a definition of *azlām* from al-Bustī's *Tafsīr*.

The casting of lots (*qurʿa*) is discussed. In some circumstances the practice is permissible (e.g. in deciding which case a judge should hear first), while in others it is forbidden (e.g. in the case of slaves to be manumitted by a man who is in his death-sickness and has no other property, for in this case the loss of rights is involved). **[228]**

The study of the stars is forbidden except to determine the direction of the qibla and the going down of the sun. (*Tajnīs wa-l-mazīd* quoted.)

Superstitions about magpies and owls are referred to. **[229]** *72A* To draw good omens is permitted by Prophetic precedent. He turned his garment during prayer asking for rain (*istisqā'*). His action was in the form of drawing good omens to beg God to alter their situation as he had turned the garment upside down. A similar hadith relates how when he was asked by Abū Hurayra to help him not to forget any hadith that he had heard from him, the Prophet asked him to open out his clothes. He then pretended to scoop with his hand and said to Abū Hurayra, 'Hold.' Abū Hurayra tells us that he never forgot a hadith after that.

Sunāmī: this kind opening, scooping, or holding of a garment is only a form of drawing good omens since knowledge is not something that can be carried in or fall from a garment. The meaning is symbolic. The Prophet gave Abū Hurayra a great deal of knowledge that can be scooped up by the two hands like a great amount of providence. Then he was told to hold it as though he were holding jewellery or pearls in his dress.

Another form of drawing good omens is when hearing someone uttering a good word. The Prophet said that there was no pessimism or infection but that he liked the good omen. He was asked about the meaning of good omen. He said, "When you hear a good word being said by your brethren." **[230]**

Sources: *TᶜAyn*
TB
Man
TM
Muḥ

CHAPTER 58
(S)
On Cooks and Cooking

This chapter deals with parts of lawful animals that are either forbidden (blood and embryos that are not fully formed) or disapproved of (ten are given, including the bladder, sexual organs, and spinal marrow.)

Food that is putrid is forbidden, as is the meat of cows that have eaten dung.

Food should not be bought or sold during the time of prayer. *Qūt al-qulūb* is quoted to show that early Muslims did not themselves sell *harīsa* or *rūs*. Instead it was sold by children or dhimmis because adult Muslims were occupied in the Fajr prayer at the time these commodities should be sold. **[231]**

Sources: *Maẓ*
QQ

CHAPTER 59
(S)
On Expressions which Make Men Unbelievers and Sinners

This long chapter *72A – 81A* **[231-254]** is a mixed bag of statements which, for the author, entail certain religious consequences. Some, covered in the first section *72A – 74A*, bespeak unbelief or monotheism that is not Islam, while others, covered in the second section *74A – 74B* bespeak heresy (references are made to cardinal beliefs of various sects such as the Qādariyya, Rawāfiḍ, Khawārij, Yazīdiyya, Najjāriyya, Mu^{c}tazila, Karrāmiyya and Jābriyya). The third section *74B – 81A* is broken down into a number of subdivisions and deals with what is expected of a Muslim and what is not.

In this third section there are references to oaths and a list of utterances, some obviously in common use, which are blasphemous, improper, or obscene. The list includes several in Persian.

This part is followed by observations on what one may say or think of the prophets, scholars and men of piety *77B – 78B*.

The next part is on faith and unbelief *78B*. Amongst other things, mention is made of clothes that may not be worn (e.g. clothes characteristic of Zoroastrians or Christians, black apparel, and women's hoods) *79A*. Items of interest include references to Muslims' entering churches and synagogues and attending shrines to obtain *baraka* from monks and priests *79A – 79B*; the practice of giving an apple in honour of the day of Nayrūz, or colouring eggs for the festival *79B*.

In a subdivision devoted to the Sharī^{c}a *79B – 80B*, it is noted that it is unbelief to declare that any science is better than that of the Sharī^{c}a. Those who maintain that intercourse with a woman during her menstrual period or that homosexuality, wine-bibbing, etc. are lawful are unbelievers *80B*.

The subdivision on the Hereafter and the Unseen *80B* contains sayings and material reflecting both popular and learned attitudes.

The next subdivision takes us back to a subject already treated, *viz*, improper glorification of sultans *80B*.

The last two subdivisions deal briefly with the kinds of things said by reprobates and depraved persons and with the sort of utterance that is made when one offers consolation during a bereavement *81A*. **[255]**

<u>Sources:</u> *N*
Jāmi^{c}?
Kash
TK
SAM
SK
Nd
Khulāṣa?
KSM
Munt
H

CHAPTER 60
(TO)
On Innovations (*Bidāʿ*) Connected with Marriage

There are various unorthodox marriage practices, and these include:

1. The practice of inviting singers and having them give a public performance. It is forbidden.
2. The practice of bringing musical instruments. It is forbidden.
3. The practice of inviting public players (*laʿābīn*) to provide entertainment. It is forbidden. *81B*
4. The practice of draping the walls with fabrics of pretty design for the purpose of decoration. In our view this is reprehensible; in Aḥmad b. Ḥanbal's it is forbidden.
5. The practice of parading through the town on horseback unnecessarily. This is reprehensible for thirteen reasons:

(i) People's time is wasted by things which do not concern them;
(ii) Pack animals are utilized to no [good] purpose;
(iii) The streets are filled and needlessly obstructed;
(iv) The purpose is to show off finery, and this is contrary to Quranic teaching (Quran quoted viii:47);
(v) There will be singers in the procession; Quran reciters **[256]** may not even recite for fear of committing an act of unbelief since what they will be doing is demeaning the Quran. It is also forbidden to recite anything else;
(vi) There will be people with drums and cymbals as well as public players;
(vii) There will be unveiling of the bride before the community – an abominable practice which is strictly forbidden ... ...[325]
(viii) The presence of engraved braziers at the contracting of a marriage is reprehensible because of the representations of living creatures, presumably, which they bear.
(ix) The prospective groom should not sit on silk, but on this there is a difference of opinion.
(x) The practice of measuring the height of the prospective groom with thread and later giving the latter to a sorcerer to cast a spell on the couple to bind them in love and affection and enable the woman to keep the man in her grasp is forbidden as is all sorcery of any kind. In the opinion of some ulama it is unbelief.
(xi) The practice of drinking from gold and silver vessels at the wedding receptions of rulers is undoubtedly forbidden.
(xii) The practice of lavishing exaggerated compliments on the couple's parents to the point of untruth by the person concluding the marriage contract is forbidden. (Quran quoted: iii:188)

---

325 From here we depart from the 13 reasons for not parading on horseback.

(xiii) The practice whereby the groom wears silk at the time of drawing up the marriage contract is unorthodox.

The use of the *duff* is authorized on the authority of the Prophet, but it may only be used at the time the marriage is contracted in order to make the marriage public, and not purely as a musical instrument. **[257]**

Sources: *BA*

CHAPTER 61
(SO)
On Unorthodox Practices Regarding Hair on One's Head

... *82A* ... ... Here the author repeats some of the observations he has already made in Chapter 41 (e.g. a slave-boy's hair being kept uncut in curls with the intention of satisfying sodomitical lust). **[258]**

There is a discussion of various terms – e.g. *ʿaqṣ*, as to whether it means tying the hair firmly or putting up the hair and fixing it with gum, or gathering it round the head as women do, or just tying it up so that it does not touch the ground during the *sujūd* (Hadith narrated by Abū Rāfiʿ quoted). Various styles that are approved or disapproved are mentioned including, the dissapproval of long hair by the author's contemporary, Ghazālī. *82B* **[259]**

Sources: *Muḥ*
Dh
Mut
Ṣiḥ
Iḥ
Saḥ

CHAPTER 62
(S)
On Religious Instructors/Admonishers (*Mudhakkirūn*) and on those who Listen to them

This chapter, which deals with such matters as concentration on lessons, contains material that is of little interest. One point, however, is worth noting: Sunāmī tells us that it was his practice when holding a *majlis al-tadhkīr* to disallow dozing, talking, drinking, and the use of a fan. **[260]**

The question whether women may attend sermons, etc. is discussed and answered in the affirmative. *83A* (Prophetic Tradition quoted from *Yawāqīt al-mawāqīt*.)

It is noted that a *mudhakkir* may not, as had been the practice in Sunāmī's day, recite rhymed couplets (*dhūbaytī*) in the pulpit. Sunāmī comments that although he had preached from the pulpit for more than thirty years, he thanked God that he had never recited such poetry from the pulpit. Rhymed couplets are classified as singing.**[261]**

Sources: *UB*
US
YM
Ṣiḥ

CHAPTER 63
(TO)
On the Instruments and Methods of Discretionary *Taᶜzīr*
and
Whether the *Dirra* Should be hung on the *Muḥtasib*'s Door

1. Pinching and slapping are permitted.
2. Punching is not permitted as it may have fatal results.
3. The use of a whip without a knot at the end is permissible. (Practice of ᶜAlī quoted.)
4. The use of a stick is permissible. (Prophet quoted.)
5. The use of a *dirra* is permitted; it should be hung on the *muḥtasib*'s door for all to see. *83B* (Prophet quoted: 'May God's mercy fall upon him who hangs his whip for his family to see.')**[262]**
6. A stripped palm branch is allowed.
7. Shoes may be used. **[263]**

Sources: *Muḥ*

CHAPTER 64
(S)
On Expulsion

Passive male effeminates and active female homosexuals may be expelled from people's houses.

A *muḥtasib* may expel a woman from a house if she has gone to express condolences and, in so doing, keens. (ᶜUmar quoted.)

Sources: *Saḥ*

Glossary of Arabic Words Used in the Translation

Note: the numbers used represent folio numbers used in the translation. See also Index of Arabic words p. 164.

2A *Birūn dāsht*. The literal translation of these words is 'projecting board' (F. Steingass, *A comprehensive Persian-English dictionary*, (London,1892): 219, 526). Sunāmī's definition is *janāḥ*, which Hamilton translates as 'projecting balcony' in his translation of the *Hidāya*.
Hamilton, *Hidāya*: 661.

2A *Sanjāt*. The plural of *sanja*, a word of Persian origin. It means 'counterbalancing weight' used on a set of scales.
Lisān al-ᶜArab:3:136.
Jawāliqī, *Muᶜatrab*:215.

2A *Faqqāᶜī*. A person who sells *fuqāᶜ*, a non-intoxicating drink. *Fuqāᶜ* can be made from barley or various fruits. The name of the drink is derived from the bubbles (*fuqāᶜāt*) which rise to the surface.
S.M. Husain, *Indian Islam* :286.
Muḥīṭ :2:1624.

2A *Tānbūl*. (See also Ṭin:15A) A word of Sanskrit origin. Sanskrit *tāmbūla* is used of the betel, i.e. the *piper betel*). Somadeva uses the word in two senses: (a) the betel in general; (b) a popular chew which was, in fact, wrapped in betel leaves. Ibn Baṭṭūṭa also gives an account of the word *tānbūl* stating that it is 'a tree which is cultivated in the same manner as the grape-vine. The betel bears no fruit and is grown solely for the sake of its bramble-like leaves.' The Indians attach immense importance to *tānbūl*, particularly in the way it is eaten. Before eating *tānbūl*, one takes an areca nut, which is broken up until it is reduced to small pellets, and places them in the mouth and chews them. Then one takes the leaves of the *tānbūl*, puts a little chalk on them, and masticates them along with the nut. *Ibn Baṭṭūṭā* (Gibb):2:387.
Somadeva Bhatta, *The Ocean of story*, being C.H. Tawney's translation of *Kathā Sarit Sāgara.* ed. N.M. Penzer (London, 1924):8:239.
Ibn Baṭṭūṭā, Riḥla:263.

2B *Najash.* Raising the price of a commodity without intending to sell it at that price but in order to force another buyer to pay more.
Lisān al-ʿArab:8:243.

2B *Taṭfīf.* Paying less for a commodity than it is worth. It can also mean any kind of cheating in weights and measures.
Lisān al-ʿArab:11:126.

3A *Laylat al-Barā'a.* The night of mid Shaʿbān, so called because it is supposed to be the night on which the fate of every human being for the coming year is decided and registered in the book of life.
It seems to be a day observed only by the Muslims of India and not of universal Muslim observance. Generally there are great rejoicings instead of the religious performances that are said to have been recommended by the Prophet to his followers. Extensive use of fireworks and the illumination of mosques are the distinguishing features of this night. This custom seems to have been influenced – like many others mentioned in the *Niṣāb* by the Hindu festivals of lights.
S.M. Husain, *Indian Islam*:264.
Hughes, *Dictionary*:36:570.

3A *Nayrūz.* New Year's Day. It is observed primarily among Persians, and normally lasts for one week.
Hughes, *Dictionary*:340.

3B *Muṣallā.* A place where prayer and other acts of worship are performed, when not performed in a mosque.
Hughes, *Dictionary*:423.

3A *Al-Mulk-li-llāh.* These words are often inscribed on various articles; one example of it on textiles can be found on p.10 of A.Schimmel's *Islamic Calligraphy* (Leiden, 1970 A.D.). It is also recorded as being used to decorate the façade of a mosque in Bukhārā.
Nāji Zayn al-Dīn, *Muṣawwar al-Khaṭṭ al-ʿArabī* (Beirut, 1974):8.

3B *Al-ʿIzz wa-l-iqbāl.* These words seem to be an abbreviation of longer words (c.f. *basmala* instead of *bism Allāh al-Raḥman al-Raḥīm*) The words are reported as being used by Indian Muslims as a charm to cure certain diseases. S.M. Husain, *Muslim Saints*:226. The word *ʿizz* is mentioned as being inscribed on marble chairs belonging to the Buwayhid Prince Abū al-Najm Badr b. Ḥasanwayh (d. 493/1047). The inscription reads as follows:

عزٌّ ونصرٌ وتأييدٌ للآمير بدر الدين بن حسنويه

Nājī Zayn al-Dīn, *Muṣawwar al-Khaṭṭ al-ᶜArabī* (Beirut, 1974):11.
*EI*²:3:258.

3B *Walīma.* It originally meant the leading of the bride to the bridegroom but it has now come to mean the wedding feast.
*EI*¹:4:1038 *s.v. ᶜUrs.*

3B *Mashāᶜkhunā.* Sunāmī often uses this word when referring to Ḥanafī scholars in general.

3B ᶜĪd. A festival or holiday which occurs twice a year, either *ᶜĪd al-Aḍḥā* and *ᶜĪd al-Fiṭr.* The common feature is a sunna prayer of two *rak'as* similar to the Friday prayer.
*EI*²:3:1007.

3B The night of mid-Shaᶜbān. See *Laylat al-Barā'a* 3A.

3B *ᶜUlamā'.* The plural of *ᶜālim*, 'scholar'. It is used as a title for Muslim doctors of divinity or law. They form the theocratic element of the government and their *fatwā*s or decisions, regulate life.

4A *Dirra.* A whip of ox-hide, or made of strips of hide on which date-stones have been stitched.
Ibn al-Ukhuwwa, *Maᶜālim*:103.

4A *Fatwā.* An opinion on a point of law. Law, in Islam, is any civil or religious matter. *Fatwās* may be given by an individual, magistrates or any other authority.
*EI*²:2:866.

4A *Bayt al-Māl.* The house of wealth or treasure. Not all state revenue belongs to the *Bayt al-Māl*, but only that which belongs to the community as a whole and the purpose for which it is used depends on the discretion of the imam or his delegate.
*EI*²:1:1141.

4B *Aʿwān.* This word has a very wide meaning in Arabic, denoting all kinds of assistance. However, Sunāmī uses the word in a more restricted sense when referring to people who aid the *muḥtasib.*

4B *Jizya.* Capitation tax levied on subjects of a different faith but who are protected.
Hughes, *Dictionary*:248.

4B *Kharāj.* A term borrowed by the Arabs from the administrative language of the Byzantines (probably Greek). Originally it meant the tribute to which unbelievers in Muslim lands were liable. By the 1st/7th century A.H. it had come to mean the tax paid on property as opposed to the poll-tax (*jizya*). The earliest record of the imposition of *kharāj* in Muslim India relates to the reign of Sultan ʿAlā' al-Dīn Muḥammad Khālidī (695–715/1296–1316).
EI[1]:2:902.
EI[2]:4:1030-56.

4B *Wālī.* In ordinary use it can mean 'protector, benefactor, companion', or 'friend'. In a religious connection the best translation would be 'saint'. A person meriting this title is thought to be free from passion, have influence with God, and to be able to work miracles.
EI[1]:4:1109.

4B *Qāḍī.* A judge in both civil and criminal law. There is now some division between secular and religious law and in this division the qadi deals with only religious matters, family law, and inheritance. The qadi is a Muslim scholar who must lead a blameless life and be conversant in sacred law.
EI[1]:2:606 *s.v.* Ḳāḍī.

4B *Ghuzāh.* The plural of *ghāzī*, which means a person who fights for Islam. It is also a title conferred by Muslim rulers upon renowned warriors.
Hughes, *Dictionary*:139.

4B *Muftī.* An officer who expounds the law. He assists the qadi or judge and supplies him with *fatwās.* He must be learned in the Quran, hadith, and in Muslim works of law.
Hughes, *Dictionary*:367.

4B *Mutaṭawwiʿ.* Sunāmī seems to be applying the idea of obligation to the volunteer *muḥtasib*, if he is involved in another contract. This idea is not in accordance with the nature of the legal qualifications required of the

volunteers. The qualifications are that he applies *ḥisba* according to his own judgment. In the case of a trustee (*mūdaʿ*), his obligation is to keep the deposit until the owner asks for it. This is based on the deposits (*wadīʿa*) contract and not on *ḥisba*.
Hamilton, *Hidāya*:471–2.

4A *Imām.* When Sunāmī uses this term he means not only the imam but also the government and its administrative officer.

5A *Taʿzīr.* A punishment intended to prevent the culprit from relapsing. Many crimes now punished by this were counted as sins in the Quran and for them there was no *ḥadd* punishment. The kind and amount of *taʿzīr* is left to the discretion of the judge.
EI[1]:4:710.
Farrā', *Aḥkām*:263–8.

5A *ʿUqūba.* Punishment or chatisement, a legal term for punishment inflicted at the discretion of the magistrate.
Hughes, *Dictionary*:655.

5A *Taṭhīr.* The purification or cleansing of anything which is ceremonially unclean. Sunāmī's usage of *taṭhīr* to mean expurgation or purification from sin is rather interesting. It hints at the nature of the *taʿzīr* punishment which purifies the Muslim soul from committed sins.
Hughes, *Dictionary*:629.

5B *Ḍamān.* In Islamic law, *ḍamān* means 'civil liability' in the widest of the term, whether it arises from the non-performance of a contract or from tort, or negligence.
EI[2]:2:105.

5B *Kaffāra.* Atonement or expiation. It usually consists of releasing a slave, fasting a number of days, or else feeding and clothing a certain number of poor people. This technical term, which is employed in the Quran four times, is said to have been borrowed from Hebrew:*kappūra.*
EI[1]:2:618.
EI[2]:4:406.

5B *Nukūl*. Failure to take an oath, a simple refusal which cannot be enforced by law except in *liʿān* and *qasāma*, where it may be enforced by imprisonment.
Schacht, *Introduction*:190, 197.

5B *Ḥadd*. Hindrance, impediment, limit, boundary, or frontier. *Ḥadd* has become to mean in a narrow, technical sense the punishment of certain acts which have been forbidden or sanctioned by punishments in the Quran and have thereby become crimes against religion.
EI[2]:3:20.

6A *Diyya*. See *s.v. Arsh* 7A; *ʿĀqila* 7B.

5A *Iʿlā'*. Continuous beating.
Ismā'īl b. Ḥammād al-Jawharī, *Ṣiḥāḥ* (Cairo, AH 1376–7):218.

6A A quotation from *Sharḥ adab al-qāḍī*, 96A [1:163].

6A *Ajnabīyya*. In this case *ajnabīyya* means a foreign lady; it includes all women who are not related to a particular man by the legal ties of marriage or ownership (on the male side only). Accordingly, the woman would still be *ajnabīyya* (by this definition) even if she were within the prohibited degrees. A man is not permitted to see from his mother or sister what he may see from his wife.

6B *Akāf*. A type of saddle which is shaped like the palm of a hand (*kaff*) and which has a buckle shaped like a pomegranate on its bow (*qarbūs*).
Sarakhsī, *Sharḥ*:1:137.

6B *ʿAmā'im* (sing. *ʿimāma*). May be used in two senses: (1) the complete turban, consisting of one or more skull-caps with a band of material rolled around them; (2) the band of material on its own. It is normally white and made of muslin, but it can be made of other materials and other colours. It is only worn by men.
Dozy, *Supplément*:305.

6B *Durrāʿa*. A woollen garment which normally distinguishes the *wazīr* from administrative or justice officers. It opens at the front to the level of the heart and is fastened with buttons and button-holes. In India it was worn by the qadis and scholars as well as by the ordinary people.
Dozy, *Supplément*:177.

6B *Shirāk*. Straps.
Muḥīṭ:2:319.

7A *Kuffār*. This word is often used by Sunāmī with reference to the Hindus.

7A *Ṣukūk*. A further feature of customary commercial law, and of Islamic law as applied in practice was its reliance on written documents. Documents are called *ṣakk* (pl. *ṣukūk*). The branch of legal science which deals with documents is called the science of *shurūṭ* (pl. of *sharṭ*), 'stipulations'.
Schacht, *Introduction*:82.

7A *Khuṭūṭ*. This word can mean 'signatures' as well as 'documents'. See Sunāmī's usage of it, 16B.

7A *Mahr*. Hebrew *mohar*, Syriac *mahāra* (bridal gift), meaning the dower or settlement of money or property on the bride without which the marriage would not be legal.
EI[1]:3:137.
EI[2]:6:78-80.
Hughes, *Dictionary*:307.

7A *Arsh*. A legal term for 'compensation'. It is a specified amount of money or goods which is due in the case of homicide or other injuries, a substitute for private vengeance. *Diyya* is compensation for homicide, while *arsh* is compensation for other offences against the body.
EI[2]:1:661, *s.v. diya*. *EI*[2] :2:340.

7A It is curious to note that the reference which Sunāmī quotes – concerning the case of a Muslim in fear of the government – is inaccurate. *Al-Kifāya al-Shaʿbiyya*, to which Sunāmī referred, does not mention the sultan. It reads as follows: 'If a person forces a man to kill...' This might suggest that Sunāmī added the word 'sultan' because of the actions of Sultan Muḥammad Tughluq in a particular case.
Kifāya, MS no. 1699, 182A.
Kifāya, MS no. 1698, 219B.

7A *Qiṣāṣ*. Literally, 'tracking the footsteps of an enemy'. It is the law of retaliation which applies to either the loss of a life or to the loss of less. In occasions affecting life, retaliation is incurred by killing a person who is

under continual protection (Muslim or dhimmi), but not an alien. Retaliation is executed by the next of kin with a lethal weapon.
Hughes, *Dictionary*:481.

7B *Zinā*. A word that means both adultery and fornication, sexual intercourse of persons not in a legal state of matrimony or concubinage. It requires the testimony of four witnesses before punishment can be administered.
EI[1]:4:1227.
Hughes, *Dictionary*:713.

7B *Shubha*. The resemblance of an unlawful act, which has been committed, to another, lawful one, and therefore, subjectively speaking, the presumption of a *bona fides* in the accused. Duress is widely recognised, particularly in the case of drinking wine or unlawful sexual intercourse.
Schacht, *Introduction*:176.

7B *^{c}Aqr*. The dowry that a Muslim should pay to a woman with whom he has had sexual intercourse by error (*subha*). *Shubha* may be in respect of the act or the subject.
Mughrib:52.
Hamilton, *Hidāya*:182.

7B *Bay^c*. Originally meant the clasping of hands on concluding an agreement. In the technical usage of Islamic law, *bay^c* (the verbal noun) means 'the contract of sale'.
EI[2]:1:1111. See also *Safḳa*:*EI*[2]:8:818.

7B *Ijāra*. The use and enjoyment of property for a time, including hire, rental and lease.
Hughes, *Dictionary s.v. ijārah*:197; 'hire':175.

7B *Fāsid*. *Fāsid* and *bāṭil* are used interchangeably, but the distinction between the two terms is the principal chracteristic of the Ḥanafī theory of nullity (*buṭlān*). *Bāṭil* denotes an act which lacks one of the elements essential for the existence of any legal activity. In the doctrine of the other three orthodox schools, the terms are synonymous. According to the Ḥanafīs, a sale is invalid (*fāsid*) when it is lawful with respect to its essence, but not with respect to its quality, while it is null (*bāṭil*) when the subject is not of an appreciable nature.
EI[2]:2:829.
Hamilton, *Hidāya*:266.

7B *Safīh.* A major who is irresponsible, for example a spendthrift.
Schacht, *Introduction*:125.

7B *ʿĀqila.* The people who pay the *diyya.* It is termed *ʿāqila* or *maʿāqil* because it restrains men from shedding blood. (*ʿAql* has many meanings including 'restraint').
Hamilton, *Hidāya*: 670.

7B *Zuhd.* Abstinence; exercising oneself in the service of God, especially in respect of eating; subduing the passions. A technical term in Muslim mysticism which implies not only the renunciation of fashionable dress, lodging and pleasant food, but also of women.
Hughes, *Dictionary*:716.
EI[1]:4:1239.

8A *Ribāṭ.* An Arab type of hostel or training centre. It is the establishment of a teacher or preacher, although not necessarily a Sufi. Sufis trained in these institutions, then founded daughter lodges in their own countries or in entirely new pasture grounds, especially India. These rarely maintained direct contact with the mother institution and became independent schools with their own characteristics and tendencies. The *ribāṭ*s were sometimes isolated but were more often associated with a mosque.
Trimingham, *Sufi Orders*:17–21.
Schimmel, *Dimensions*:232.

8A *Khanqā.* See *Ribāṭ* above. Similar to *ribāṭ,* but originated in Persia or Khurasan. They are more like hostels and less like training centres than the *ribāṭs*, and were important centres in Muslim commerce. During the thirteenth century A.D. many Sufis fled to remote corners of the Muslim world. The migrants to the Hindu environment acquired an aura of holiness, which attracted Indians to them rather than to formal Islam. The *khānqās* were in a special sense the focal points of Islam and functional as centres of holiness, fervour, ascetic exercise, and Sufi training. Contrary to the Arab institutions bearing the name, the Indian *khānqās* grew up around a holy man and became associated with his method of discipline. A *khānqā* normally consisted of a central courtyard, having cloisters along the sides, within which were situated the cells of the Sufis. On one side was the main hall, where their common devotional exercises took place. This was generally simple in construction. In front of the *miḥrāb* there was the sheepskin of the shaykh upon which he reclined during the ceremonies and

receptions. Over the niche was engraved the name of the founders and some religious phrases such as the *shahāda*. Frequently there was a separate mosque, whilst kitchens and other offices, and sometimes a bath-house, were attached. Trimingham, *Sufi Orders*: 5, 22, 23, 69, 169.
Schimmel, *Dimensions*:232.

8B *Ghalabāt*. Rapture, ecstasy.
Trimingham, *Sufi Orders*:4.

8B *Jawāliqiyyūn*. A Sufi order, probably a branch of the Qalandārī order, which was introduced into India by Khiḍr Rūmī during the time of Iltutmish (ruled 607 – 633/1211 – 1236). The Qalandarīs share two distinctive features with the *Jawāliqiyyūn*, which may suggest a similar origin. These characteristics are shaving off the beard and wearing the *jawāliq*, which is a practice which Sunāmī mentions (8B). Moreover, Maqrīzī in his *Khiṭaṭ* mentions a Sufi who established a Qalandarī *zāwiya* in Egypt. This man was Ḥasan al-Jawāliqī (d. 722/1322). C.E. Bosworth suggests that he was the founder of the Jawāliqiyya order.
Trimingham, *Sufi Orders*:268.
Maqrīzī, *Khiṭaṭ*:301.
Bosworth, *Islamic Underworld*:114.

9A *Muraqqa*ᶜ. A patched garment worn by an alleged saint. This patched garment is also worn by women.
Dozy, *Supplément*:189.

9A *Samā*ᶜ. The problem of *samā*ᶜ, 'hearing', was a major cause of differences among the scholars. There were complicated problems as to whether 'listening to music' and 'dancing movements' are genuine utterances of mystical states or illegitimate attempts to gain by one's own effort a state that can only be granted by God. *Samā*ᶜ is the most widely known expression of mystical life in Islam. *Samā*ᶜ *khānqā*s, houses in which Sufis could listen to music and let themselves be drawn into the ecstatic state, were founded in Baghdad as early as the second half of the ninth century A.D. The orthodox were scandalised by the sight of what took place there. They objected to the rending of garments that frequently happens in *samā*ᶜ. The authors of the tenth and eleventh centuries A.D. devoted long chapters to the dangers inherent in *samā*ᶜ. In India *samā*ᶜ was advocated by the Chishtī order.
Schimmel, *Dimensions*:179, 185.

9A *Kabīra.* The feminine of great (*kabīr*). It is a term used in theological books for *junḥa kabīra*, 'a great sin', i.e. a sin which is clearly forbidden in the law, and for which punishment has been ordained by God.
Hughes, *Dictionary*:259.

9A *Al-Hawā.* Desire, love, hankering after. A term used by the Sufi mystics for lust or unholy desire.
Hughes, *Dictionary*:169.

9A *Dhikr Allāh. Dhikr* is the distinctive worship of a Sufi which consists of the constant recollection of God. This can be performed either silently or aloud. Its advantage is that it is permitted in any place and at any time; its practice is restricted neither to the exact hours of ritual prayer nor to a ritually clean place. It is based on the Quranic order xiii:24.
Schimmel, *Dimensions*:84, 167.
*EI*²:2:223.

9B *Wajd.* This word is normally translated 'ecstasy'. It is a Sufi term for the fifth stage of the mystical journey, when the spiritual traveller finds God and becomes quiet and peaceful in finding Him.
Schimmel, *Dimensions*:178.
Hughes, *Dictionary*:663.

9B *Ikhwān.* 'Brothers', the members of a Sufi order.
Trimingham, *Sufi Orders*:27, 175, 304.

9B *Qawwāl.* The leader of the *samāᶜ*.
Trimingham, *Sufi Orders*:309.

10A *Mutabarraka.* The recipient of God's *baraka* or spiritual power and it has come to mean not just a gift, but something that can be passed on and inherited. God can implant an emanation of *baraka* in the person of His prophets and saints. Muḥammad and his descendants are especially endowed therewith. Contrary to the orthodox Islamic view, the Sufis believe that these sacred personages, in their turn, may communicate the effluvia of their supernatural potential to ordinary men, either during their lifetime or after their death. The manner of the transmission varies greatly and may sometimes be very strange and unIslamic. People often make pilgrimages to various saints, certain that the spiritual power of the saints will help them. God, however, can withold His *baraka*.

EI[2]:1:1032.
Trimingham, *Sufi Orders*:24, 84.
Schimmel, *Dimensions*:82, 217.

10A *Mizmār*. In the generic sense it refers to any instrument of the woodwind family, i.e. reed, pipe, or flute, but normally to the reed pipe, which is conical or cylindrical in shape, pierced with finger-holes, and played with a single or double beating reed.
EI[1]:3:339.
EI[2]:7:206–209.

10A *Ghabb*. A period of time equivalent to one day and one night. However, some say that it is equal to one day and two nights.
Lisān al-ʿArab:2:126.

10B *Iqrār*. Acknowledgement, confession. A theological term used for the admission of a sin. The limit of the *mūḥtasib*'s authority, which Sunāmī suggests here has been enforced by many succeeding scholars who wrote on the subject of *ḥisba*. For examples see Māwardī, *Aḥkām*:242; Farrā', *Aḥkām*:270.
Hughes, *Dictionary*:215.

11A *Ḍarūra*. Necessity. In the works of *fiqh* it has a narrow meaning when used to denote what may be called the technical state of necessity. A person finding himself in a dangerous position is permitted to do something normally forbidden.
EI[2]:2:163.

12A *Rasātīq*. The plural of *rustāq*, a Persian word for a group of houses or a small village.
Jawālīqī, *Muʿarrab*:158.

12B *Muʿtadda*. A woman during the period of *ʿidda*, which is the term of probation incumbent on a woman after the dissolution of her marriage. After divorce the period is three months, and after the death of her husband, four months and ten days, both periods being enjoined in the Quran (ii:228; ii:234). During the period of *ʿidda* a woman is not permitted to remarry. The reason for this is to avoid any problems in deciding the paternity of any children. If the woman is pregnant, then the *ʿidda* ends with the accouchement, but if in the case of a widow this occurs less than four

months and ten days after the death of her husband, then she must wait the remainder as a time of mourning for her husband.
Hughes, *Dictionary*:190.
EI[2]:3:1010.

12B *Ḥinna'*. Henna, the shrub (*Lawsonia alba*), whose leaves possess medicinal properties and are also used as a dye. The flower was used to make a scented oil. It is a native of Iran and Western India, but widely grown throughout the Middle East. It is widely used as a cosmetic, the dried leaves being ground and mixed to a paste with water. This is used by old men to dye their beards, by both men and women to dye their hair, and also by women to dye their nails, hands and feet on festive occasions. It is commonly used by both bride and bridegroom before a wedding.
EI[2]:3:461, *s.v. Hinna.*
Hughes, *Dictionary*:175.

12B *Qaṣab.* Spun gold and silver thread, gold silk thread.
Dozy, *Supplément*:353.

13B *Muḥrima.* The pilgrim in a state of *iḥrām*, i.e. after he has assumed the pilgrim's garb.
Hughes, *Dictionary*:418, *s.v. muḥrim.*

14A *Niqāb.* A woman's veil in which there are two holes. It is normally black but can also be red, white, or blue. 'The women wear in front of their face a piece of material with two holes through which they can see.'
Dozy, *Dictionary*:424.

14B *Khiyānat al-ʿayn.* This is the Quranic term describing the eye of the beholder when it involves him in seeing prohibited sights. See Quran xl:19 'God knows the tricks which deceive the eye'.

15A *Ṭīn.* There are various kinds of *ṭīn*.
Ṭīn armīnī. Widely known in Egypt and sold in the bazaars as a tonic desiccative and styptic. It is still used in many skin disease ointments.
Ṭīn khūzī or *ṭin makhlūm.* It is recommended as a styptic or as an enema for dysentery.
Ṭīn rūmī or *ṭīn qimlūya* : *Terre cimolée.* This is thought to be a kind of chalk.
H. Isaacs, *A critical edition of the 'Kitāb al-Hummayyāt' by Isaac Israeli* (Ph.D. thesis, Manchester, 1969):195.

Dozy, Supplément:2:81.
Mūsā b. ᶜUbayd Allāh al-Isrā'īlī, *Sharḥ asmāᶜ al-ᶜUqqār*, ed. Max Meyerhof (Baghdad, 1940):20.

15A *Majūs.* The Magians. They formerly possessed a revelation from God which they have since lost. They devote their time to the study of heavenly bodies. They are supposed to have worshipped a deity under the emblem of fire. They held in the greatest abhorrence the worship of images, and considered fire the purest symbol of the Divine Being. This religious sect was reformed by Zoroaster in the sixth century B.C. They are now known as Parsees (Persians) in India.
Hughes, *Dictionary*:310.

15A *Zalla.* The food which a guest can take away with him from a dinner party to a relative at home.
Lisān al-ᶜArab:13:326.

15B *Arbaᶜat ᶜashar.* Fourteen:a board game which is called in Persian *shahardah*, which again means 'fourteen'. Ibn ᶜUmar is reported to have smashed a fourteen board.[326] Fourteen has been identified with the game *hizza* mentioned in Shāfiᶜī's *Kitāb al-umm.* Ibn Ḥajar al-Haythami says, '*Hizza* is a piece of wood in which there are three rows of holes into which small pebbles are put for playing. It may also be called fourteen.' In Egypt it is called *manqila.* In the *Taqrīb* of Sulaym (a Shāfiᶜī treatise by Sulaym b. Ayyūb al-Rāzī, d. 447/1055), it is explained as a board in which there are twenty-eight holes, fourteen on one side and fourteen on the other, for playing.[327] F. Rosenthal also states that all such descriptions are likely to refer to games similar in principle and played according to different rules.

15B *Qimār.* Games of chance, prohibited by the Quran when it prohibited wine. The pagan Arabs used to stake their family and property in games of chance, especially lotteries with arrows. As regards chess, certain forms of this game involve the use of dice and can therefore, be regarded as games of chance.
EI[1]:2:1009 *s.v. Ḳimar.*

---

326 F. Rosenthal, *Gambling in Islam* (Leiden, 1975): 43–4.
327 Ibn Ḥajar al-Haythamī, *Zawājir*, cited by *ibid.*: 44.

15B *Ijmāᶜ*. The unanimous consent of the learned doctors (*mujtahidūn*). *Ijmāᶜ* is the collective opinion, while *ijtihād* is the deduction made by a single *mujtahid*.
Hughes, *Dictionary*:197.

16A *Ḥamām*. A collective substantive which includes pigeons and turtledoves. In the restrictive sense, *ḥamām* denotes domestic pigeons. Medieval writers in Arabic devoted much of their work to the pastime of pigeon-keeping. The hobby was pursued with great passion in Baghdad, Basra, Damascus and Cairo. Pigeon-flying, like falconry, enjoyed great popularity from the second/eighth until seventh/thirteenth century among all the Muslim peoples. Skilful use was made of the valuable properties of the homing pigeon. The pigeon post declined in the ninth/fifteenth century.
EI²:3:108.

16B *Daʿwa khāṣṣā*. An invitation to a private party. The number of guests at a private party should be small. Some jurists hold that the maximum number of guests should be ten.
Sharḥ adab al-qāḍī:35A.

16B *Sijill*. A register, the records of a court of justice, the decree of a judge, and the written statement of a contract.
Hughes, *Dictionary*:582.

17A *Qassām*. The person who applies the *qisma*.
Qisma is the partition which involves a separation, in articles of weight measurement of capacity.[328] It applies to joint property in whatsoever manner it be obtained or acquired. It more immediately relates to the distribution of inheritance.[329] The judge according to Ḥanafī law should refer to the *qisma* if one of the partners requests it.[330] The magistrate must appoint a public partitioner (*qassām*) and appoint him a salary. The partitioner must be just, skilful, and possess a knowledge of that particular business. However, it must not always be the same person. The qadi must not compel the people always to accept one particular person as their partitioner because the transactions which pass between the partners and the

328 Hamilton, *Hidāya*: 565; Marghinānī, *Hidāya*: 4:41.

329 Hamilton's commentary on the *Hidāya*: 565

330 Hamilton, *Hidāya*: 566; Marghinānī, *Hidāya*: 4:41.

partitioner are a kind of contract and it is not lawful to compel any person to enter into a contract.[331]

18A *Ṣalāt al-janāza*. The funeral prayer, which is said not at the graveyard but either at a mosque or in an open space near the home of the deceased. The *nīyya* is made to perform four *takbīrs*. The imam says, 'God is great', and then he and the congregation recite the *subḥān* in a low voice with their hands folded right over left below the navel. Then follows the second *takbīr*, 'God is great,' followed by the *taḥiyyāt*. The third 'God is great' is followed by the *duᶜa*, and finally comes the fourth *takbīr* which consists of 'God is great' and then turning the head to the right and pronouncing, 'Peace and mercy be to thee' and then to the left and again pronouncing, 'Peace and mercy be to thee'. Following this the congregation pray silently for the soul of the deceased.
Hughes, *Dictionary*:561 *s.v.* 'Burial of the dead':44.

18B *Bīᶜa*. A synagogue or church. In modern Arabic *kanīsa* is a church while *kanīs* is a synagogue. *Kanīsa* can also mean a pagan temple.
Hughes, *Dictionary*:42, 261.
*EI*²:2:717.

18B *Khuṭba*. The sermon or oration delivered on Fridays at the time of *ẓuhr* or noon prayer. It is also delivered at the ᶜĪd prayer. It must be given in Arabic. It can also be given at services at the time of drought or eclipse. In the Friday prayer it precedes the *ṣalāt* but in other services *ṣalāt* comes first. The following are obligatory: *ḥamdala*, prayer for the Prophet, admonitions of piety, prayers of the faithful, and recitation of the Quran. The following observances are sunna: the *khaṭīb* should be on a pulpit or elevated place, to salute the congregation when addressing them, to sit until the *adhān* is completed, lean on a bow, sword or staff, pray on behalf of Muslims, and make the *khuṭba* short.
*EI*¹:2:980.
*EI*²:5:74.
Hughes, *Dictionary*:274.

19B *Siwāk* or *miswāk*. A term denoting both 'toothbrush' and 'toothpick'. The more usual term is *siwāk*, which means also the act of cleansing the teeth. The instrument consists of smooth wood, the end of which is incised so as to make it similar to a brush.

---

331 Hamilton, *Hidāya*: 566; Marghinānī, *Hidāya*: 4:42

EI[1]:3:527.

19B *Muʿtakif.* A person who is in seclusion in a mosque. The seclusion (*iʿtikāf*) should not occur in a mosque when the five prayers are being held.
Marghinānī, *Hidāya*:1:32.

20A *Jiṣṣ.* Plaster and stucco (made of a mixture of lime and marble or powdered egg-shell, or else of pure gypsum and dissolved glue) are both of interest as the facings of exteriors and interiors. The plaster is smoothed and painted or else sculptured with an iron tool. This necessitates a slow setting plaster, which is obtained by the addition of gum or salt. Later, moulding was used but this gives less delicacy.
EI[2]:2:5 *s.v. djiṣṣ.*

20A *Mulāzama.* This term means the continual personal attendance on a debtor by creditors. They must not prevent him from transacting business or travelling.
Hamilton, *Hidāya*:532.

20B *Quṣṣāṣ.* The plural of *qāṣṣ*, 'storyteller'. 'The function of the *quṣṣāṣ* in the Muslim world resembles that of the friars in medieval Christendom, whose very origin was an attempt to bridge the gulf which had grown up between a materially well-endowed but spiritually distant ecclesiastical establishment, and a populace in need of educational and devotional guidance on their own level.' Bosworth, *Islamic Underworld* (Leiden, 1976):1:26–7.

20B *Bidʿa.* A novelty or innovation in religion; heresy or schism; a belief or practice for which there is no precedent in the time of the Prophet. Some Muslims feel that every innovation must be wrong but some allowance has to be made between a *bidʿa* which is 'good' (*ḥasana*) and one which is 'bad' (*sayyi'a*).
Hughes, *Dictionary*:42.
EI[2]:1:1199.

20A *Ahl al-Ṣuffa.* A group of the Prophet Muḥammad's Companions, mentioned chiefly in ascetic or mystical writings, where they have come to typify the ideal of poverty and piety. The factual grounds of the evidence are slight. The lists include the names of persons who were either poor or pious but not necessarily both. They were those men who had no home or friends in Madina and consequently lived in a part of the mosque at Madina.
EI[2]:1:266.

21B *Sujūd al-tilāwa*. The fourteen places in the Quran where a Muslim has to prostrate himself when reciting them. He has to do this even if he hears someone else reciting them. The places are vii:206, xiii:15, xvi:50, xvii:109, xix:58, xxii:77, xxv:60, xxvii:21, xxxii:15, xxxviii:24, xli:38, liii:62, lxxxiv:21, xcvi:19.
Marghinānī, *Hidāya*:1:78.

22A *Ghina'*. Song, singing. This word covers all types of song – whether simple or elaborate, folk, popular or art. At the birth of Islam singing was not prohibited; this occurred during the time of the four Orthodox Caliphs. As a result, the rigid school of Iraq prohibited it, while that in Madina allowed it.
EI[2]:2:1072.

22A *Ṣadr*. The chief judge, especially charged with the settlement of religious grants and the appointment of law officers. Sunāmī may have meant the most important member of the congregation.
Hughes, *Dictionary*:554.

22B Sherbat. A Popular drink, which is made of perfumed sugar and water.
S.M. Husain, *Indian Islam*:286.

23A *Salaf*. Ancestors, men of piety and faith in past generations.
Hughes, *Dictionary*:561.

23A Sūrat al-Ikhlāṣ. The title of the 112th sura of the Quran.

24A *Tasjiya*. To cover a grave with a winding sheet. This practice is necessary in Ḥanafī law for women before putting in grave bricks (*libn*). It is necessary because, as Marghinānī writes in his *Hidāya*, 'woman's nature requires her to be covered'.
Marghinānī, *Hidāya*:1:93.

24B *Ṭaylasān*. This is a simple veil or cloak which is thrown over the head and shoulders or just the shoulders. It is a characteristic of *faqir*s and teachers of theology. It is similar, not only in this respect, but also in origin to the Western academic robes and hoods.
Dozy, *Supplément*:278.
Mughrib:20.

26A Quoted from Sarakhsī, *Sharḥ*:2:503.

27A *Bayt*. Also 27B *Dār*. There is an important difference between *bayt* and *dār* and their implications. *Dār* is a serai with an enclosure. If a person purchases a *dār*, he is entitled to the upper storeys and the offices because the term *dār* signifies a place comprehended within an enclosure, which is considered as the original subject and of which the upper storey is a component part. *Bayt*, on the contrary, simply signifies any place of residence normally suitable for one family, as the covered shelter where one may spend the night. Contrary to the *dār*, the upper storey of a *bayt* cannot be included in the purchase of a house, unless by an express specification. If a person purchases a *bayt* in a *dār*, he is not entitled to the use of the road unless he has stipulated the rights and appendages, or the great and small accoutrements belonging to it.
Marghinānī, *Hidāya*:3:66–7.
Hamilton, *Hidāya*:294.
EI[2]:1:139.

27A *Milk*. Possession, property. Not Quranic but in regular use in later *fiqh* terminology, denoting ownership.
EI[1]:3:497.
EI[2]:7:60.

27B *Ḍayʿa*. Generally means a rural property of a certain size, usually, but not always, owned by townspeople.

27B *Ḥākim*. A just ruler.
Hughes, *Dictionary*:160.

28A *Amīn*. He to whom something is entrusted, an overseer or administrator. The more technical usage denotes the holders of various positions of trust, particularly those whose functions entail economic or financial responsibility. In legal works the term means 'legal representative.'
EI[2]:1:437.

28A House doors in streets – fig 1.

29A Party wall repair – fig 2.

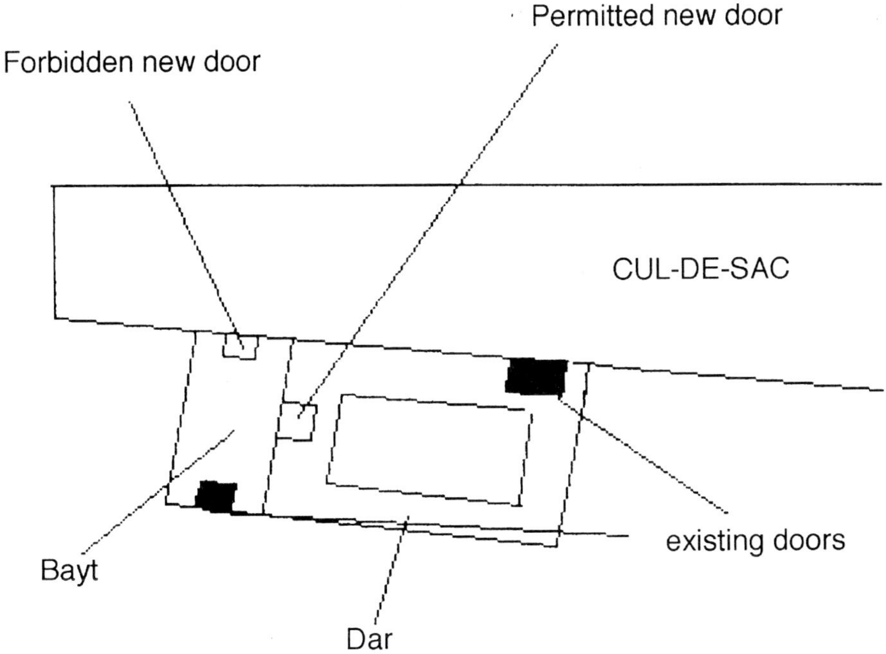
Permitted new door
Forbidden new door
CUL-DE-SAC
existing doors
Bayt
Dar

Figure1

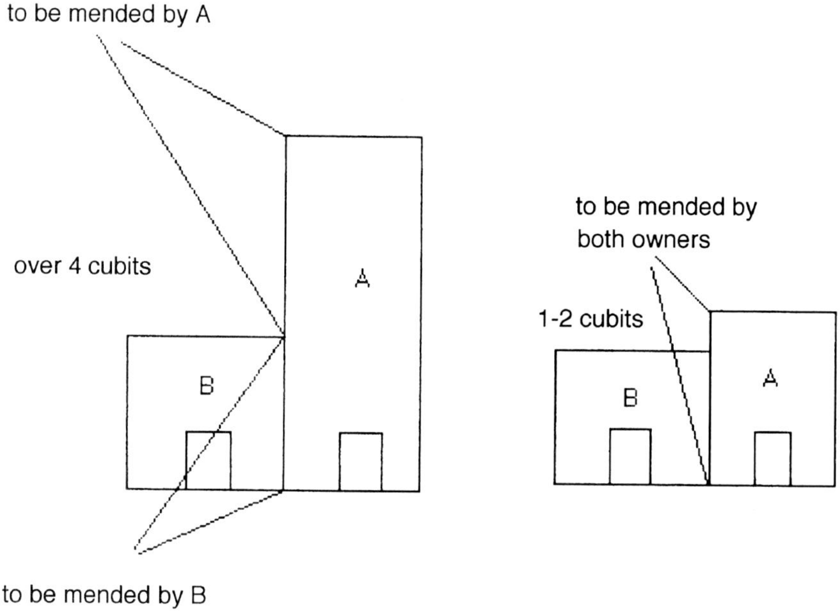
to be mended by A
over 4 cubits
A
B
to be mended by B
to be mended by
both owners
1-2 cubits
B
A

Figure 2

35B *ʿInnīn*. A general term for any man who is sexually impotent.
Muḥīṭ:2:1487.

36B *Dār al-Islām*. The territory over which the law of Islam prevails.
EI[2]:2:127.

36B *Dār al-ḍarb*. The mint, an indispensable institution in the life of medieval Middle Eastern society owing to its highly developed monetary economy. Its principal function was to supply coins. The large quantities of precious metals stored there helped to make them ancillary treasuries. Agents of the legal authorities assisted in the minting to ensure the validity of the coinage. Coins were struck of gold, silver, or copper.
EI[2]:2:117.

37A *ʿIlj*. A fat donkey or zebra.
Muḥīṭ:2:1453.

37B *Zuyūf*. Dirhams such as are not accepted at the public treasury, but which passed amongst merchants.
Hamilton, *Hidāya*:433.

37B *Nabharja*. A Persian word equivalent to Arabic *bahraj* (Hamilton seems to have made a mistake in writing *binhirja*), which is a kind of dirham worse than *zuyūf* in that it does not pass amongst merchants.
Marghinānī, *Hidāya*:3:110.
Jawāliqī has the following definition: 'Dirhams which are not minted in the government minting house'.
Jawāliqī, *Muʿarrab*:50.
Hamilton, *Hidāya*:432

37B *Mukaḥḥala*. I have been unable to trace exactly what kind of money this was. However, one cannot help feeling that this and black tanka may be the same. J. Burton-Page describes black tanka as follows: 'Black tanka was issued during the reign of Muḥammad b. Tughluq. It contained silver valued at one-eighth of the old silver tanka. Black tanka was the same size as silver tanka, the same dies could be – and were – used for both.'
EI[2]:2:120: *s.v. Dār al-ḍarb*.

37B *Sattūqa*. According to Jawāliqī the origin of the word is *sattūq*, which means three layers (Jawāliqī, *Muʿarrab*:203). Hamilton defines it as 'the

worst of all (the kinds of dirhams) in which the mixture of base metal prepondarates'.
Hamilton, *Hidaya*:433.
Muḥīṭ:1:922.

37B *Tijāriyya.* These coins could be among the kinds of token which were turned out in thousands by local artisans during Muḥammad b. Tughluq's reign, when he forced the introduction of brass tokens.
Muḥīṭ:2:120 *s.v. dār al-ḍarb.*

37B *Barbaṭ.* The lute. Arabic authors do not distinguish between *barbaṭ* and *ʿūd*, but the *barbaṭ* had the sound-box and neck in one graduating piece while the *ʿūd* had a separate sound-box and neck. The *barbaṭ* was the older type, the *ʿūd* being introduced in the eighth century. It probably had four strings.
EI[2]:1:1040 *s.v. ʿūd.*
EI[1]:4:985.

38A *Miṣr.* A common name denoting a town; it is used especially in connection with early Islamic settlements that developed out of the armed camps and the cities of the conquered provinces.
EI[1]:3:520.
EI[2]:7:146.

38A *Buyūt al-nīrān.* See the introduction to this book. (Protected People).

38B *Maḥalla.* Among the structural patterns of Delhi, *maḥalla* is mentioned as defined areas of residential and commercial activity. It is a social unit like a small village that relates to the occupation, trade, language, religion, or geographical origin of its inhabitants.
R. Ronseca, 'The walled city of old Delhi', *Ekistics* (January, 1971):75.

39A *Ṭanbūr.* A musical instrument similar to the lute but having a long neck. The word is of Persian origin.
Jawāliqī, *Muʿarrab*:223.

39A *Mufāwaḍa.* One form of partnership which can take three other forms. According to the *Hidāya*, these are partnership in traffic (*sharikat ʿinān*), partnership in arts (*sharikat ṣanā'iʿ*), and partnership upon personal credit (*sharikat wujūh*). It is curious to note that Sunāmī objected to only the first

two forms of partnership. The *mufāwaḍa* partnership, or partnership by reciprocity, is where two men, being the equals of each other in terms of property, privileges, and religious persuasion, enter into a contract of co-partnership.
Hamilton, *Hidāya*:217.
Marghinānī, *Hidāya*:3:3.
Udovitch, *Partnership and profit in mediaeval Islam* (Princeton, 1970):274.
EI^2:9:348.

39A *ʿInān*. The partnership in traffic (*sharikat al-ʿinān*) is contracted by each party respectively becoming the agent of the other but not his bail. This species of partnership is where two persons become partners in any particular traffic, such as clothes or wheat, or where they become partners in all manners of commerce indifferently.
Hamilton, *Hidāya*:223.
EI^2:9:348.

39A *Jawāliq*. An Arabicized Persian word (*gowāl*(e)), meaning 'a sack'.
Jawāliqī, *Mu'arrab*:110.
Dozy, *Supplement*:1:209.
EI^2:2:490.

42A *ʿAyn*. 'Evil eye' Belief in the evil eye is well established in Islam. The Prophet is reported to have confirmed the reality of the evil eye.
EI^2:1:786.

42A *Ratīma*. A piece of thread which is wound around a finger to jog the memory about something.
Hamilton, *Hidāya*:598.

42A *Tawla*. The magic beads which women sometimes use as aphrodisiacs to force their husbands to love them.
Muḥīṭ:1:176.

42B *Muḥtasib al-mamālik*. The chief *muḥtasib* of the kingdom. He appoints deputies to act on his behalf, to ensure that the guild sell their goods at the fixed prices.
EI^2:3:491.

43A *ʿIlm al-kalām*. The term *kalām* literally means 'speech' or 'word' and is used in Arabic translations of the works of Greek philosophers as a

rendering of the word *logos* in its various senses, including 'reason' and 'argument'. *Kalām* can be used for any branch of learning, although more specifically we can say that *kalām* means theology as distinct from *fiqh* (jurisprudence). It is the discussion of these articles of faith that constitutes *kalām*.
H.A. Wolfson, *The Philosophy of the Kalām.* (London, 1976):1:4.

43A *Tawḥīd.* Applied theologically to the oneness of Allāh.
EI[1]:4:704.

43B *Muᶜtazila.* The tenets of this group did not make them a sect in the strict sense of the word, but rather a group of thinkers who could count adherents in most of the sects proper. They rejected the traditional interpretation of the Quran and the dogma of the orthodox schools and claimed the right to judge revelation in the light of reason and philosophy. The main founders of the Muᶜtazilī theological position were four men: Muᶜammar (d. AD 830). Abū al-Hadhayl (d. AD 841), al-Naẓẓām of Basra (d. AD 846), and Bishr b. al-Muᶜtar of Baghdad (d. AD 825).
A. Guillaume, *Islam* (Harmondsworth, 1971):125.
Watt, *Philosophy*:58.

43B *Zindīq.* A term now used to denote a person in a hopeless state of infidelity. It is possibly derived from the *Zends*, i.e. the Zoroasterian commentaries on the Avesta.
Hughes, *Dictionary*:713.
The term used in Muslim law for a heretic whose teachings become a danger to the state. This crime is liable to capital punishment.
EI[1]:4:1228 *s.v. zindīḳ.*

44A *Akhdha.* A magic spell which renders a man sexually impotent.
Muḥīṭ:363.
Muḥammad Murtaḍā al-Zabīdī, *Tāj al-ᶜarūs* (Kuwait, 1971):9:365.

44B *Luqṭa.* Treasure-trove or property which a person finds lying on the ground and takes away for the purpose of preserving it in the manner of a trust. The finder must advertise it for a year before he can claim it as his own. If he is wealthy, he should give it to the poor.
Hamilton, *Hidāya*:208.
Hughes, *Dictionary*:302 *s.v. luqṭah.*

44B *Banj*. An Arabicized Persian word which originally came from Sanskrit. Probably *Hyoscyamus muticus*. In modern language it is used for every type of narcotic.
*EI*²:1:1014 *s.v. bandj*.

45A *Khabar al-wāḥid*. A term used in *ʿilm al-ḥadīth* for the traditions related by a single person and handed down by a chain of narrators. According to the generally accepted definition, *khabar al-wāḥid* is a report which falls short of the predicate *mutawātir*. Most Muslim scholars agree that *khabar al-wāḥid* can be considered as conveying a probability (*ẓann*) but not definite knowledge (*ʿilm*). Various traditionists, however, hold the opinion that those contained in the collections of Bukhārī and Muslim also convey (*ʿilm*) to the exclusion of all others.
*EI*¹:2:859.
*EI*²:4:896.
Here Sunāmī uses the term to apply to the consensus.

46B *Ḥarīr*. Silk, synonymous with *ibrīsam* and *qazz*. A group of traditions forbid the use of silk to men but allow it to women. The use of silk in garments for men is allowed only in appliqué work, or in a border not more than two fingers wide.
*EI*²:3:209.

46B *ʿAsalī*. Literally a garment which although having been once white has now become the colour of honey. Nuwayrī states that in AH 235 al-Mutawakkil ordered dhimmis to wear yellow *ṭaylasāns*. Later he adds that he ordered their women to wear yellow coats when going out.
Dozy, *Supplément*:436.

46B *Qalansuwwa*. This is variously described by Arabic writers but would appear to be a cap worn under a turban, equivalent to the modern *ṭarbūsh*. Zamakhsharī translates *qalansuwwa* as *kalāt*, which is the Persian word for a cap. Arabic authors frequently mention that oriental hermits wear *qalansuwwa*s.
Dozy, *Supplément*:365.

46B *Mūy band*. A Persian hair-band.
F. Steingass, *Dictionary* (London, 1930):201, 1349.

47B *ʿAlam*. A shred which is attached to a dress to distinguish it from others.
al-Muʿjam al-wasīṭ:2:624.

47B ᶜ*Adl*. An adjective which is derived from the word ᶜ*adāla* (justice). Various definitions have been established by the different schools of law. According to Māwardī's definition, 'It is a person in a perfect religious and moral state'. Another author observes that ᶜ*ādil* is a person who obeys the moral and religious law. This last definition is the one which has come to be accepted. The antonym of ᶜ*adl* is *fisq*.
*EI*²:1:209.

48A *Mukaᶜab*. Embroidered clothes.
Muḥīṭ:2:1820.

48A *Nasīj*. Cloth, fabric. Fabric of silk with gold stitching or brocade. Dozy, *Supplément*:2:666.

48A *Qabā'*. A long jacket closed at the front with buttons, brightly coloured in red, white, purple, blue or black. It is sometimes made of satin or silk. A *jubba* is worn underneath. The *qaba'* was worn at the time of the Prophet. Dozy, *Supplément*:352.

48A ᶜ*Azl*. *Coitus interruptus*. This was known to Arabs in the time of the Prophet Muḥammad and not forbidden by him. It may be practised with slaves without conditions, but when practised with a wife, her permission may be necessary. It is permitted if one is afraid that the large number of children may cause hardship, or with less justification to enable the husband to continue enjoying marital rights.
*EI*²:1:826.

49B *Talaqqī al-rukbān*. Meeting a caravan. A term which refers to an abominable practice of some traders. They meet a caravan at a distance from the city with a view to purchasing the grain brought by the merchant in order to sell it to the people of the city at an enhanced price.
Hamilton, *Hidāya*: 278.

49B *Muwaḍaᶜa*. Selling a selected female slave for the purpose of sex. These women are normally chosen because they are beautiful and healthy.
Aḥmad Saᶜid al-Mujaylidī, *Al-taysīr fī aḥkām al-tasᶜīr* (Algiers, 1970):95.

51A *Mustaᶜmin*. A protected person according to an *amān*. *Amān* in Islamic religious law is a safe conduct or pledge of security by which a *ḥarbī* or enemy alien, i.e. a non-Muslim belonging to the enemy country (*dār al-*

ḥarb), becomes protected by the sanction of the law with respect to his life and property for a limited period. Every free Muslim man or woman, who is of age and, according to most doctrines, even a slave, is qualified to give a valid *amān*.
EI[2]:1:429 *s.v. amān*.

51A *Istiḥsān*. Literally 'approving'. A term used in the exegesis of the Quran and of the hadith. It implies the rejection of *qiyās* and the admission of the law of expediency. For example, it is a law of Islam that everything that is washed must be squeezed like a cloth; but, as it is impossible to squeeze a vessel, it is evident that it must be cleaned without squeezing. The name is given to the method of argument used in the Ḥanafī school to settle *fiqh* rules in conformity with the requirements of everyday life, or social conditions. It is note worthy that Shāfiᶜī fundamentally rejects *istiḥsān*, seeing it as a loophole for arbitary decision-making.
Hughes, *Dictionary*:221.
EI[1]:2:561; *EI*[2]:4:255–258.

51A *Qiyās*. Comparison, deduction by analogy; one of the roots of *fiqh*. Analogical reasoning of the learned with regard to the Quran, hadith and *ijmāᶜ*.
Hughes, *Dictionary*:482.
EI[1]:2:1051 *s.v. ḳiyās*.

51A *Mamālīk*. Used in law for a bond-slave, *ᶜabd*, meaning a servant of God.
Hughes, *Dictionary*:312.

51A *Rāya*. A metal ring which is placed around a runaway slave's neck like a collar.
Muḥīṭ:1:847.

52B *Maḍrabā*. Quilt, comforter.
Muḥīṭ:2:1240.
Wehr, *Dictionary*:540.

52B *Tasnīm*. Anything convex and shelving at both sides.
Hughes, *Dictionary*:629

53A *Laḥd*. The hollow made in a grave on the *qibla* side in which the corpse is placed. It is made the same length as the grave and is as high as would allow a person to sit up in it.

Hughes, *Dictionary*:282.

53A *Muwārāt* (n.), *wārā* (v.). To conceal, by a screen either of cloth or another material.
Lisān al-ᶜArab:15 :388.

53A *Shufᶜa*. The power of possessing property which is for sale. It only applies to immovable property. It applies first to a co-owner, then to a sharer in the appendages of the property (e.g. right of water), and then to a neighbour. Hughes, *Dictionary*:582.

53A *Wars*. Believed to be the Latin *Brasilum.*
Wars has no meaning other than (a) *Memecylon tenetorium*; and (b) *Fleningia rhodocarpa*, both of which seem to be used in the production of dyes that are basically yellow.
J.D. Latham, 'Arabic into mediaeval Latin', *Journal of Semitic Studies*, vol. XVII (1972): 64.
Wars is also described as a kind of plant, similar to the sesame.
Muḥīṭ:267

55B *Tashrīq*. A name given to the three days after the sacrifice at Makka during the pilgrimage, because the flesh of the slaughtered animals is being dried in the sun.
Hughes, *Dictionary*:628.
R. Paret (*EI*[1]:4:691) gives the dates as 11th-13th *Dhū al-Ḥijja*, but states that the story about the drying of the meat is of doubtful origin.

73B *Qadariyya*. A name commonly used by Islamists to denote a group of theologians who represented, in one form or another, the doctrine of free will in the early period of Islam (from about 70/690) prior to the definitive concatenation of the Muᶜtazila at the beginning of the third/ninth century. The root of the doctrine of free will is the conviction that God is just. He cannot condemn men for actions for which they are not responsible. *Qadariyya* is derived from *qadar* (determination) and is usually applied to God's determination of events. The term *Qadariyya* was actually a nickname which every sect tried to fasten on its opponents. The earliest document of the free will movement that we have is of al-Ḥasan al-Baṣrī, composed between AH 75-90 (AD 694-699).
Watt, *Philosophy*:31.
EI[2]:4:368.

73B *Yazīdiyya.* It is more likely that Sunāmī meant *Zaydiyya*, the followers of Zayd b. ^{c}Alī b. al-Ḥusayn b. ^{c}Alī b. Abū Ṭālib, who revolted against the Umayyads in AD. 740. It is not likely that Sunāmī meant Yazīdiyya, the Kurdish 'devil-worshippers' who as such are considered *kāfirs* and not part of Islam.
Watt, *Philosophy*: 25 – *Zaydiyya*, 105 – *Yazīdiyya*.

73B *Rawāfiḍ* or *Rāfiḍiyya.* A name used for a Shi^{c}ī sect by their opponents which means 'deserters'. Hishām b. al-Ḥakam from Baghdad (d. AD 825) was one of the group's leaders. Their chief doctrine was that ^{c}Alī b. Abū Ṭālib had been clearly designated imam for the Muslim community by the Prophet in succession to himself.
Watt, *Philosophy*:52.

74B *Jabriyya.* The people who believe in the theory of compulsion (*jabr*) in which a man has no power to act or will. They think the power he has is only the power to perform the act and not its opposite. Al-Ash^{c}arī (d. AD 935) considered that this idea of compulsion (*jabr*) gave man sufficient responsibility for him to be justly punished or rewarded on the Day of Judgment.
Watt, *Philosophy*: 88.

74B *Najjāriyya.* The followers of Ḥusayn b. Muḥammad al-Najjār (d. 250 AH) a contemporary of Naẓẓām, and representative of the Mu^{c}tazilī sect. The *Najjāriyya* denied God's attributes (*ṣifāt*) as did the Mu^{c}tazila. These attributes are based on seven of God's names mentioned in the Quran and are: knowing, powerful, willing, living, hearing, seeing and speaking.
^{c}Abd al-Qāhir al-Baghdādī, *Al-milal wa-l-niḥal*, ed. A.N. Nādir (Beirut, 1970): 142.
Watt, *Philosophy*:63.

74B *Karrāmiyya.* A sect which flourished in the central and eastern parts of the Islamic world, and especially in the Iranian regions from the third/ninth century until the Mongol invasion, founded by Muḥammad b. Karrām (d. 255/869). Ibn Karrām considered that God was a substance (*jawhar*) and, therefore, approached the belief that He has a body (*jism*) finite in certain directions when He comes into contact with the throne.
EI^{2}:4:667.

Index of Arabic Words

Books Mentioned in the Text

The numbers indicate the folio page on which the book is cited for the first time.

Adab al-qāḍī 62B =*AQ*	By Al-Khaṣṣāf Abū Bakr Aḥmad b. ᶜUmar who died in 261/874–5. Luknawī:129 Quṭlūbughā:7 *GAL*:80
Aḥkām al-Qur'ān 8A =*AḥQ*	By Abū Bakr al-Rāzī, al-Jaṣṣāṣ Aḥmad b. ᶜAlī who died in 370/980–1. Luknawī:28 Quṭlubughā:6 *GAL*:1:204
Al-aḥkām al-sulṭāniyya 1A =*AḥS*	There are two works with this title, one by ᶜAlī b. Muḥammad al-Māwardī al-Shāfiᶜī, Abu al-Ḥasan who died in 450/1058–9. The second is byMuḥammad b. al-Ḥusayn al-Farrā' al-Ḥanbalī who died in 458/1065–6. H.Kh., *Kashf*:19 *GAL*:1:483, Sup:1:686
Al-ajnās 25B =*Aj*	On Ḥanafī *furūᶜ*, by Aḥmad b. Muḥammad al-Ḥanafī al-Nāṭifī who died in 446/1054–5. Quṭlūbughā:61 Luknawī:36 H.Kh., *Kashf*:11
ᶜAwārif al-maᶜārif 9A =*AM*	A work on Sufism by ᶜUmar b. Muḥammad b. ᶜAbd Allāh al-Suhrawardī, also known as Shaykh al-Shuyūkh, who died in 632/1234–5 in Baghdad. *GAL*:1:569 H.Kh., *Kashf*:1177, *Al-munjid*:276
ᶜAyn al-maᶜānī fī tafsīr al-sabᶜ al-mathānī	See *Tafsīr ᶜayn al-maᶜānī*

Bustān al-ʿārifīn 4A =*BA*	A work on Ḥanafī law by Abū al-Layth al- Samarqandī Naṣr b. Muḥammad who died in 373/983–4 or 393/1002–3. Quṭlūbughā:79 Luknawī:221 *GAL*:1:211
Al-dhakhīra 4A =*Dh*	A work on Ḥanafī law by Maḥmūd b. Tāj al-Dīn Aḥmad b. al-Ṣadr al-Shahīd who died in 616/1229–20. This work is a summary of the author's work *Al-muḥīṭ*, together with some practical cases which occurred during his legal career in Samarqand. Luknāwī:205-7 H.Kh., *Kashf*:823
Fatāwā Abī al-Layth 8A =*FAL*	By Abū al-Layth al-Samarqandī, Naṣr b. Muḥammad who died in 373/983–4 or 393/1002–3. H.Kh:*Kashf* 1220 Luknawī:221
Fatāwā ahl Samarqand 10A =*FS*	All that it has been possible to discover about this work is that it was mentioned in *Al-tajnīs wa-l-mazīd* and some other works. H.Kh., *Kashf*:352, 1221
Fatāwā al-Bayhaqī 45B =*FB*	There is no book with this title in the references available. However, al-Bayhaqī, Ismāʿīl al-Ḥusayn b. ʿAbd Allāh (d. 402/1011–2) composed a book on the *fatāwā* of Ḥanafī law. This book is entitled *Al-shāmil*. *GAL*:1:183 H.Kh., *Kashf*:1024 Ziriklī:1:308
Fatāwā al-Faḍlī 28B =*FF*	Two books of *fatāwā* bear this title: (a) *Fatāwā al-Faḍlī* by Muḥammad b. al-Faḍl who died in 381/991–2. Luknawī:184 H.Kh., *Kashf*:353 (b) *Fatāwā al-Faḍlī* by Abū ʿAmrū ʿUthmān b. Ibrāhīm al-Ḥanafī who died in 508/1114–5.

H.Kh., *Kashf*:1227
The first *Fatāwā* is probably the one to which Sunāmī referred, because Luknawī states that the title of *Faḍlī*, if used alone refers to the first author.
Luknawī:246

Al-fatāwā āl-khāniyya
3B
=*FKh*

No treaty appears to have this title. It would appear likely that Sunāmī referred to the work entitled *Fatāwā Qāḍī Khān* by Qāḍī Khān Ḥasan b. Manṣūr al-Awzajandī who died in 592/1195–6.
Luknawī:64–5
Quṭlubūgha:22
H.Kh., *Kashf*:1227
Sunāmī seems to put the word *Khān* after Qāḍī Khān's work in order to distinguish it from similar works by other authors; see *Al-jāmiᶜ al-ṣaghīr al-khānī*. However, this may not be true and *Fatāwā al-khāniyya* and *Al-jāmiᶜ al-ṣaghīr al-khānī* may be completely different works.

Al-fatāwā al-Nasafiyya
29A
=*FN*

This treatise on Ḥanafī law was composed by ᶜUmar b. Muḥammad al- Nasafī (461 – 537/1068–9 – 1142–3). It includes the answers to all the questions that had been put to him.
H.Kh., *Kashf*:1230

Al-fatāwā al-Ẓahīriyya
12B
=*FẒ*

By Ẓahīr al-Dīn Abū Bakr Muḥammad b. Aḥmad al-Qāḍī, the *muḥtasib* of Bukhārā who died in 619/1222–3.
H.Kh., *Kashf*:1226

Gharīb al-riwāya
70A
=*Gh*

By Ibn Shujāᶜ.
H.Kh., *Kashf*:352

Al-hidāya
8B
=*H*

A book on Ḥanafī law by Burhān al-Dīn ᶜAlī b. Abī Bakr al-Marghinānī who died in 593/1196–7.
This work is in fact a commentary on a work by the same author, *Bidāyat al-mubtadī*. The *Hidāya* was translated into English by C. Hamilton (see bibliography).

H.Kh., *Kashf*:2031
GAL:Sup:1:644

Al-īḍāḥ
64B
=*IMN*

Many books have this title. Sunāmī probably meant *Īḍāḥ al-maḥajja fī kawn al-ᶜaql hijja* by Maymūn b. Muḥammad al-Nasafī al-Ḥanafī who lived 418 – 508/1027–8 – 1114–5. The author was originally from Samarqand and lived in Bukhārā for some time.
Luknawī:216
Quṭlubughā:78
Īḍāḥ : 3:156
Alternatively, *Al-īḍāḥ* may be the title of a commentary on the work entitled *Al-tajrīd*, both written by the same author, Abū al-Faḍl ᶜAbd al-Raḥmān b. Muḥammad al-Karmānī (457 – 543/1064–5 – 1148–9).
Quṭlubughā:33

Iḥyā' ᶜulūm al-dīn
82A
=*Iḥ*

A treatise on ethics and Sufism by Al-Ghazāli, Abū Ḥāmid Muḥammad b. Muḥammad (450 – 505/1058–9 – 1111–2).
H.Kh., *Kashf*:23
GAL:1:539

Imlā'
37B
=*Im*

Many scholars have given this title to their works.
It seems, however, that Sunāmī referred to *Amālī* by Abū Yūsuf, which was narrated by his student Bishr. It is curious that Sunāmī chose to call this work *Imlā'* (a dictation) instead of the correct title *Amālī*, which is the plural ('dictations'). The probable reason is that he only used one chapter from the book. The only other alternative is the existence of another book by Abū Yūsuf which was also narrated by Bishr. This does not appear in any of the references available.
Luknawī:55
Samᶜānī, *Ansāb*:523B – 524A

Al-jāmiᶜ
72B

Sunāmī gave no more details of the book to which he referred. However, he probably meant *Al-jāmiᶜ li-aḥkām al-Qur'ān*. This work is a Quranic commentary

	by Al-Qurṭubī, Abū ᶜAbd Allāh Muḥammad b. Aḥmad, who died in 671/1273. *GAL*:Sup:1:737 H.Kh., *Kashf*:537
Al-jāmiᶜ al-ṣaghīr 25B =*JṢ*	A work on Ḥanafī law by Muḥammad b. al-Ḥasan al-Shaybānī who died in 187/802–3. The work contains all Shaybānī learnt from Abū Yūsuf on Ḥanafī legal views. There are many commentaries on this work including those by Ṭaḥāwī (d.321/933) and Abū Bakr al-Rāzī al-Jaṣṣāṣ, (d.370/980–1). H.Kh., *Kashf*:561–4
Al-jāmiᶜ al-ṣaghīr al-khānī 6A =*JṢKh*	This work, like *Al-fatāwā al-khāniyyā*, does not appear to fit any of the works in the references available. It seems therefore, to be a special term used by Sunāmī to identify the commentary on *Al-jāmiᶜ al-ṣaghīr*. This commentary was composed by Qāḍi Khān Ḥasan b. Manṣūr al-Awzajandī who died in 592/1195–6. Luknawī:65 Quṭlūbughā:22 *Al-jāmiᶜ al-ṣaghīr* was written by Muḥammad b. al-Ḥasan al-Shaybānī.
Al-kashshāf ᶜan ḥaqā'iq al-tanzīl 43B =*Kash*	By Al-Zamakhsharī, Abū al-Qāsim Jār Allāh Maḥmūd, who died in 538/1143–4. *GAL*:Sup:1:507 H.Kh., *Kashf*:1475
Al-kashshāf 10A	It has not been possible to trace this work. It is apparently not Zamakhsharī's *Kashshāf*, because I was not able to find Sunāmī's quotations in it.
Al-kaysāniyyāt 60B =*K*	A work on Ḥanafī law by Muḥammad b. al-Ḥasan al-Shaybānī. Luknawī:163 Quṭlūbughā:54 *GAL*:Sup:1:291
Khānī	See *Al-jāmiᶜ al-ṣaghīr al-khānī*.

Al-khāniyya	See *Al-fatāwā al-khāniyya.*
Khulāṣat al-fatāwā 19A *=KhF*	By Ṭāhir b. ᶜAbd al-Rashīd al-Bukhārī who died in 542/1147 – 8. It would appear that Sunāmī refers to this work as both *Khulāṣat al-fatāwā* and as *Khulāṣa.* Luknawī:84 *GAL*:1:462, Sup:1:641
Khulāṣat al-mukhtaṣar wa-naqāwat al-muᶜtaṣar 16A *=Khul*	By Al-Ghazālī, Abū Ḥāmid Muḥammad b. Muḥammad (450 – 505/1059-9 – 1111–2). This is a work on Shāfiᶜī *fiqh*. A.R. Badawī, Mu'allafāt al-Ghazālī (Cairo, 1961):30
Al-kifāya al-Shaᶜbiyya 4A *=KSh*	This is a work on Ḥanafī law by Al-Shaᶜbī, Maḥmud b. ᶜUmar Abū Jaᶜfar. *Īḍāḥ*:4:372 Levy, *Catalogue*:277
Kitāb al-diyyāt *=KD*	There is no evidence of what Sunāmī intended by this title. It is possible, however, that he meant the chapter on *diyyāt* in one of Ṭaḥāwī's books. Alternatively, he may have meant the book on *diyyāt* by Abū Bakr Aḥmad b. Muḥammad b. ᶜAmrū al-Nabīl al-Shaybānī al-Ẓāhirī who died in 287/900. Y.A. Sarkīs, *Muᶜjam al-maṭbūᶜāt al-ᶜarabiyya wa-l-muᶜarraba*, (Cairo, 1346/1927):col. 1220
Kitāb al-istiḥsān 34A see also 28A	No book appears to have been written by Abū al-Layth with this title. It is, therefore, probable that Sunāmī meant a chapter in one of Abū al-Layth's books.
Al-Mabsūṭ 5A *=Mabs*	A treatise on Ḥanafī law by Muḥammad b. Aḥmad al-Sarakhsī Shams al-A'imma who died in 483/1090–1. The author composed this work while in prison. Luknawī:159 *GAL*:1:460 H.Kh., *Kashf*:1580

Al-manāhī 22B =*Man*	It has not been possible to trace this work in the references available.
Al-manẓūma 72A =*Maẓ*	By Abū Ḥafṣ ᶜUmar b. Muḥammad Aḥmad al-Nasafī al-Ḥanafī who died in 537/1142–3. A poetic treatise comprising ten chapters written according to Ḥanafī law. The author completed the work in Safar, 504/1110. H.Kh., *Kashf*:1867 *GAL*:1:549 – 50
Maᶜrifat al-ṣaḥāba 60A =*MM*	A biography of the Prophet's Companions by Al-Mushtaghfirī, Abū al-ᶜAbbās Jaᶜfar b. Muḥammad, who lived betweeen 350 and 432/961–2 and 1040–1. H.Kh., *Kashf*:1739 Ziriklī:123
Al-mughrib fī tartīb al-muᶜrab 1A =*Mugh*	This is a dictionary of Ḥanafī law and is considered a standard work of Ḥanafī reference. It was composed by Nāṣir b. ᶜAbd al-Sayyid al-Muṭarrizī who died in 610/1213–4. H.Kh., *Kashf*:1748 *GAL*:1:352
Al-muḥīṭ 4A =*Muḥ*	There are two Ḥanafī books of law with this title: (a) *Al-muḥīṭ al-burhānī fī al-fiqh al-nuᶜmānī* by Maḥmūd b. Tāj al-Dīn Aḥmad b. al-Ṣadr al-Shahīd who died in 616/1219–20. (b) *Muḥīṭ al-Sarakhsī* by Muḥammad b. Aḥmad al-Sarakhsī who died in 483/1090–1. The first of these works is probably the one to which Sunāmī referred, since both Luknawī and Ḥājjī Khalīfa agree that whenever the work *Muḥīṭ* is used in Ḥanafī works it refers to the first of these two books. Luknawī:246 H.Kh., *Kashf*:1619–20 *GAL*:1:464, Sup:1:642
Muttafaq 82A	A work on Ḥanafī *furūᶜ* by Abū Bakr ᶜAbd Allāh al-Jawzaqī, 307 – 388/919–20 – 998.

=*Mut*	H.Kh., *Kashf*:1585 Ziriklī:7:99 *Tadhkirat al-ḥuffāẓ*:3:1013
Al-multaqaṭ fī al-fatāwā al-Ḥanafiyya 3B =*MN*	By Nāṣīr al-Dīn Muḥammad al-Samarqandī who died in 556/1160–1. The author composed this work during 549/1154–5. *GAL*:1:475 H.Kh., *Kashf*:1812
Al-muntaqā 19B =*Munt*	This may be either of the two following texts: (a) *Al-muntaqā* on the *furūᶜ* of Ḥanafī law by Muḥammad b. Muḥammad b. Aḥmad al-Balkhī al-Shahīd or al-Ḥākim who was killed in 334/945 – 6. (b) Muntaqā al-marfuᶜ by Burhān al-Dīn ᶜAlī b. Abū Bakr ᶜAbd al-Jalīl al-Farghānī al-Marghiyānī who died in 593/1196–7. H.Kh., *Kashf*:1852
Al-nawādir 46A =*Nd*	This treatise was originally the work of Muḥammad b. al-Ḥasan al-Shaybānī. It was, however, compiled by his student Abū Bakr Ibrāhīm b. Rustum al-Marwazī who died in 211/826–7. Luknawī:10 Quṭlubughā:54
Al-nawāzil min al-fatāwā 13B =*N*	A treatise on law which includes both Ḥanafī and non-Ḥanafī elements. It was written by Abū al-Layth al-Samarqandī who died in either 373/983–4 or 393/1002–3. H.Kh., *Kashf*:198 *GAL*:1:210
Qūt al-qulūb fī muᶜāmalat al-maḥbūb 20A =*QQ*	This is a treatise on Sufism by Muḥammad b. ᶜAlī b. ᶜAṭiyya al-Makkī who died in 386/997–8 in Baghdad. H.Kh., *Kashf*:1361 *GAL*:1:217

Al-rawḍa 30B =*R*	Many works bear this title. Sunāmī may have been referring to any one of the following: (a) *Rawḍat al-ᶜulamā'* by Ḥusayn al-Zandawaysitī who died c. 400/1009–10. Ismāᶜīl Bāshā al-Baghdādī, *Hadiyyat al-ᶜārifin* (Istanbul, 1951):5:307 Quṭlubughā:69 (b) *Rawḍat al-ṭālibīn* by Muḥammad b. Muḥammad al-Ghazālī. *Īḍāḥ*:2:595 (c) *Rawḍat al-quḍāṭ fī ādāb al-qaḍa'* by ᶜAlī b. Aḥmad al-Samnānī al-Ḥanafī who died in 499/1105–6. *Īḍāḥ*:2:596
Al-ṣalāt al-masᶜūdiyya 61A	The author is unknown. H.Kh., *Kashf*:1081
Ṣaḥīḥ al-Bukhārī, also known as *Al-jāmiᶜ al-ṣaḥīḥ* 5B, 41B =*Ṣaḥ*	By Abū ᶜAbd Allāh Muḥammad Ismāᶜīl al-Juᶜfī al-Bukhārī who died in 256/869–70. H.Kh., *Kashf*:541 *GAL*:1:163, Sup:1:260
Al-ṣalāt al-nasafiyya 70B =*SN*	No book with this title appears in the references available.
Al-ṣārim al-maslūl ᶜalā shātim al-rasūl 75B =*SAM*	By Taqī al-Dīn Amad b. Taymiyya al-Ḥanbalī who died 728/1327–8. It was written because of a Christian named Ibn ᶜAsāq who swore at the Prophet in 693/1293–4. It gives legal points concerning people who swear at the Prophet. H.Kh., *Kashf*: 1069
Sharḥ adab al-qāḍī 5B =*ShAQ*	A commentary on *Adab al-qāḍī* by Aḥmad b. 'Umar al-Khaṣṣāf (261/874–5). The author was Aḥmad b. ᶜAlī al-Jaṣṣāṣ who lived between 305 and 307/917–8 and 980–1.

Sharḥ al-awrād
22B
=*ShA*

It has not been possible to trace this work in the references available.

Sharḥ al-Karkhī
4A
=*ShK*

ᶜUbayd Allāh b. Ḥusayn Abū al-Ḥasan al-Karkhī (260 – 340/874–5 – 951–2) wrote commentaries on two books. Sunāmī does not mention to which he of these refers.
The two books are:
(a) *Al-jāmiᶜ al-ṣaghīr* by Muḥammad b. al-Ḥasan al-Shaybānī.
(b) *Al-jāmiᶜ al-kabīr* by Muḥammad b. al-Ḥasan al-Shaybānī.
Luknawī:108
Ziriklī:347
Kaḥḥāla, *Muᶜjam*:6:239

Sharḥ al-manẓūma
6A
=*ShMaẓ*

It is difficult to ascertain which commentary (*sharḥ*) Sunāmī referred to, as there are several bearing this title.
GAL:1:459-50, Sup:1:761

Sharḥ al-shāfiya
45B
=*ShSH*

Sunāmī is not very clear as to which book or commentary he refers. There is a book entitled *Al-Shāfiya* by ᶜUthmān b. ᶜUmar known as Ibn al-Ḥājib. This is a work on the science of conjugation (*taṣrīf*).
H.Kh., *Kashf*:1020
GAL:1:305, Sup:1:535

Sharḥ al-siyar al-kabīr
26A
=*ShSK*

This is a commentary on *Al-siyar al-kabīr* by Muḥammad b. al-Ḥasan al-Shaybānī.
The commentary is written by Sarakhsī, Muḥammad b. Aḥmad, who died in 483/1090–91. He finished the work in Jumādā al-awwal, AH 480.
H.Kh., *Kashf*: 1014

Sharḥ al-Ṭaḥāwī
13A
=*ShṬ*

A commentary on *Al-jāmiᶜ al-ṣaghīr* by Muḥammad b. al-Ḥasan al-Shaybānī (see also *Sharḥ al-Ṭaḥāwī al-kabīr*). *Sharḥ al-Ṭaḥāwī* is by Aḥmad b. Amad b. Muḥammad Abū Jaᶜfar *al-Ṭaḥāwī* (229–321/843-4 – 933).

	Luknawī:32 Quṭlubughā:8
Sharḥ al-Ṭaḥāwī al-kabīr 14B =*ShTK*	A commentary on *Al-jāmi*ᶜ *al-kabīr* by Muḥammad b. al-Ḥasan al-Shaybānī. The commentary is by Aḥmad b. Muḥammad Abū Jaᶜfar al-Ṭaḥāwī (229 – 321/843–4 – 933). Luknawī:32 Quṭlūbughā:8
*Shir*ᶜ*at al-Islām* 8A =*ShI*	A treatise on Ḥanafī law and Sufi conduct by Muḥammad b. Abī Bakr, also known as Imām Zāda of Bukhārā. He died in 573/1117–8. H.Kh., *Kashf*:1044 Luknawī:161
Al-ṣiḥāḥ 1A =*Ṣiḥ*	A dictionary of Arabic language by Ismāᶜīl b. Ḥammad al-Jawharī. He died while attempting to fly with a pair of wings in 393/1002–3. H.Kh., *Kashf*:1071
Siyar al-atqiyā' 49A =*SA*	It has not been possible to trace this work in the references available.
Al-siyar al-kabīr 26A =*SK*	A treatise on Ḥanafī international law by Muḥammad b. al-Ḥasan al-Shaybānī. This work has been commented on by various scholars. Sunāmī appears to have been referring to the commentary by Muḥammad b. Aḥmad b. Abū Sahl al-Sarakhsī who died in 483/1090–1. *GAL*:1:179 Luknawī:159 H.Kh., *Kashf*:1014
Tafsīr Abī al-Layth 57A =*TA*	By Abū al-Layth al-Samarqandī Naṣr b. Muḥammad who died in either 373/983–4 or 393/1002–3. H.Kh., *Kashf*:441 Luknawī:220

Tafsīr ᶜayn al-maᶜānī or *Tafsīr al-Sajjāwandī*
19A
=*TᶜAyn*

By Muḥammad b. Ṭayfūr al-Sajjāwandī who died in 560/1164–5.
GAL:1:519
H.Kh., *Kashf*:1182

Tafsīr al-Bastī
57A
=*TB*

A commentary on the Quran by Nāṣir al-Dīn Muḥammad b. Muḥammad b. Jaᶜfar, also known as Ibn Ḥibban al-Bastī, who died in 354/965.
H.Kh., *Kashf*:437, 444

Al-tafsīr al-kabīr
73A
=*TK*

By Fahkr al-Dīn ᶜUmar al-Rāzī who died in 606/1209 – 10. This commentary on the Quran is incomplete and other scholars have attempted to finish the work. The work is otherwise known as *Mafātīḥ al-ghayb.*
H.Kh., *Kashf*:1756
GAL:1:667

Al-tajnīs wa-l-mazīd
8B
=*TM*

On the subject of *fatāwā* by Burhān al-Dīn ᶜAlī b. Abū Bakr al-Marghinānī al-Ḥanafī who died in 593/1196–7.
H.Kh., *Kashf*:352
GAL:Sup:1:649

Tadhkirat al-awliyā'
59A
=*Tadh*

By Abū Ḥāmid Muḥammad b. Ibrāhīm, otherwise known as Farīd al-Dīn al-ᶜAṭṭār who died between 617/1220–1 and 628/1230–1 at an advanced age. His death may have been at the hands of the Mongol invaders of Persia. The traditional account that he was born in 513/1119–20 and murdered in 628/1230–1 is now generally rejected.
Arberry, *Muslim Saints*:1
EI^2:1:752

Tanbīh al-ghāfilīn
21A
=*TGh*

By Abū al-Layth al-Samarqandī Naṣr b. Muḥammad b. Aḥmad.
H.Kh., *Kashf*:441
Luknawī:220
GAL:Sup:1:348

Uṣūl al-Bazdawī 32B =*UB*	A treatise on the subject of *uṣūl al-fiqh*, written by ᶜAlī al-Bazdawī b. Muḥammad Fakhr al-Islām (400–482/1010–1089). Many commentaries have been written on this book on account of the difficulty in its comprehension. H.Kh., *Kashf*:112 Luknawī:124 *GAL*:1:460, Sup:1:637
Uṣūl al-Sarakhsī 82B =*US*	By Muḥammad b. Aḥmad al-Sarakhsī who died in 383/993–4. H.Kh., *Kashf*:112 Luknawī:158 *GAL*:1:460
Wāqiᶜāt al-nāṭifī 59A =*WN*	A Ḥanafī law book by Aḥmad b. Muḥammad b. ᶜUmar al-Nāṭifī who died in 446/1054–5. Luknawī:36 H.Kh., *Kashf*:1998
Wāqiᶜāt al-Ṣadr al-Shahīd 29A =*WSS*	By ᶜUmar b. ᶜAbd al-ᶜAzīz al-Bukhārī al-Ḥanafī who died in 536/1141–2 otherwise known as Al-Ṣadr al-Shahīd. This book is a selection from the *Nawāzil*, *Al-ḥusāmī*, and *Al-ajnās* written by Abū al-Layth, *Wāqiᶜāt al-Nāṭifī*, and *Fatāwā al-Faḍlī* by Muḥammad b. al-Faḍl. H.Kh., *Kashf*:1998 *GAL*:1:374
Yawāqīt al-mawāqīt 7B =*YM*	By Najm al-Dīn ᶜUmar al-Nasafī who lived between 461 and 537/1068–9 and 1142–3. Luknawī:149 H.Kh., *Kashf*:2054 *GAL*:Sup:1:762

Biographies of People Mentioned in the Text

Al-ᶜAbbās b. ᶜAbd al-Muṭṭalib
66B

51BH – AH32/573–4 – 552–3.
The Prophet's uncle. He was one of the elite of Makka prior to Islam. He became a Muslim secretly and remained in Makka when the rest of the Muslim community emigrated to Madina. He narrated 34 hadiths in the two *Ṣaḥīḥ*s.
Ṣifat al-ṣafwa:1:510
Ziriklī:4:35

ᶜAbd Allāh
41B

Sunāmī would appear to mean ᶜAbd Allāh b. Abū Bakr al-Anṣarī who died in 35/665–6.
Badr al-Dīn Maḥmud b. Aḥmad al-ᶜAynī, *ᶜUmdat al-qārī*, (Cairo, AH 1348):14:252
Tahdhīb al-tahdhīb:5:65

ᶜAbd Allāh b. ᶜAbbās b. ᶜAbd al-Muṭṭalib
20A

3BH – AH 61/618–9 – 680–1.
He was called the doctor (*ḥibr*) because of his doctrine of Quranic exegesis. He established his doctrine at a time when it was necessary to bring the Quran into accord with the demands of society which had undergone a profound transformation.
EI^2:1:40
Tadhkirat al-ḥuffāẓ:1:40

ᶜAbd Allāh b. Abū Salūl b. Ubayy
53B

He died in 6/627–8.
The person who began the controversial dispute about the Prophet's wife, ᶜĀ'isha. Salūl was his grandmother's name.
Ṣifat al-ṣafwa:2:23
Ziriklī:4:188

ᶜAbd Allāh b. Mūsā b. Jaᶜfar
75B

128 – 183/745–6 – 799–800.
Son of Mūsā al-Kāẓim, who was the sixth imam according to the Imāmī Shīᶜa who believe in the twelve selected imams. These imams should be the oldest male descendants of the Prophet. Thus ᶜAbd Allāh, being a younger son, was not entitled to be imam after his father,

	who was in fact succeeded by ʿAbd Allāh's brother ʿAlī al-Riḍā (153–203/770–818–9). A.M. Subḥī, *Naẓariyyāt al-imāma ʿinda al-Shīʿa* (Cairo, 1969):384,386
ʿAbd Allāh b. Rawāḥa 52A	He died in 8/629–30. One of the Prophet's Companions. He was one of the poets of whom the Prophet approved, an early convert to Islam who was later appointed governor of Madina. He was killed in the battle of Mu'ta. Ibn Qudāma, *Istibṣār*:108–12 *Ṣifat al-ṣafwa*:1:480 *Ḥilyat al-awliyā'*:1:118
ʿAbd Allāh b. ʿUmar b. al-Khaṭṭāb 14A	10BH – AH73/ 613–4 – 692–3. He was converted to Islam with his father when still a boy in Makka. An outstanding *muftī* and traditionist for some 60 years. *Ṣifat al-ṣafwa*:1:563–82 *Tadhkirat al-ḥuffāẓ*:1:37
ʿAbd Allāh b. Salūl	See ʿAbd Allāh b. Abū Salūl b. Ubbay.
ʿAbd al-ʿAzīz al-Tirmidhī 45A	It has not been possible to trace this name in the references available.
ʿAbd al-Jabbār al-Rāzī, Abū al-Ḥasan al-Hamadānī 43B	He died in 415/1024–5. He was the Shaykh of the Muʿtazilīs. He was first Ashʿarī and then changed to Muʿtazilī. Towards the end of his life he went to Rayy where he was appointed as *qāḍī quḍāt*. He wrote several books to present his views on *iʿtizāl*. *Ṭabaqāt al-Muʿtazila*:112 Ibn Ḥajar, *Lisān*:3:386
ʿAbd al-Mālik b. Maysara 14B	He died 145/762–3. He related traditions from Anas b. Mālik, ʿAṭā', Saʿīd b. Jubayr and others. Among his students of hadith were Thawrī and Ibn al-Mubārak. He was a contemporary of ʿAmrū b. Dinār.

Mīzān al-iʿtidāl:2:144
Tahdhīb al-tahdhīb:6:396–8

ʿAbd al-Raḥmān b. Abū Bakr
11A

He died in 54/673–4.
A son of the Prophet's well-known Companion, Abū Bakr, and a brother of ʿĀ'isha, the Prophet's wife. He narrated eight hadith concerning the Prophet. He died six miles from Makka, and was carried to Makka to be buried.
Tahdhīb al-asmā':1:295
Iṣāba:2:399

ʿAbd al-Raḥmān b. ʿAwf b. Kilāb
32A

44BH – AH32/580–1 – 652–3.
He was one of the six people selected by ʿUmar after he was stabbed, to choose a caliph from among themselves.
Ḥilyat al-awliyā':97–100
Ziriklī:4:95

ʿAbd al-Raḥmān b. Ghanam al-Ashʿarī
32A

He died in 78/697–8.
The son of a Prophet's Companion. ʿAbd al-Raḥmān was the faqih in Shām and Palestine. He narrated hadith from ʿUmar and Muʿādh b. Jabal.
Tadhkirat al-ḥuffāẓ:151
Tahdhīb al-tahdhīb:6:250
Iṣāba:2:410

ʿAbd al-Wahhāb b. al-Ḥakam al-Warrāq
37A

He died in 251/865–6.
A Sufi friend of Aḥmad b. Ḥanbal. It is said that Bishr (150–227/767–8–841–2) was seen in a dream after his death, and said that ʿAbd al-Wahhāb and Aḥmad b. Ḥanbal were both happy and enjoying God's rewards.
Ṣifat al-ṣafwa:2:370
Tahdhīb al-tahdhīb:6:448

Abū al-ʿĀliya Rafīʿ al-Riyāḥī
33B

He died in 90/708–9.
A well-known transmitter of hadith. He transmitted from Abū Bakr, Ubayy b. Kaʿb, Ibn ʿAbbās, Abū Hurayra and others.
Tadhkirat al-ḥuffāẓ:1:62

Ṣifat al-ṣafwa:3:112
Tahdhīb al-asmā':2:251

Abū ᶜAbd Allāh al-Khwārizmī, Muḥammad b. Aḥmad 70A	He died in 387/997–8. An encyclopaedic writer of Khwārizm. He lived during the reign of Nūḥ al-Sāmānī (AH365–387). *GAL*:Sup:1:434 Ziriklī:6:204 H.Kh., *Kashf*:1756
Abū ᶜAlī al-Daqqāq, Aḥmad b. Muḥammad b. ᶜAbd al-Raḥmān 70A	He died in 340/951–2. He taught Ḥanafī law in Baghdad. Luknawī:146 Quṭlūbugha:89
Abū Bakr 66B	Since Sūnāmi did not give any further details, it has not been possible to trace this man.
Abū Bakr al-Aᶜmash, Muḥammad b. Saᶜīd 5A	He died in 340/951–2. A Ḥanafī scholar and a faqih. His teacher was Muḥammad b. Aḥmad Abū Bakr al-Iskāf who died in 333/944–5.
Abū Bakr al-ᶜAyyaḍ, Muḥammad b. Aḥmad b. al-ᶜAbbās 16A	He died in 361/971–2. A Ḥanafī scholar who also had a fair knowledge of mathematics and astronomy. His great-grandfather was said to have been Saᶜd b. ᶜUbāda, a Companion of the Prophet. Luknawī:156 Samᶜānī, *Ansāb*:403B
Abū Bakr al-Faḍlī	See Al- Faḍlī.
Abū Bakr al-Iskāf Muḥammad b. Aḥmad al-Balkhī 4A	He died in 333 or 336/944–5 or 947–8. He was a teacher of Abū Bakr al-Aᶜmash. Samᶜānī gave his date of death as 263/876–7. Luknawī:160 Samᶜānī, *Ansāb*:35A
Abū Bakr al-Jaṣṣāṣ	See Al-Jaṣṣāṣ.

Abū Bakr al-Shiblī, Dulaf b. Jaḥdar or Ja^{c}far
62A

He died in 334/945–6 at the age of 87.
He was of Khurāsānī origin but was born in Sāmarrā'.
He was the son of a court official and was himself prominent in the Imperial Service in Baghdad. He became a Sufi and joined the circle of al-Junayd. He was a leading figure in the stormy history of al-Ḥallāj. Sunāmī appears to have made a mistake when he wrote that Abū Bakr al-Shiblī met al-Mu^{c}taṣim, since they were not contemporaries. It is probable that he meant either Muwaffaq (d. 261/874–5) or Mu^{c}taḍiḍ (d. 289/901–2).
Ṣifat al-ṣafwa:2:467
Arberry, *Muslim Saints*:277

Abū Bakr al-Ṣiddīq, ^{c}Abd Allāh b. Abū Quḥāfa
1B

A well-known Companion of the Prophet and the first Muslim Caliph. He is said to have been three years younger than the Prophet, but there is some disagreement about this.
Tadhkirat al-ḥuffāẓ:1:2
Abū ^{c}Umar Yūsuf b. ^{c}Abd Allāh al-Qurṭubī, *Al-isti^{c}āb fī asmā' al-aṣḥāb* (Cairo, 1939/1358):4:18

Abū Bakr al-Zāhid b. Ismā^{c}īl al-Ismā^{c}īlī
18B

He died c. 264/877–8.
He was a Ḥanafī scholar who when asked his opinion about giving money to the poor in a mosque replied, 'Each dirham which is given represents a sin which requires seventy dirhams to be given in charity as expiation'.
Quṭlūbughā:84
Luknawī:18

Abū Bashīr al-Anṣārī, Qays b. ^{c}Ubayd
41B

He died in 40/660–1.
Some biographers contend that his date of death was later than this. He was a Companion of the Prophet and transmitted some hadiths.
Ibn Qudāma, *Istibṣār*:338
Tahdhīb al-tahdhīb:12:22
Iṣāba:4:21

Abū Burda, Hānī b. Niyār b. ʿUbayd b. Kilāb 5B	He died in 42/662–3. A Companion of the Prophet who narrated four hadiths. *Tahdhīb al-asmā''*:2:178 *Iṣāba*:4:19 Ibn Qudāma, *Istibṣār*:338
Abū al-Dardā', ʿUwaymir b. Zayd 30A	He died in 32/652–3. A narrator of hadiths and a Companion of the Prophet. He was appointed as a judge in Damascus by Muʿāwiya b. Abū Sufyān. *Ṣifat al-ṣafwa*:1:627–43 *Tadhkirat al-ḥuffāẓ*:1:24 *Tahdhīb al-asmā'*:2:228
Abū Dharr, Jundub b. Qatāda, or Janāda Ghifārī 46B	He died in 32/652–3. A Companion of the Prophet who emigrated to Shām after the Prophet's death. There he incited the poor people against the rich. As a result ʿUthmān expelled him to Rabdha where he lived until his death. *Ṣifat al-ṣafwa*:1:584–99 Ibn Saʿd, *Ṭabaqāt*:2:354 *Tadhkirat al-ḥuffāẓ*:1:17
Abū Ghiyāth al-Zāhid 62B	Nobody in the references available bears this name. We know from the *Niṣāb* that he was a contemporary of Naṣr b. Sahl b. Aḥmad al-Sāmānī (293–331/905–6–942–3). It might be useful to note here that Ibn Ḥajar in his *Lisān al-mīzān* stated that Abū Ghiyāth was an unknown person who narrated hadiths to a person from Bukhārā. Ibn Ḥajar, *Lisān*:7:90
Abū Ḥanīfa, al-Nuʿmān b. Thābit 5B	80–150/699–700–767–8. He was a theologian and religious lawyer, the eponym of the Ḥanafī school. He studied with Ḥammād b. Abū Sulaymān. He also attended lectures given by ʿAṭā' b. Rabāḥ. He refused the frequent offers of the position of qadi. He did not compose any works on religious law, but discussed his opinions with his students, who

	included them in their books. He died in a Baghdad prison. *EI*²:1:123 *Al-kuna wa-l-alqāb*:1:284 *GAL*:Sup:1:284
Abū al-Ḥasan	See Abū al-Ḥasan al-Karkhī.
Abū al-Ḥasan al-Ashᶜarī ᶜAlī b. Ismāᶜīl 43B	260 – 324/873–4 – 935–6. Abū al-Ḥasan was born in Baṣra and initially followed the ideas of Ashᶜarī. He later went against their beliefs and wrote in criticism of them. *GAL*:Sup:1:345 *EI*²:1:696
Abū al-Ḥasan al-Isfarā'īnī al-Isfandiyānī 43A	A Muᶜtazili scholar mentioned by al-Jubbā'ī (235 – 303/849–50 – 915–6), who described him as 'a well-built room', meaning that his knowledge was limited but well organized. *Ṭabaqāt al-Muᶜtazila*:99 Abū Qāsim al-Balkhī, *Faḍl al-iᶜtizāl wa-ṭabaqāt al-muᶜtazila* (Tunis, 1974/1393):309
Abū al-Ḥasan al-Karkhī ᶜUbayd Allāh b. al-Ḥusayn 24A	260 – 340/873–4 – 951–2. A Ḥanafī lawyer and scholar who was among the leading Ḥanafī figures of his time. He composed several books, including *Sharḥ al-jāmiᶜ al-ṣaghīr*. Luknawī:108 *GAL*:Sup:1:295
Abū Hurayra, ᶜAbd Allāh (al-Raḥmān?) al-Dawsī 13A	He died in 58/677–8 at the age of 78. He was known as Abū Hurayra because he kept a kitten to play with. He is noted as a narrator of Prophetic traditions; 3,500 such traditions are credited to him. *Ṣifat al-ṣafwa*:1:685–95 Ibn Saᶜd, *Ṭabaqāt*:1:362 *Tadhkirat al-ḥuffāẓ*:1:32
Abū Isḥaq al-Fizārī Ibrāhīm b. Muḥammad	He died in 188/803–4. He was born in Kūfa and travelled to Shām where he

56A	practised the profession of *ᶜālim* for a short time. He then went to Baghdad where he was received by Hārūn al-Rashīd with great respect and veneration. *Ḥilyat al-awliyā'*:8:254 *Al-kuna wa-l-alqāb*:3:28 *Tadhkirat al-ḥuffāẓ*:1:274
Abū Jaᶜfar 44B	Sunāmī may have meant Abū Jaᶜfar al-Astarūshanī Muḥammad b. Muḥammad or Abū Jaᶜfar al-Ṭaḥāwī (see Sharḥ al-Ṭaḥāwī).
Abū Jaᶜfar al-Astarūshanī Muḥammad b. Muḥammad 79A	A Ḥanafī scholar who was a student of Abū Bakr Muḥammad b. al-Faḍl (d.381/991–2). He was also a student of al-Jaṣṣāṣ (305 – 370/917–8 – 980–1). Luknawī:57–8 Quṭlūbughā:91
Abū Jahl, ᶜAmrū b. Hishām al-Qurā 3B	He died in 2/634–5. A leader of the Quraysh tribe to which the Prophet belonged. Abū Jahl was a great opponent of the Prophet when the latter began his proclamation of the new religion. He was killed in the battle of Badr. Ziriklī:5:262
Abū al-Layth al-Samarqandī, Naṣr b. Muḥammad 4A	He died in 373/983–4 or 393/1002–3. A well known Ḥanafī faqih and scholar. He composed several books, including: *Tafsīr al-Qur'ān* *Al-nawāzil* *Al-fatāwā* *Bustān al-ᶜārifīn* *Tafsīr juz' ᶜamma* *Tanbīh al-ghāfilīn* *Sharḥ al-jāmiᶜ al-ṣaghīr* Luknawī:221 *GAL*:Sup:1:347 H.Kh., *Kashf*:441 Quṭlūbughā:79

Abū Manṣūr al-Māturīdī Muḥammad b. Muḥammad 24B	He died in 33/944–5. A well known theologian originating from Samarqand. He was an outstanding lawyer. He died in Samarqand. Luknawī:195 *GAL*:1:209;Sup:1:396
Abū Miḥjin al-Thaqafī ᶜAmru b. Ḥabīb b. ᶜAwf 57A	He died in 30/650–1. He was well known before Islam as a poet and warrior. He was converted to Islam in A.H. 9 and participated in the battle of Qādisiyya. The story which *Niṣāb al-iḥtisāb* relates is also told with a difference in the name of the Muslim army leader. The *Niṣāb* gives his name as Khālid b. al-Walīd, while his real name was Saᶜd b. Abū Waqqāṣ. Ziriklī:5:243
Abū Mujāhid 73A	Sunāmī, or the copyist, seems to have made a mistake with this name. There is a Quranic reader (*qari'*) named Abū Mujāhid (245 – 324/859–60 – 935–6) (Ziriklī:1:246). However, Qurṭubī, in his *Tafsīr al-Qur'ān*, did not mention Abū Mujāhid, only Mujāhid (see Mujāhid). Qurṭubī: *Tafsīr*:12:150
Abū Naṣīr al-ᶜAyyāḍi, Aḥmad b. al-ᶜAbbās 19A	He died in 333/944–5. A Ḥanafī faqih who studied *fiqh* with Abū Manṣūr al-Māturīdī. His son Naṣīr al-ᶜAyyāḍī, was also a faqih, who gained his knowledge from his father. Luknawī:23:220
Abū Naṣr al-Dubbūsī 66B	It has not been possible to trace this name, but it is probably a corruption of Abū Zayd al-Dubbūs ᶜUbayd Allāh b. ᶜUmar (430/1039). He was a Ḥanafī scholar and theologian, who is considered to be the founder of *ᶜilm al-khilāf* or the science of religious debate between various schools of thought. Luknawī:109 Quṭlūbughā:86 *GAL*:1:184, Sup:1:296

Abū al-Qāsim	See Naṣīr al-Dīn al-Samarqandī, Abū al-Qāsim Muḥammad b. Yūsuf. *Niṣāb al-iḥtisāb*:29A
Abū al-Qāsim al-Ḥakīm, Isḥāq b. Muḥammad al-Samarqandī 63A	He died in 342/953–4. A student of Abū Manṣūr al-Māturīdī, a well-known Ḥanafī scholar. He is called al-Ḥākīm because of his reputed wisdom. Luknawī:44 Samᶜānī, *Ansāb*:172B
Abū Qulāba, ᶜAbd Allāh b. Zayd al-Juramī 17B	He died in Shām c. 104/722–3. He transmitted hadith from Anas b. Mālik and other Companions. He was visited before he died by ᶜUmar b. ᶜAbd al-ᶜAzīz. *Tahdhīb al-tahdhīb*:5:223 *Ṣifat al-ṣafwa*:3:238
Abū al-Qāsim al-Ṣaffār Aḥmad b. ᶜIsma 41B	He died in 336/947–8. A Ḥanafī imam and scholar. He lived in Balkh. Luknawī:26 Kaḥḥāla:*Muᶜjam*:8:104 H.Kh., *Kashf*:113
Abū Rāfiᶜ al-Qibṭī Ibrāhīm Aslam 82A	He died c. 35/655–6. A slave of the Prophet, who was given his freedom when Abū Rāfiᶜ told him the good news of his uncle ᶜAbbās's conversion to Islam. He narrated hadith from many people including Ḥasan b. ᶜAlī. *Iṣāba*:4:68 *Tahdhīb al-tahdhīb*:12:93 Ibn Māja, *Sunan*:1:330
Abū Saᶜīd al-Khudarī Saᶜd b. Mālik b. Sinān 59A	He died at the beginning of 74/693–4 at the age of 86. A transmitter of many hadith from whom many of the Prophet's Companions learned.
Abū Shaḥma b. ᶜUmar b. al-Khaṭṭāb, ᶜAbd al-Raḥmān	The brother of ᶜAbd Allāh. He drank wine and was whipped for it by ᶜUmar b. al-ᶜĀṣ, the governor of Egypt. He was whipped again in Madina by his father,

60A

the Caliph ᶜUmar. He died one month after this whipping.
Tahdhīb al-asmāᶜ:1:300

Abū Sufyān b. al-Ḥārith b. ᶜAbd al-Muṭṭalib
23A

He died in 32/652–3 at about 90 years of age.
A leading figure in Makka prior to Islam and cousin of the Prophet; he became a Muslim when Makka was conquered by the Muslims and then became a Companion of the Prophet.
Ṣifat al-ṣafwa:1:521
EI^2:1:151
Iṣāba:2:172

Abū Ṭālib al-Makkī Muḥammad b. ᶜAlī b. ᶜAṭiyya
64A

He died in 386/996–7.
A well-known Sufi of Makkan origin.
GAL:1:217, Sup:1:359
Samᶜānī, *Ansāb*:541A
Al-kuna wa-l-alqāb:1:11
H.Kh., *Kashf*:1758

Abū Thaᶜlaba al-Khushanī, Jurham or Jurthūm
31B

He died in 75/694.
A Companion of the Prophet who transmitted hadith from the Prophet himself and from companions like Muᶜādh b. Jabal. He also taught Saᶜīd b. al-Musayyab and ᶜAṭā' b. Yasid.
Tahdhīb al-asmā':2:199
Tahdhīb al-tahdhīb:1:49

Abū Umāma, Suday b. ᶜAjlān
56A

He died in 81/700–1.
A Companion of the Prophet, who narrated 250 hadith recorded in the *Ṣaḥīḥayn*.
Tahdhīb al-tahdhīb:4:420
Iṣāba:2:175

Abū al-Yusr al-Bazdawī Muḥammad b. Muḥammad Fakhr al-Islām, called Ṣadr al-Islām
43A

He died in 493/1098–9.
He is called 'the easy' (*Abū al-Yusr*) (contrary to his brother ᶜAlī al-Bazdawī (see below) who is called 'the difficult' (*Abū al-ᶜUsr*)).

Abū Yūsuf Yaᶜqūb b. Ibrāhīm al-Anṣārī 5B	He died in 182/798–9. One of the founders of the Ḥanafī school of law. He was appointed qadi to Baghdad and held this appointment until his death. His treatise on public finance, taxation, criminal justice and other subjects is entitled *Kitāb al-kharāj*. *EI*[2]:1:164
Abū Zayd, al-Dubbūs ᶜUbayd Allāh, b. ᶜUmar	He died in 430/1038–9. His *kunya* is derived from the village of Dubbūsiya in Samarqand. He is buried in Bukhārā, and Samᶜānī wrote in his *Ansāb* that he had visited the grave. Quṭlūbughā:86 Luknawawī:109 Samᶜānī, *Ansāb*:221 B ᶜAbd Allāh Muṣṭafā al-Marāghī, *Al-fatḥ al-mubīn fī ṭabaqāt al-uṣūliyīn* (Cairo, n.d.):1:248 *GAL*:1:184, Sup:1:296
Abū Zayd, Saᶜīd b. Aws b. Thābit al-Anṣārī 73A	He died in 215/830–1 at 93 years of age. He was one of the leading figures in the science of Arabic language. He wrote a book on the languages of the Quran (*Lughāt al-Qur'ān*). Ziriklī:3:144 Muḥammad b. ᶜImrān al-Marzubānī, *Nūr al-qabas al-mukhtaṣar min al-muqtabas fī akhbār al-nuḥāt*, ed. R. Sellheim (Wiesbaden, 1964)):1:108
Abū al-Zinād, Abū ᶜAbd al-Raḥmān b. ᶜAkwān al-Madanī al-Qurashī 47B	63 – 131/682–3 – 748–9. A transmitter of hadith from Anas b. Mālik, ᶜAbd al-Raḥmān al-Aᶜraj, and Saᶜīd b. al-Musayyab. He taught hadith to Mālik b. Anas. *Tadhkirat al-ḥuffāẓ*:1:135 *Tahdhīb al-asmā'*:2:234
Adam 30B	The Prophet.
Aḥmad 37A	Sunāmī is not very clear as to which Aḥmad he referred, but he probably meant Aḥmad b. Ḥanbal al-Shaybānī.

Aḥmad b. Ḥanbal al-Shaybānī
37A

163 – 241/780–1 – 855–6.
The eponym of the Ḥanbalī school of law. He was whipped during the caliphate of Al-Ma'mūn because of the crisis over whether the Quran was created or not.
Ṣifat al-ṣafwa:1:336
EI^2:1:272

ʿĀ'isha bint Abū Bakr
11A

9BH – AH58/613–4 – 677–8.
A wife of the Prophet, daughter of his close friend and Companion Abū Bakr. She was his favourite wife amongst those to whom he was married at the time. She is considered as an important figurehead. She narrated more hadith than any other woman.
Ziriklī:4:5

ʿAlī b. Abū Ṭālib
14B

23BH – AH40/599–600 – 660–1.
The Prophet's cousin, son-in-law and the fourth orthodox Caliph.
Ḥilyat al-awliyā':1:66
Ziriklī:5:107

ʿAlī al-Bazdawī b. Muḥammad Fakhr al-Islām
82B

400 – 482/1010 – 1089.
An eminent Ḥanafī scholar. He is called 'the difficult' (*Abū ʿUsr*) because of the difficulties his readers had in understanding his works which displayed such depth of knowledge. His brother, Muḥammad b. Muḥammad, was the exact opposite in this respect and was known as 'the easy' (*Abū al-Yusr*). ʿAlī al-Bazdawī wrote several works including his well-known *Uṣūl*.
Luknawī:124, 235
GAL:1:460, Sup:1:637
H.Kh., *Kashf*:112

ʿAlī b. Mūsā b. Jaʿfar, also known as al-Riḍa
75B

He is considered as the eighth candidate for the Imāma according to the Imāmī Shīʿītes.
The Caliph Ma'mūn respected him greatly and acknowledged him as his successor.
Aḥmad Maḥmūd Subḥī, *Naẓariyyāt al-Imāma ʿind al-Shīʿa*, (Cairo, 1969):386–9
Ziriklī:5:178

ᶜAlī al-Razī 25B	Sunāmī probably meant ᶜAlī b. Mujāhid b. Muslim b. Rafiᶜ al-Rāzī who died in 180/796–7. He was a traditionalist and a historian who visited Baghdad and narrated hadith there. This person would appear to be the man who met Muḥammad al-Shaybānī, the author of *Al-Jāmiᶜ al-ṣaghīr*, who died in 189/804–5. He was born in Iraq where he lived for most of his life. Kaḥḥāla: *Muᶜjam*:7:175 H.Kh., *Kashf*:26 *Tahdhīb al-tahdhīb*:7:377–8
ᶜAlqama b. Qays b. ᶜAbd Allāh 73A	He died in 62/681–2. He was a faqih during the life of the Prophet. He died in Kūfa. *Tahdhīb al-tahdhīb*:7:276 Ziriklī:5:48
ᶜĀmir al-Shaᶜbī, b. Sharāḥīl 4A	19 – 103/640 – 721–2. An eminent traditionist who met 34 Companions of the Prophet. He was the organizer of a famous study circle for hadith. He died in Kūfa. Samᶜani, *Ansāb*: 334 A *Tahdhīb al-tahdhīb*:5:65 *Ḥilyat al-awliyā'*:4:10
ᶜAmrū b. Dīnār al-Jamḥī 14B	46 – 126/666–7 – 743–4. He was a *muftī* in Makka of Persian origin. He is an authenticated traditionist. *Tahdhīb al-tahdhīb*:8:28–30 Ziriklī:5:245
Anas b. Mālik al-Anṣārī 24A	10BH – AH 93/612–3 – 711–2. A Companion of the Prophet, who narrated 2,286 hadith in the *Ṣaḥīḥayn*. He died in Basra. *Ṣifat al-ṣafwa*:1:710–714 Ziriklī:1:365
Al-Aᶜraj ᶜAbd al-Raḥmān b. Hirmiz	He died in 117/735–6. A narrator of hadith who studied with Abū Hurayra and

47B	Abū Saᶜīd al-Khudarī. His students were Zuhrī and Abū al-Zinād. He died at Alexandria in Egypt. *Tahdhīb al-tahdhīb*:6:148 Ziriklī:3:340
ᶜĀṣim b. ᶜUmar b. al-Khaṭṭāb 49A	6 – 70/627–8 – 690–1. A poet and the grandfather of ᶜUmar b. ᶜAbd al-ᶜAzīz. *Iṣāba*:356 Ibn Sa'd, *Ṭabaqāt*:5:15 *Mīzān al-iᶜtidāl*:2:355
ᶜAṭā' 16A	Sunāmī is not very clear as to whom he meant by ᶜAṭā'. He may have meant ᶜAṭā' b. Abī Rabāḥ (see below) or ᶜAṭā' b. Dīnār (d. 126/743–4). The latter was an Egyptian scholar who was taught by Saᶜīd b. Jubayr (45 –95/665–6 – 713–4). He was an expert in hadith and wrote a book on the subject. *Tahdhīb al-tahdhīb*:7:198 *Mīzān al-iᶜtidāl*:2:197
ᶜAṭā' b. Abū Rabāḥ 34A	27 – 114/647–8 – 732–3. Born in Yemen but lived in Makka where he became a leading figure in both *fiqh* and hadith. *Mīzān al-iᶜtidāl*:2:197 *Tahdhīb al-tahdhīb*:7:199 *Ṣifat al-ṣafwa*:2:211 Ibn Saᶜd, *Ṭabaqāt*:5:470 *Ḥilyat al-awliyā'*:3:310–62
ᶜAṭā' b. Yasār al-Hilālī 51B	He died in 103/721–2. He owned Maymūna (one of the Prophet's wives), before she was freed and married the Prophet. He narrated hadith from many people, but his ability has been questioned. *Tahdhīb al-tahdhīb*:7:218
Al-Azharī, Abū Manṣūr Muḥammad b. Aḥmad 42A	282 – 370/895–6 – 980–1. An Arab lexicographer who was born and died in Herat. He received most of his education in grammar from Nifṭawayh in Iraq, but was also slightly influenced by

Ibn Durayd. Since most of his teachers were Shāfiᶜī, it is probable that he had a thorough knowledge of Shāfiᶜī law.
EI[2]:1:822
GAL:1:134, Sup:1:197

Bādiya bint Ghaylān
b. Salama
4A

One of Abū Bakr's wives who bore him one daughter named Juwayriyya. Hīt, the effeminate, described her to another man in the Prophet's presence, who then forbade him the company of women.
Ibn Saᶜd, *Ṭabaqāt*:3:128
Ibn al-Athīr, *Kāmil*:2:268

Al-Bayḍāwī, ᶜAbd Allāh
b. ᶜUmar
72B

He died in either 685/1286–7 or 692/1292–3.
A Shāfī'ī scholar who is well known for his commentary on the Quran known as *Tafsīr al-Bayḍāwī* or *Anwār al-tanzīl w-asrār al-ta'wīl.*
H.Kh., *Kashf*:186
Tāj al-Dīn Nāṣir b. ᶜAbd al-Wahhāb b. ᶜAlī, *Ṭabaqāt al-Shāfiᶜiyya al-kubrā*, ed. M. Ṭanahī (Cairo, 1964–74):8:157
Kaḥḥāla, *Muᶜjam*:6:97
EI[1]:1:590

Bilāl b. Rabāḥ al-Ḥabashī

His date of death is variously given as 17, 18, 20 and 83A21/638–642. He was the Prophet's *mu'adhdhin* and kept the *Bayt al-Māl*. After the Prophet's death he acted as *mu'adhdhin* for Abū Bakr, but refused to do so for ᶜUmar. He died in Syria.
EI[2]:1:1215
Ziriklī:2:49

Bilāl b. Saᶜīd, al-Muzanī
32A

He died in 60/679–80 at the age of 80.
A Companion of the Prophet, who entered Islam in AH5.
Tahdhīb al-asmā':1:135
Abū ᶜUmar Yūsuf b. ᶜAbd Allāh al-Qurṭubī, *Al-istiᶜāb fī asmā' al-aṣḥāb* (Cairo, 1939):1:150
Ḥilyat al-awliyā':5:319–20

bint Ghaylān	See Bādiya bint Ghaylān.
Bishr 58A	Sunāmī may have intended either of the two mentioned below, since they were both contemporaries of Ma'mūn. However, he probably referred to Bishr b. Walīd, since he was a Ḥanafī theologian.
Bishr b. al-Ḥārith al-Ḥāfī 37A	150 – 227/767–7 – 841–2. A Sufi who had gained his knowledge of hadith from many sources such as Wakī^{c}, Abū Bakr al-^{c}Ayyāsh, Mālik b. Anas, Ibn al-Mubārak, al-Mu^{c}āfa b. ^{c}Imrān and al-Fuḍayl b I^{c}yāḍ. He never wore shoes and was thus nicknamed 'the barefoot'. Aḥmad b. Muḥammad b. Khallikān, *Wafayāt al-a^{c}yān wa anbā' abnā' al-zamān*. (Beirut 1968–72):1:274 *Al-kuna wa-l-alqāb*:2:167 Arberry, *Muslim saints*:80
Bishr b. al-Walīd b. Khālid al-Kindī 37B	He died in 218/833–4. He studied *fiqh* with Abu Ḥanīfa, but his main teacher was Abū Yūsuf whose books and lectures he narrated (*amālī*). He was appointed judge during Mu'taṣim's reign. Luknawī:55 Sam^{c}ānī, *Ansāb*: 523B – 524A
Bustī	See Nāsir al-Dīn al-Bustī
Al-Ḍaḥḥāk b. Muzāḥim al-Khurāsānī 73A	He died in 105/723–4. A Quranic commentator who also taught children (*mu'adib*). *Mīzān al-i^{c}tidāl*:1:471 Ziriklī:3:310
Dāwūd, al-Ẓāhirī, b. ^{c}Alī b. Khalaf al-Iṣbahānī 24B	201 – 270/816–7 – 883–4. He is said to have been the leader of the Ẓāhirī group which refers to the apparent meaning of Muslim sources of law. Ibn Ḥajar, Lisān:2:422 Ziriklī:3:8

Durra bint Abū Lahab b. ᶜAbd al-Muṭṭalib b. Hāshim 30B	She died in 20/640–1. She was married to Zayd b. Thābit, a Companion of the Prophet. She narrated one or two hadith from the Prophet. Ibn Sa'd, *Ṭabaqāt*:3:45; 8:50 Ziriklī:3:15
Al-Faḍlī, Abū Bakr al-Kumārī Muḥammad b. al-Faḍlī 6B	He died in 381/991–2. A Ḥanafī scholar who apparently possessed considerable importance. Luknawī states that 'whenever the *kunya* al-Faḍlī is mentioned it refers to this man.' Luknawī:184, 246
Al-Faqīh Abū Jaᶜfar al-Ṭaḥāwī Aḥmad b. Muḥammad 14B	229 – 321/843–4 – 933. A leading Ḥanafī authority in Egypt. He wrote many books on Ḥanafī law, including *Sharḥ al-jāmi al-ṣaghīr*, *Sharḥ al-jāmiᶜ al-kabīr*, and *Kitāb al-shurūṭ*. Luknawī: 31–34 Quṭlūbughā: 8
Fāṭima bint Muḥammad 13A	18BH – AH 11/605–6 – 632–3. The youngest of the Prophet's daughters. She married ᶜAlī and they were the parents of Ḥasan and Ḥusayn. Ṣifat al-ṣafwa:2:9–15 Ziriklī :5:329
Firᶜawn 61B	Pharaoh.
Al-Fuḍayl b. ᶜIyāḍ al-T mīmī 37A	He died in 187/802–3. A Sufi traditionist who was born in Khurāsān. Prior to his conversion to Sufism, he is reputed to have been a highwayman. After becoming a Sufi, he went to Kūfa and later to Makka where he resided for several years. Arberry, *Muslim saints*: 52 *Tadhkirat al-ḥuffāẓ*:1:245 *Ḥilyat al-awliyā'*:8:84–140
Al-Ghazālī, Abū Ḥāmid	450 – 505/1058–9 – 111–2.

Muḥammad b. Muḥammad. 16A	A well-known Sufi philosopher and lawyer who wrote a total of 200 works including *Iḥyā' ʿulūm al-dīn* and *Khulāṣat al-mukhtaṣar.* Ziriklī:7:247–8 *GAL*:1:535, Sup:1:744 A.R. Badawī, *Mu'allafat al-Ghazālī*, (Cairo, 1961):30
Al-Ḥajjāj b. Yūsuf al Thaqafī 32A	41 – 95/661–2 – 713–4. He was the most able and most famous Ummayad governor. He put an end to ʿAbd Allāh b. Zubayr's Makkan revolt on Jumādā 73/October 692. He was a governor, first of Makka and then of Iraq. It is recorded that he was the first governor to mint coins inscribed with the *shahāda.* EI^2:3:39–42 *Tahdhīb al-tahdhīb*:2:10
Al-Ḥākim	See Muḥammad b. Muḥammad b. Aḥmad al-Balkhī al-Shahīd.
Ḥamīd al-Dīn al-Ḍarīr, ʿAlī b. Muḥammad al-Rāmishī al-Bukhārī al-Quhandizī 44B	He died in 66/1267–8. He taught many scholars and wrote many treatises on Ḥanafī *fiqh*, including *Al-fawā'id* (a commentary on the *Hidāya*), *Sharḥ al-manẓūma al-Nasafiyya* and *Sharḥ al-jāmiʿ al-kabīr.* Luknawī:125 Quṭlūbugha:46 *GAL*:Sup:1:519 H.Kh., *Kashf*:2031
Ḥammād b. Shākir 44A	It has not been possible to trace this man in the references available. From the *Niṣāb* we know that he was contemporary with Naṣūḥ b. Wāṣil al-Wararānī (q.v.) and that he probably taught him.
Hārūn b. ʿImrān 61B	The Biblical Aaron, son of Amran.

Hārūn al-Rashīd b. Muḥammad b. al-Mahdī	149 – 193/766-7 – 808–9. A well-known ʿAbbasid Caliph. He was born in Rayy where his father was *wālī*. He became Caliph in AH 170. His relationship with King Charlemagne of France was particularly good. His own reign extended over 23 years and 2 months. A large part of his fame was due to his wars against the Byzantines. *EI^2*:3:232–4 Ibn al-Athīr, *Kāmil*:6:96
Al-Ḥasan 64A	Whenever Al-Ḥasan is mentioned in Quranic interpretation, it means Al-Ḥasan al-Baṣrī. Whenever Al-Ḥasan is mentioned in a Ḥanafī work, it means Al-Ḥasan b. Ziyād al-Lu'lu'ī. Luknawī:248 The reference to Al-Ḥasan on 64A is unclear and could mean any of the three mentioned below.
Al-Ḥasan b. ʿAlī b. Abī Ṭālib 34A	3 - 49/624-5 - 669-70. A grandson of the Prophet, being ʿAlī and Fāṭima's son. He was the fifth orthodox Caliph, and second Imam according to the Shīʿīs. He ruled for 6 months and 5 days. *Ṣifat al-ṣafwa*:762 Ziriklī:2:214
Al-Ḥasan al-Baṣrī 24B	21 – 110/641–2 – 728–9. A *Tabiʿī* who met many Companions of the Prophet. He was born in Madina and died in Basra. He was a well-known Sufi. Arberry, *Muslim saints*:19 *GAL*:Sup:1:102
Al-Ḥasan b. Ziyād al-Luʿluʿī 24B	He died in 204/819 – 20. A friend of Abū Ḥanīfa who was appointed as judge to Kūfa in 194/809 – 10. He wrote two books: *Amālī* and *Mujarrad*. Luknawī:60 Quṭlūbughā:22

Ḥātim al-Aṣamm b. Yūsuf ᶜUnwān 39B	He died in 237/851–2. A native of Balkh, who was taught by Shaqīq al-Balkhī. They were both prominent Sufis. He was called 'the deaf' (*aṣamm*) because of his habit of pretending to be deaf in front of a woman who broke wind. *Ḥilyat al-awliyā'*:8:73–84 Arberry, *Muslim saints*:150–3 *Al-kuna wa-l-alqāb*:2:40 ᶜAbd al-Ra'ūf al-Munāwī, *Al-kawākib al-durriyya fī tarājīm al-sāda al-Ṣūfiyya* (Cairo, 1952):1:96
Hishām b. ᶜAbd Allāh al-Rāzī 64B	A Ḥanafī scholar who studied with Abū Yūsuf and Muḥammad b. al-Ḥasan al-Shaybānī. The latter died in his house. Luknawī:223 Ismāᶜīl Bāshā al-Baghdādī, *Hadiyyat al-ᶜārifīn* (Istanbul, 1951):2:508
Hishām b. ᶜUrwa b. al-Zubayr b. al-ᶜAwwām 15B	61 – 146/680–1 – 763–4. He was born in Madina and became a leading imam there in the science of hadith. He died in Baghdad while visiting the Caliph al-Manṣūr. *Mīzān al-iᶜtidāl*:3:255 Ziriklī:9:85–6
Hīt 4A	An effeminate man of Madina, who was expelled from the company of women after the Prophet heard him describing a woman in a lusty manner. Ibn Māja:613 *Mughrib*:277 *Lisān al-ᶜArab*:2:412 Ibn al-Athīr, *Kāmil*:2:268
Hūd b. ᶜAbd Allāh b. ᶜĀd 46B	An Arab prophet. Surat Hūd in the Quran was revealed concerning him. Ziriklī:9:110, 111

Ḥudhayfa b. al-Yamān 30B	He died in 36/656–7. A Companion of the Prophet, who was later appointed as governor of Madā'in in Persia. He narrated 225 hadith from the Prophet. *Ṣifat al-ṣafwa*:1:610–616 Ibn Sa^{c}d, *Ṭabaqāt*:6:15
Al-Ḥulwānī	See Shams al-A^{c}imma al-Ḥulwānī.
Humā (both of them) 45B	Sunāmī uses this term, which is common among Ḥanafī scholars, to indicate Abū Yūsuf and Muḥammad b. al-Ḥasan al-Shaybānī. Luknawī:248
Al-Ḥusayn, ^{c}Alī b. Abū Ṭālib 34A	4 – 61/625 – 680. A grandson of the Prophet, being ^{c}Alī and Fāṭima's son. He is famous on account of his revolt which ended tragically at Karbalā' during Muḥarram. *EI^{2}*:3:607
Iblīs 33B	The proper name of the Devil. Various other etymologies have been given for the word. *EI^{2}*: 3 : 667–70
Ibn ^{c}Abbās 1B	See ^{c}Abd Allāh b.^{c}Abbās.
Ibn Durayd, Muḥammad b. al-Ḥasan al-Azdī 1A	223 – 321/837–8 – 933. An Arabic philologist and lexicographer who was born in Basra. *EI^{2}*:3:757 Ibn Ḥajar, *Lisān*:7:20 *GAL*:Sup:1:172
Ibn Khaṭl 75B	He was killed during the conquest of Makka in 8/629–30 He was among the inhabitants of Makka whom the Prophet ordered to be killed even if he was holding the coverings of the Kaaba. This was done by men who wished to escape death by their enemies. He was eventually killed by Abū Bazra.

Ibn Saʿd, *Ṭabaqāt*:2:139, 141

Ibn Masʿud, ʿAbd Allāh b. Ghāfil
4B

He died in 32/652–3.
A famous Companion of the Prophet and reciter of the Quran. He died in Madina.
EI^2:3:873
Ṣifat al-ṣafwa:1:395
Ibn Saʿd, *Ṭabaqāt*:6:13

Ibn al-Mubārak, ʿAbd al-Wahhāb b. Aḥmad al-Anmāṭī
59B

462 – 535/1069–70 – 1140–41.
He narrated hadith from Abū Muḥammad al-Surayfīnī, the teacher of Ibn al-Jawzī who wrote *Ṣifat al-ṣafwa*.
Ṣifat al-ṣafwa:2:498

Ibn al-Mubārak, Abū al-Rahmān al-Marwazī al-Ḥanẓalī
37A

He died in 118/736–7.
He was very fond of *ṭanbūr* playing until he saw in a dream the Quranic verses inviting him to become a good believer. After this he devoted his life to mysticism.
GAL:Sup:1:256
Arberry, *Muslim saints*:124

Ibn Rāfiʿ
82A

Sunāmī, or the copyist, appears to have made a mistake in this man's name. The name of the man who transmitted the hadith is Abū Rāfiʿ rather than *Ibn* Rāfiʿ, according to Ibn Māja's *Sunan*. (See Abū Rāfiʿ)
Ibn Māja:1:330

Ibn Rawāḥa

See ʿAbd Allāh b. Rawāḥa.

Ibn Rustam, Abū Bakr Ibrahīm al-Marwazī
7A

He died in 211/826–7.
A Ḥanafī lawyer who is reputed to have been a qadi during Maʿmun's reign. He died in Nīsāpūr. He was the author of *Al-nawādir*. Samʿānī states that he died in AH 281.
Quṭlūbughā:3
Luknawī:10
Samʿānī, *Ansāb*: 523 B

Ibn Shabrama, ʿAbd Allāh al-Ẓabbī

He died in 144/761–2.
A jurist who became judge of Kūfa during Manṣūr's

56A	reign. Ibn Sa^{c}d, *Ṭabaqāt*:6:350 *Tahdhīb al-asmā'*:1:272
Ibn Shajara, Aḥmad b. Kāmil al-Baghdādī 33A	260 – 350/873–4 – 961–2. A well-known Quranic commentator who was taught hadith by Abū Qulāba among others. Ibn Ḥajar, *Lisān*:1:249 Ziriklī:1:190
Ibn Shihāb, Muḥammad b. Muslim b. ^{c}Abd Allāh, also known as al-Zuhrī 47B	45 – 124/665–6 – 741–2. It is interesting to note that Sunāmī referred to this man also by the name Ibn Shihāb while quoting a hadith transmitted by him from Bukhārī. Bukhārī, however, calls him al-Zuhrī. This suggests that Sunāmī was writing from memory. *GAL*:Sup:1:102 *Tahdhīb al-asmā'*:1:90–92 *Ḥilyat al-awliyā*:3:359–360
Ibn Sīrīn, Abū Bakr Muḥammad 35A	He died in 110/728–9. The first renowned Muslim interpreter of dreams who was also a traditionist and imam of great scholarship and piety. He was a friend of Al-Ḥasan al-Baṣrī and they died in the same year. *EI*^{2}:3:947 *Tahdhīb al-tahdhīb*:9:214 *GAL*:Sup:1:102
Ibn ^{c}Umar	See ^{c}Abd ^{c}Allāh b. ^{c}Umar.
Ibrāhīm 34B	Sunāmī is unclear, but he may have meant Ibrāhīm b. Yazīd al-Nakh^{c}ī (q.v. al-Nakh^{c}ī)
Ibrāhīm al-Khalīl 9B	The Prophet Abraham, called *Khalīl* (friend) of God according to the Quranic verse iv: 125.
Ibn Umm Salama	See ^{c}Umar b. Abū Salama.

ᶜIkrima
35B

25 – 105/645–6 – 723–4.
A slave of ᶜAbd Allāh b. ᶜAbbās. He was released from slavery on his master's death. He learnt *fiqh* from Ibn ᶜAbbās and was also a good traditionist.
Tahdhīb al-tahdhīb:7:270
Ṣifat al-ṣafwa:2:105
Ḥilyat al-awliyā':3:326

Al-imām, or Al-imām al-Aᶜẓam — See Abū Ḥanīfa.

Al-imām al-Zāhid al-Ṣaffār — See Abū al-Qāsim al-Ṣaffār.

ᶜĪsā
9A

The Arabic name for Jesus.

Isfarā'īnī — See Abū al-Ḥasan al-Isfarā'īnī.

Isḥāq al-Kindī — See Kindī.

Ismāᶜīl al-Zāhid
76A

He died in Shaᶜbān 402/March 1012.
He was the leading authority on *fiqh* and *usūl*. He studied with Abū Bakr al-Faḍlī Muḥammad b. al-Faḍl who died in 381/991.
Luknawī:46

Jābir b. ᶜAbd Allāh al-Anṣārī
14B

16BH – AH 78/607 – 697–8.
A Companion of the Prophet who narrated numerous hadith; in the *Ṣaḥīḥayn* alone there are 1,540.
Tahdhīb al-tahdhīb:2:42
Ibn Qudāmā, *Istibṣār*:151–2
Iṣāba:1:214

Al-Jaṣṣāṣ, Abū Bakr al-Rāzī Aḥmad b. ᶜAlī
6A

305 – 370/917–8 – 980–1.
A Ḥanafī jurist and scholar who composed many books, including his commentaries on Khaṣṣāf's *Adab al-qāḍī* and *Aḥkām al-Qur'ān*. During his life he was a leading figure among Ḥanafī scholars. His name is derived from the process of making plaster (*juṣṣ*).
Samᶜānī, *Ansāb*:130B

Quṭlūbughā:6
Luknawī:27–28
GAL:1:204

Jibrīl
22A

The angel Gabriel.

Al-Jubbā'ī, Muḥammad
b. ʿAbd al-Wahhāb
b. Salām
43B

235 – 303/849–50 – 915–6.
The eponym of a group of Muʿtazilīs who call themselves al-Jubbā'iyya. He was originally from Juba near Baṣra in Iraq. He composed a commentary on the Quran which was severely criticized by Al-Ashʿari.
Al-kuna wa-l-alqāb:2:142
Aḥmad b. Muḥammad b. Khallikān, *Wafayāt al-aʿyān wa anbā' abnā' al-zamān*. (Beirut, 1968–72):1:48
Ṭabaqāt al-muʿtazila:96

Al-Junayd b. Muḥammad
b. Junayd al-Baghdādī
9B

He died in 298/910–1.
His family was originally from Nāhawānd (South Iran) although he was born and lived in Baghdad. An eminent Sufi who studied *fiqh* with Al-Shāfiʿī.
Ṣifat al-ṣafwa:2:416
Ziriklī:2:138
Ibn al-Athīr, *Kāmil*:8:62

Kaʿb b. al-Ashraf,
al-Ṭā'ī
75B

He was killed in 3/624–5.
An Arab poet who wrote many defamatory poems about the Prophet and other Muslims. The Prophet ordered that he should be killed; this was carried out by five Muslims who brought his head back to Madina.
Ziriklī:6:79
Ibn al-Athīr, *Kāmil*:2:143, 146
Ibn Saʿd, *Ṭabaqāt*:2:31

Al-Kaʿbī, Abū al-Qāsim
ʿAbd Allāh b. Aḥmad
al-Balkhī
43B

A leader of the Muʿtazilīs, particularly the Kaʿbiyya sect.
Ibn Ḥajar, *Lisan*:3:255
GAL:Sup:1:343
Ṭabaqāt al-muʿtazila:93

Kamāl al-Dīn al-Sunāmī al-Badhawī 44B	See Introduction.
Khalaf b. Ayyūb 18B	He died in 205/820–1. A Ḥanafī scholar who was a Companion of Muḥammad b. al-Ḥasan. He said, 'The legal testimony of one who gives charity in a mosque is not accepted'. Luknawī:71
Khālid b. al-Walīd	He died in 21/641–2. An outstanding army general both before and after his conversion to Islam which occurred in AH 7. *Ṣifat al-ṣafwa*:1:650–4 Ibn Saᶜd, *Ṭabaqāt*:3:202 *Ḥilyat al-awliyā'*:1:412–15
Al-Khaṣṣāf, Abū Bakr Aḥmad b. ᶜUmar 62B	He died in 261/874–5. A Ḥanafī faqih and scholar who composed many books on Ḥanafī law, such as *Adab al-qāḍī.* Luknawī:129 Quṭlūbughā:7 *GAL*:1:80
Al-Khaṭṭābī, Ḥammād b. Muḥammad b. Ibrāhīm 75B	319 – 388/931–2 – 998. A traditionist and faqih who composed several treatises on hadith and a Quranic commentary. Ziriklī:2:304
Khwāharzāde 65B	According to Quṭlūbughā (p.91), this title when used alone by a Ḥanafī scholar refers to Muḥammad b. al-Ḥusayn al-Bukhārī who died in 483/1090–1. The meaning of the title is 'the Nephew of the *ᶜĀlim*'. Luknawī, however, states that the title can also be used for Muḥammad b. Maḥmūd al-Kurdurī who died in 656/1258. *GAL*:Sup:1:296 H.Kh., *Kashf*:1580 Quṭlūbugha:62, 91 Luknawī:164

Al-Kindī, Ya^cqūb b. Isḥāq 43A	He died in 260/873–4. An Arab philosopher, born in Baghdad. There he became famous in many fields including medicine, philosophy, music and engineering. The author of numerous works, he was whipped during the reign of Mutawakkil because of his philosophic ideas. Ibn Ḥajar:*Lisān*:6:305 *GAL*:1:230, Sup:1:372
Luqmān 61B	A prophet who was well known for his wisdom, which became enshrined in a collection of fables. *Tahdhīb al-asmā'*:1:71
Makḥūl b. Abī Muslim Shahrāb 55B	He died in 112/730–1. An eminent traditionist who was also the jurist of Shām. *Tahdhīb al-tahdhīb*:10:289 *Mīzān al-i^ctidāl*:3:198
Mālik 62B	The angel keeper of Hell.
Mālik b. Anas 48B	93 – 179/711–2 – 795–6. The eponym of the Mālikī school of law. He was born and died in Madina. His *Muwaṭṭa'* is an outstanding treatise on law. *Ṣifat al-ṣafwa*:2:177 *Tahdhīb al-tahdhīb*:10:5 *GAL*:1:184, Sup:1:297
Mālik b. Dīnār 32A	He died c.130/747–8. The son of a Persian slave, Mālik b. Dīnār became a disciple of Ḥasan of Baṣra. He is mentioned as a reliable traditionist who transmitted hadith to early authorities such as Anas b. Mālik and Ibn Sīrīn. *Ṣifat al-ṣafwa*:3:273 *Ḥilyat al-awliyā'*:2:357–87 *Tahdhīb al-tahdhīb*:10:14

Al-Ma'mūn, Caliph
16B

170 – 218/786–7 – 833–4.
He succeeded to the caliphate after his brother al-Amīn in 198/813–4.
Ziriklī:4:287

Marwān b. al-Ḥakam
b. Abū al-Āṣ
30B

2 – 65/623–4 – 684–5.
An Umayyad Caliph who ruled for 9 months after Mu^{c}āwiya b. Yazīd.
Iṣāba:3:409
Ziriklī:8:94

Masrūq b. al-Ajda^{c}
b. ^{c}Abd al-Raḥmān
56A

He died in 63/682–3.
He was kidnapped as a child, which is the reason for his name Masrūq (the kidnapped). He was a traditionist who transmitted from ^{c}Umar, ^{c}Alī and Ibn Mas^{c}ūd amongst others.
Ṣifat al-ṣafwa:3:26
Tadhkirat al-ḥuffāẓ:1:50

Mis^{c}ar b. Kidām b. Ẓahīr
al-Dīn
14B

He died in 152/768–9.
An authenticated narrator of hadith who taught Muḥammad b. Ḥasan al-Shaybānī. He transmitted about 1,000 hadith, including some from ^{c}Abd al-Mālik b. Maysara.
Tahdhīb al-tahdhīb:1:115
Tahdhīb al-asmā':2:89
Mīzān al-i^{c}tidāl:4:99

Mu^{c}ādh b. Jabal
b. ^{c}Amrū
19B

20 BH – AH 18/603–4 – 639–40.
He taught hadith to ^{c}Abd al-Raḥmān b. Ghanam and Masrūq. He died of bubonic plague.
Tadhkirat al-ḥuffāẓ:1:19
Ziriklī:8:166
Ṣifat al-ṣafwa:1:489 – 502

Al-Mu^{c}āfā b. ^{c}Imrān
al-Mawṣilī
37A

He died in 184/800–1.
A traditionist who transmitted from Thawrī and Mis^{c}ar. He taught hadith to Bishr al-Ḥāfī amongst others.

	Tadhkirat al-ḥuffāẓ:1:288 *Ṣifat al-ṣafwa*:4:181
Mu^{c}ammar, b. ^{c}Abbād al-Sulamī 74A	He died in 215/830–1. A Mu^{c}tazilī of Basra. He lived in Baghdad and was involved in a theological dispute with al-Naẓẓām (185 – 221/801–2 –835–6). *Tahdhīb al-tahdhīb*:10:243 Ziriklī:8:190
Mu^{c}āwiya b. Abū Sufyān 32B	20BH – AH 60/603–4 – 679–80. A Companion of the Prophet and his copyist. The first Umayyad Caliph and the one who made the caliphate hereditary. *Tahdhīb al-asmā'*:32:102 *Iṣāba*:3:412 Kaḥḥāla, *A^{c}lām*:8:172
Al-Mubarrad, Muḥammad b. Yazīd 71A	210 – 286/825–6 – 899–900. The leading authority in Arabic grammar of his time. He composed many works, including his *Kāmil.* *Tahdhīb al-tahdhīb*:9:530
Al-Mughīra b. Shu^{c}ba, b. Abū^{c} Āmir b. Mas^{c}ūd 34A	20 BH – AH 50/603–4 – 670–1. A Companion of the Prophet. Later he was appointed by ^{c}Umar as the governor of Baṣra and Kūfa where he eventually died. Ibn Sa^{c}d, *Ṭabaqāt*:6:20 *Tahdhīb al-tahdhīb*:10:262
Muḥammad	See Muḥammad b. al-Ḥasan al-Shaybānī.
Muḥammad b. ^{c}Alī b. al-Ḥusayn; also known al-Bāqir 75B	57 – 114/676 – 732–3. The fifth Imam according to the Imāmī Shī^{c}a. *Tahdhīb al-tahdhīb*:9:350 Ziriklī:7:153
Muḥammad b. al-Faḍlī	See Al-Faḍlī.

Muḥammad b. al-Ḥasan al-Shaybānī 5B	131 or 135 – 189/748 or 752–3 – 804–5. An outstanding Ḥanafī scholar who studied *fiqh* with Abū Ḥanīfa. He composed many works on Ḥanafī law. When the word Muḥammad occurs in the books of Ḥanafī law it always means this man. He was appointed as qadi in Raqqa by al-Rashīd. Luknawī:6:163 Quṭlūbughā:54 *GAL*:Sup:1:288–9
Muḥammad b. al-Hayṣam 43B	He died in 407/1016–17. A theologian of the Hayṣamiyya sect which is a subdivision of the Karrāmiyya sect established by Muḥammad b. Karrām. EI^2:4:668 Ibn Ḥajar, *Lisān*:5:354 ^{c}Abd al-Karīm al-Shahrāstānī, *Al-milal wa-l-niḥal* (Cairo, AH 1321):146
Muḥammad b. Karrām 74A	190–255/805–6 – 868–9. The eponym of the the Karrāmiyya sect which flourished in the central and eastern parts of the Islamic world. Ibn Ḥajar, *Lisān*:5:354 EI^2:4:667–9
Muḥammad b. Muḥammad b. Aḥmad al-Balkhī al-Shahīd al-Ḥākim 3A	He was killed in 334/945–6. He was appointed as a qadi to Bukhārā. The author of many books, including *Al-muntaqā*, *Al-mukhtaṣar* and *Al-kāfī*. *GAL*:1:182, Sup:1:294, 638 H.Kh., *Kashf*:1378, 1851 Luknawī:185 Sam^{c}ānī, *Ansāb*:341B
Muḥammad b. Muqātil al-Rāzī 3B	He died in 248/862–3. A Ḥanafī scholar and friend of Muḥammad b. al-Ḥasan al-Shaybānī. He narrated hadith from Wakī^c b. al-Jarrāḥ. Luknawī:201

Muḥammad b. Salāma Abū ʿAbd Allāh 18A	192 – 278/807–8 – 891–2. A Ḥanafī faqih. Luknawī: 168
Muḥammad b. Tamīm al-Dārī 60A	Probably the son of Tamim al-Dārī (q.v.).
Mujāhid b. Jabr al-Makkī 35A	21 – 104/641–2 – 722–3. An outstanding Quranic reader and commentator who studied *tafsīr* with Ibn ʿAbbās and narrated hadith from him, Ibn ʿUmar, Jābir, and Abū Saʿīd al-Khudarī. His students included ʿAṭā' and Ṭāwūs. He died in Makka. Ibn Saʿd, *Ṭabaqāt*:5:466–7 *Ḥilyāt al-awliyā'*:8:266–279
Mūsā 40B	The prophet Moses.
Al-Muṣawwar b. Makhramā 33B	2 – 64/623–4 – 683–4. A Companion of the Prophet. When young, he related traditions from the orthodox Companions. He was killed by a catapult stone during a campaign in Africa. *Ṣifat al-ṣafwa*:1:772 *Tahdhīb al-asmā'*:2:94 *Iṣāba*:3:400 Ziriklī:8:123
Al-Mustaghfirī, Abū al-ʿAbbās Jaʿfar b. Muḥammad 44A	350 – 432/961–2 – 1040–1. The preacher of Nasaf, who also taught many scholars. He is the author of *Maʿrifat al-Ṣaḥāba.* H.Kh., *Kashf*:1739 Samʿānī, *Ansāb*:528B Luknawī:57
Al-Muʿtaṣim, Muḥammad b. Hārūn al-Rashīd, Caliph 62A	179 – 227/795–6 – 841–2. He became Caliph in AH 218 on the death of his brother Ma'mūn, who recommended him as his successor. He built the town of Sāmarrā' in AH 222. His reign lasted for eight years and eight months.

	Ibn al-Athīr, *Kāmil*:6:439, 524–8 Ziriklī:7:351
Al-Nakhᶜī, Ibrāhīm b. Yazīd 42A	46 – 96/666–7 – 714–5. A well-known faqih of Kūfa who also narrated hadith. He died while hiding from Hajjāj. *Ṣifat al-ṣafwa*:3:86 Ibn Saᶜd, *Ṭabaqāt*:6:270 *Tadhkirat al-ḥuffāẓ*:1:73
Al-Nasafī, Najm al-Dīn ᶜUmar b. Muḥammad 60A	461 – 537/1068–9 – 1142–3. A Ḥanafī scholar who was taught by Muḥammad al-Bazdāwī (d. AH 493). He wrote *Yawāqīt al-mawāqīt* and *Fatāwā al-Nasafiyya*. Luknawī:149 H.Kh., *Kashf*:2054 *GAL*:Sup:1:762
Nāṣir al-Dīn al-Bustī Muḥammad b. Ḥibbān 16B	He died in 354/965 at the age of about 60. He was born in Bust, a town in Sijistan. He became a judge and also wrote many books on hadith. *Tadhkirat al-ḥuffāẓ*:3:920–24
Nāṣir al-Dīn al-Samarqandī, Muḥammad b. Yūsuf, Abū al-Qāsim 3B	He died in 556/1160–1. A Ḥanafī scholar who composed many books, including *Al-nāfiᶜ* and *Al-multaqaṭ*. H.Kh., *Kashf*:565 *GAL*:1:475, 526, Sup:1:733 Luknawī:219–20
Naṣr b. Muḥammad al-Marwazī, whose real name was Muḥammad b. Naṣr al-Marwazī 66A	202–294/817–8 – 906–7. A friend of Abū Hanīfa and eminent traditionist and theologian. He composed many treatises, including one concerning the differences of opinion between Abū Ḥanīfa, ᶜAlī, and Ibn Masᶜūd. *Tahdhīb al-tahdhīb*:9:489 *GAL*:Sup:1:258, 305 *Ṣifat al-ṣafwa*:4:147–8

Naṣr b. Sahl b. Aḥmad al-Samānī 62B	293 – 331/905–6 – 942–3. He was appointed as prince of Khurāsān after his father's assassination. Ibn al-Athīr, *Kāmil*:8:401 Samᶜānī, *Ansāb*:466B
Al-Naẓẓām, Ibrāhīm b. Sayyār al-Baṣrī 43B	185 – 221/801–2 – 835–6. He was known as Al-Naẓẓām because of his job stringing beads. He became the leader of a sect of Muᶜtazila of which he became the eponym (Naẓẓāmiyya). This sect is supposed to believe in fatalism. *Ṭabaqāt al-Muᶜtazila*:49 Abū al-Ḥasan al-Ashᶜarī, *Maqālāt al-Islāmiyyīn wa-ikhtilāf al-muṣallīn*, ed. Helmut Ritter (Wiesbaden, 1963):660 ᶜAbd Allāh Musṭafa al-Marrāghī, *Al-fatḥ al-mubīn fī ṭabaqāt al-uṣūliyyin* (Cairo, n.d.):148–9.
Al-Qāḍī	See Abū Yūsuf Yaᶜqūb b. Ibrāhīm.
Al-Qaddūrī, Aḥmad b. Muḥammad 46B	362 – 428/972–3 – 1036–7. A jurist who was born and died in Baghdad where he was the leading Ḥanafī of his time. His manual on Ḥanafī law (*Mukhtaṣar al-Qaddūrī*) is very well known. Luknawī:30 Samᶜānī, *Ansāb*:444B H. Kh., *Kashf*:1631 *GAL*:1:183
Al-Qāsimī, al-Ḥasan b. Aḥmad b. Muḥammad b. Jaᶜfar	409 – 491/1018–9 – 1097–8. A contemporary of Al-Mustaghfirī, who was one of the leading authorities on hadith of his time. Ziriklī:2:194
Qatāda 29B	Many people have this name but Sunāmī probably referred to Qatāda b. Diᶜāma b. Qatāda (61 – 118/680–1 – 736–7). This is because Sunāmī said that Qatāda met Saᶜīd b. al-Musayyab and Qatāda b. Diᶜāma b. Qatāda was his contemporary. Qatāda b. Diᶜāma b. Qatāda was

a Quranic commentator, traditionist and grammarian. He died in Wāsiṭ.
Tahdhīb al-tahdhīb:8:351
Ziriklī:6:27

Al-Qurṭubī, Abū ᶜAbd Allāh Muḥammad b. Aḥmad
73A

He died in 671/1273.
The author of a well-known commentary on the Quran entitled *Jāmiᶜ aḥkām al-Qurᶜān*, or *Tafsīr al-Qurṭubī*.
H.Kh., *Kashf*:537
GAL:1:Sup:737

Al-Qutaybī, ᶜAbd Allāh b. Muslim al-Marwaẓī
42A

213 – 276/828–9 – 889–90.
A grammarian who was appointed as judge to Daynūr. He composed many books on Arabic language and a Quranic commentary.

Quṭb al-Dīn Ḥaydar
8B

He died in 618/1221–2.
The establisher of a Sufi order known as Haydariyya. He met Ibn Baṭṭūṭa and rewarded him with a Sufi gown (*khirqa*). His shaykh was Muḥammad b. Yūnus al-Qalandarī.
Ibn Baṭṭūṭa, *Riḥla*:388
Trimmingham, *Sufi Orders*:39,199
Maqrīzī, *Khiṭaṭ*:3:205–6

Quṭrub, Muḥammad b. al-Mustanīr b. Aḥmad
36A

He died in 206/821–2.
A grammarian from Basra who believed in the views of the Naẓẓāmiyya sect of Muᶜtazila. Quṭrub is a nickname given to him by his teacher Sībawayh.
Muḥammad b. ᶜImrān al-Marzubānī, *Nūr al-qabas al-mukhtaṣar min al-muqtabas fī akhbār al-nuḥāt*. ed. R.Sellheim (Wiesbaden,1964):1:174

Ruḍwān
62B

The angel keeper of Heaven

Saᶜd b. Abū Waqqāṣ b. Mālik b. Kilāb
53A

23 BH – AH 55/599–600 – 674–5.
He entered Islam at the age of 17. He became a great army general and a Companion of the Prophet.
Ṣifat al-ṣafwa:1:356–61

	Tadhkirat al-ḥuffāẓ:1:22 *Iṣāba*:2:30
Sa^c^d b. ^c^Ubāda 54A	He died in 14/635–6. A leading figure of the Anṣār (people of Madina). He was called the perfect because of his ability to shoot, swim and write. *Iṣāba*:2:28 *Ṣifat al-ṣafwa*:1:202
Saddī, Ismā^c^īl b. ^c^Abd al-Raḥmān 33A	He died in 128/745–6. A Quranic commentator and historian. He is cited as an authority in many history books, e.g. Al-Ṭabarī. Jamāl al-Dīn Yūsuf b. Taghrībirdī, *Al-Nujūm al-zāhira fī mulūk Miṣr wa-l-Qāhira.* (Cairo, 1972) :1:308 Ziriklī:1:313 Sam^c^ānī, *Ansāb*: 294B Ṭabarī:1:numerous references, 2:290
Ṣadr al-Islām	See Abū al-Yusr al-Bazdawī.
Ṣadr Jihān Bukhārā 44B	Ṣadr Jihān was a title given by faqihs to a man as a sign of respect (Luknawī:239). According to Barthold, it means 'the pillar of the world'. Bosworth, however, suggests that Ṣadr means 'the eminent'. Ibn al-Athīr states that Ṣadr Jihān Bukhārā was Muḥammad b. Aḥmad b. ^c^Abd al-^c^Azīz the leader of Ḥanafī scholars in Bukhārā. He is reported to have passed through Baghdad on his way to the pilgrimage in 603/1206–7. Sunāmī was of the opinion that Ṣadr Jihān Bukhārā was a contemporary of Ḥamīd al-Dīn al-Ḍarīr (d.666/1267–8) (*Niṣāb*:44B). This statement leads us to believe that Sunāmī might have meant Aḥmad II b. Muḥammad, who was the last of the family who carried the title Ṣadr. He was driven out of Bukhārā during the popular movement which broke out in 636/1238. Ibn al-Athīr, *Kāmil*:12:207–8 Barthold, *Turkistan*:354 C.E. Bosworth, art. "Al-e Borham", *Encyclopaedia Iranica* (New York, 1985):1:753–4.

Ṣadr al-Shahīd, Ḥusām al-Dīn ^{c}Umar b. ^{c}Abd al-^{c}Azīz b. Māza 22B	483 – 536/1090–1 – 1141–2. A Ḥanafī scholar who studied *fiqh* with his father. He was killed in the battle of Qaṭwān in Samarqand. He composed many treatises on Ḥanafī law, including *Al-waqi^{c}āt.* Luknawī:149 *GAL*:1:461–462, Sup:1:639 Ziriklī:5:210
Sahl b. Sa^{c}d al-Sā^{c}idī b. Ka^{c}b al-Anṣārī 47B	He died in 91/709–10 at 100 years of age. He was a Companion of the Prophet and narrated 188 hadiths in the *Ṣaḥīḥayn*. He said to have been the last of the Companions of the Prophet when he died. Tabarī:1:12, 13, 2:329, 855 Ziriklī:3:210 Ibn Qudāma, *Istibṣār*:105 *Iṣāba*:2:87
Saḥnūn al-Mālikī ^{c}Abd al-Salām b. Sa^{c}īd 75B	160 – 240/766–7 – 854–5. A judge and faqih who was the leading Mālikī authority in the Muslim West during his lifetime. Ziriklī:4:129
Sa^{c}īd	See Sa^{c}īd b. Al-Musayyab, b. Ḥazn.
Sa^{c}īd b. Abū al-Ḥasan al-Baṣrī	He died c. 98/716–7. He is mentioned as a narrator of hadith from Ibn ^{c}Abbās. He was the brother of Al-Ḥasan al-Baṣrī, (21 – 110/641–2 – 728–9). Ibn Sa^{c}d, *Ṭabaqāt*:7:179
Sa^{c}īd b. Jubayr al-Wālibī 34A	45 – 95/665–6 – 713–4. An outstanding *muftī* from Kūfa who was killed by Ḥajjāj after a fierce dispute with him. *Tadhkirat al-ḥuffāẓ*:1:76 Ibn Sa^{c}d, *Ṭabaqāt*:6:256–8 *Ḥilyat al-awliyā'*:4:272–310

Saᶜīd b. al-Musayyab b. Ḥazn 29B	13 – 94/634–5 – 712–3. An eminent narrator of hadith and an outstanding faqih from Madina. He transmitted hadith from ᶜUthmān and ᶜAlī. He is reported to have met Qatāda b. Diᶜāma b. Qatāda. *Tadhkirat al ḥuffāẓ*:1:56 *Ḥilyat al-awliyā'*:3:161–176
Salmān al-Fārisī Abū ᶜAbd Allāh 13A	He died in 36/656–7. A Companion of the Prophet who was originally from Iṣfahān in Persia. He was appointed as governor of Madā'in by ᶜUmar and he died there. Some reports suggest that he lived for 250 years. *Ṣifat al-ṣafwa*:1:523–55 Ibn Saᶜd, *Ṭabaqāt*:4:75, 93 *Ḥilyat al-awliyā'*:1:185
Al-Sāmirī 40B	The Samaritan, mentioned in the Quran xx:85, 87, 95.
Sarakhsī, Muḥammad b. Aḥmad, otherwise known as Shams A'imma 11A	He died in 483/1090–1. A Ḥanafī scholar who studied with al-Hulwanī. He composed his book *Al-mabsūṭ* while in prison. Luknawī:159 *GAL*:1:460, Sup:1:638
Ṣaᶜṣaᶜa b. Ṣawḥān b. Ḥajar 32B	He died in 60/679–80. A supporter of ᶜAlī and fighter on his side in the Battle of the Camel. He narrated a few hadith. He was expelled by Muᶜāwiya to Kūfa where he died. Ibn Saᶜd, *Ṭabaqāt*:6:221 *Mīzān al-iᶜtidāl*:2:315 *Iṣāba*:2:192
Al-Shaᶜbī	See ᶜĀmir al-Shaᶜbī.
Al-Shāfiᶜī, Muḥammad b. Idrīs	150 – 204/767–8 – 819–20. The eponym of the Shāfiᶜī school who was born in

6A	Gaza. He was extraordinarily skilled in archery in addition to his exalted intellectual ability. He was the author of a large number of books. *Ṣifat al-ṣafwa*:2:248 *Tahdhīb al-tahdhīb*:9:25 *GAL*:1:188, Sup:1:303
Shams al-A'imma	See Sarakhsī, Muḥammad b. Aḥmad.
Shams al-A'imma al-Awzajandī, Maḥmūd b. ᶜAbd al-ᶜAzīz 19A	A Ḥanafī scholar who was the grandfather of Qāḍi Khān (d. 592/1195–6). He was taught *fiqh* by Sarakhsī (d. 483/1090–1). Luknawī:209
Shams al-A'imma al-Ḥulwānī 15A	He died in 448/1056–7. He was a leading Ḥanafī scholar who taught many other scholars including Sarakhsī. He is considered to be from the category of scholars who are able to apply analogy. He wrote several books including *Al-mabsūṭ.* Luknawī:7:96 Quṭlūbughā:35 *GAL*:Sup:1:638
Shams al-Islām Awzajandī	Sunāmī probably made an error writing this man's name. Instead of Shams al-A'imma al-Awzajandī, he wrote Shams al-Islām Awzajandī.
Shaqīq b. Ibrāhīm al-Balkhī 39A	He died in 194/809–10. A man of wide learning who began his career as a merchant but later turned to the Sufi way of life. He narrated hadith and was a friend of Ḥātim al-Aṣamm. *Ṣifat al-ṣafwa*:4:159 *Ḥilyat al-awliyā'*:8:58–73 Arberry, *Muslim saints*:133–7
Al-Shaykh ᶜAbd al-Karīm 21A	It has not been possible to trace this man with certainty in the references available. Sunāmī may have meant ᶜAbd al-Karīm b. Muḥammad Abū al-Qāsim al-Rāfiᶜī (557 – 623/1161–2 – 1226). Rāfiᶜī was from Qazwīn where he had a public

	study circle for the Quran and hadith. He wrote a number of books. H.Kh., *Kashf*:205 *GAL*:1:493, Sup:1:678 Ziriklī:4:179
Al-Shaykh Abū Bakr 36A	Sunāmī is not very clear when he mentions this person. He might have meant Abū Bakr al-Rāzī who is also known as Al-Jaṣṣāṣ (305 –370/917–8 – 980–1), (q.v.).
Al-Shaykh Muḥammad b. Ibrāhīm. ᶜAlī al-Rāzī 22B	He died in 615/1218–9. A Ḥanafī scholar who composed some treatises on Ḥanafī law, including his commentary on Qaddūri's manual. Quṭlūbughā:59 H.Kh., *Kashf*:1631–2 Kaḥḥāla, *Muᶜjam*:8:218
Shaykh al-Shuyūkh 67A	See *ᶜAwārif al-maᶜārif*..
Shuᶜayb 61B	The Prophet sent to the people of Madyan. Quran vii:85
Sufyān al-Thawrī b. Saᶜīd 16A	97 – 161/715–6 – 777–8. A narrator of hadith and a mystic. He studied first with his father and then with other learned men including Aᶜmash. *Tahdhīb al-tahdhīb*:4:111, 115 *Ḥilyat al-awliyā'*:7:143–4?
Sulaymān b. ᶜAbd al-Mālik, Caliph 60B	45 – 99/664–5 – 717–8. An Umayyad Caliph who was born in Damascus. He became Caliph in AH 96 and his reign lasted for two years and eight months. Ibn al-Athīr, *Kāmil*:5:11, 37 Ziriklī:3:192

Tamīm al-Darī b. Aws b. Khārija 57B	He died in 40/660. A story-teller during ᶜUmar's time and a Christian convert to Islam. *Ṣifat al-ṣafwa*:1:737–9 ᶜAbd al-Raḥmān b. al-Jawzī *Kitāb al-quṣṣās wa-l-mudhakkirīn*, ed. M.L. Swartz (Beirut, 1971):22, 23, 32 Ziriklī:2:71
Ṭāwwūs b. Kaysān 35B	33 – 106/653–4 – 724–5. He narrated hadith from many Companions of the Prophet, including Ibn ᶜAbbās. He taught hadith to Mujāhid, ᶜAṭā', ᶜAmrū b. Dīnār, Wahb b. Munabbih and many others. He died in Makka. *Tahdhīb al-tahdhīb*:5:8 *Ṣifat al-ṣafwa*:2:284 *Ḥilyat al-awliyā'*:4:4–23
Al-Thaᶜālibī 33B	Sunāmī is not very clear when he mentions this man. He might have meant ᶜAbd al-Mālik b. Muḥammad b. Ismāᶜīl Abū Manṣūr al-Thaᶜālibī (350 – 429/961–2 – 1037–8). This man was an eminent grammarian and philologist and the author of many books. *GAL*:1:337, Sup:1:499 Ziriklī:4:311
Thawrī	See Sufyān al-Thawrī.
Thumāma b. Athāl b. al-Nuᶜmān al-Ḥanafī 50B	He died in 12/633–4. He was a leader of the people of Yamāma and he became a Muslim. He prevented food from reaching Makka by blocking the important caravan route from Yamāma. Sunāmī contradicts this report when he says that Thumāma did not boycott the Makkans. Ibn Saᶜd, *Ṭabaqāt*:5:550 Ibn al- Athīr, *Kāmil*:2:354–5 *Iṣāba*:1:204
ᶜUbāda b. al-Ṣāmit b. Qays 33B	38 BH – AH 34/586–7 – 654–5. A traditionist who narrated 181 hadith, 6 of which are reported by the *Ṣaḥīḥayn*.

	Ibn Sa^cd, *Ṭabaqāt*:3:546 *Tahdhīb al-tahdhīb*:5:111
Ubayy b. Ka^cb, Abū al-Mundhir 30B	He died in 30/650–1. One of the people who gave *fatwās* when the Prophet was alive. He was also an expert in Quranic recitation. *Ṣifat al-ṣafwa*:1:474 Ibn Sa^cd, *Ṭabaqāt*:3:498
Ubayy b. Rāfi^c, the Jew 75B	It would appear that Sunāmī made a mistake in writing this name, or else it has become corrupted. His real name is Abū Rāfi^c Salām b. Ubayy, the Jew. He was killed in AH 3. Ibn al-Athīr, *Kāmil*:2:146–8
^cUmar b. ^cAbd al-^cAzīz 30A	61 – 101/680–1 – 719–20. An Umayyad Caliph who is considered to have been as just as his grandfather ^cUmar b. al-Khaṭṭāb. He was Caliph from AH 99 to 101. *Tahdhīb al-tahdhīb*:7:475
^cUmar b. Abū Salama b. ^cAbd Allāh 4A	2 – 83/623–4 – 702–3. The son of the Prophet's wife Umm Salama, he was fostered by the Prophet. He narrated some hadith included in the *Ṣaḥiḥayn*. He was appointed as governor of Baḥrayn. *Iṣāba*:2:512 Ibn Sa^cd, *Ṭabaqāt*:1:297 Ziriklī:5:211
^cUmar b. al-Khaṭṭāb. 6A	40 BH – AH 23/584–5 – 643–4. The second orthodox Caliph. *Tadhkirat al-ḥuffāẓ*:1:5–8 *Ḥilyat al-awliyā'*:1:3
Umm Ḥabība, Ramla bint Abū Sufyān b. Ḥarb 23A	25 BH – AH 44/599–600 – 664–5. A wife of the Prophet; they were married in AH 7. She was Mu^cāwiya's sister. *Ṣifat al-ṣafwa*:2:47 Kaḥḥāla, *A^clām*:3:61

Umm Kulthūm bint ᶜAlī b. Abū Ṭālib 34A	She was born before the Prophet's death in 9/630–1. She married ᶜUmar b. al-Khaṭṭāb. After his death, she married his brother, Muḥammad b. Jaᶜfar. Following his death in 37/657–8, she married a third brother, ᶜAbd Allāh b. Jaᶜfar (1 – 80/622–3 –699–700). The date of her death is not recorded, although she was still alive in AH 61 but died before her third husband. *Iṣāba*:4:468 Kaḥḥāla, *Aᶜlām*:4:255–60
Umm Salama, Hind bint Abū Umayya 4A	28 BH – 62 AH/596–7 – 681–2. A wife of the Prophet; they were married in AH 4. *Ṣifat al-ṣafwa*:2:41–42 Kaḥḥāla, *Aᶜlām*:9:104
ᶜUrwa, b. al-Zubayr b. al-ᶜAwwām 15B	22 – 93/642–3 – 711–2. The son of a very well-known Companion of the Prophet and Abū Bakr's daughter Asmā'. He narrated hadith from both his father and ᶜAlī. *Ṣifat al-ṣafwa*:2:88 Kaḥḥāla, *Aᶜlām*:9:104
Usāma b. Zayd b. Ḥāritha 71A	7BH – AH 54/615–6 – 673–4. A Companion of the Prophet, who regarded him as a son. He narrated 218 hadith in the *Ṣaḥīḥayn*. Iṣāba:1:46 Ziriklī:1:282
ᶜUthmān, b. ᶜAffān 18A	47 BH – AH 35/577–8 – 655–6. The third orthodox Caliph. *Ḥilyat al-awliyā'*:1:55–61 Ziriklī:4:371
Wuhayb b. al-Ward al-Makkī 37A	He died in 153/770. His name was originally ᶜAbd al-Wahhāb, which was changed to the diminutive form. He was a contemporary of ᶜAṭā' b. Abū Rabāḥ and he narrated some Traditions. Among his students were Ibn al-Mubārak and Fuḍayl b. ᶜIyāḍ. *Tahdhīb al-tahdhīb*:11:170

	Ḥilyat al-awliyā':8:140–62 *Ṣifat al-ṣafwa*:2:218
Wakīᶜ b. al-Jarrāḥ al-Kūfī 16A	He died in 192/807–8. A student of Abū Ḥanīfa, who also studied hadith with Abū Yūsuf and Zufar. He was a good scholar but is often criticised because his Arabic grammar was not always accurate and he had some Shīᶜī tendencies. Luknawī:222 *Mīzān al-iᶜtidāl*:3:270
Yamān b. Riāb 57A	A narrator of hadith, of Khurasani origin. It has been reported that he was not accurate in transmitting hadith. It is also reported that he was one of the Khawārij theologians. *Mīzān al-iᶜtidāl*:4:460 Abū al-Ḥasan al-Ashᶜarī, *Maqālāt al-Islāmiyyīn wa-ikhtilāf al-muṣallīn*, ed. Helmut Ritter (Wiesbaden, 1963):120
Yaᶜqūb 53A	The prophet Jacob.
Yazīd b. Ḥabīb Abū Rajā' al-Azdī 35B	53 – 128/672–3 – 745–6 A narrator of hadith who studied with ᶜAṭā' b. Abū Rabāḥ. He was one of the people who were permitted to give *fatwā*s in his time. *Tahdhīb al-tahdhīb*:11:318 *Tadhkirat al-ḥuffaẓ*:1:129
Yawshaᶜ b. Nūn 30A	The prophet Joshua, the successor of Moses. *Ṭabarī*:1:448
Yūsuf b. Asbāṭ, al-Shaybānī 56A	He died in 192/807–8. A Sufi who narrated hadith and who studied with Sufyān al-Thawrī. He is described as 'not an authority of hadith'. *Mīzān al-iᶜtidāl*:4:462 ᶜAbd al-Raᶜūf al-Munāwī, *Al-kawākib al-durriyya fī tarājim al-sāda al-ṣūfiyya* (Cairo, 1952):1:182

Ḥilyat al-awliyā':8:237–53

Al-Zāhid

See Abū al-Qāsim al-Ṣaffār.

Zamakhsharī, Abū al-Qāsim Jār Allāh Maḥmud b. ᶜUmar
43B

467 – 538/1075–1143–4.
A leading scholar in the subjects of Quranic interpretation and Arabic language. He was a Muᶜtazilī who was well-known for his opposition to the Sufis. He composed many books, including *Al-kashshāf ᶜan ḥaqā'iq al-tanzīl.*
Ibn Ḥajar, *Durar*:6:4
GAL:1:344
Ziriklī:8:55

Zayd b, Thābit b. al-Ḍaḥḥak

11 BH – AH 45/612–3 – 665–6.
A Companion of the Prophet and one of the scribes who wrote down the Quran. He narrated 92 hadith which are all recorded in the *Ṣaḥīḥayn.*
Ṣifat al-ṣafwa:1:704–707
Ziriklī:3:96

Al- Zubayr, b. al-ᶜAwwām al-Asadī
73B

28 BH– AH 36/596–7 – 656–7.
A distinguished Companion of the Prophet. He was killed shortly after the Battle of the Camel, which took place near Baṣra between ᶜAlī and ᶜĀ'isha in AH36. He narrated 36 hadith recorded in the *Ṣaḥīḥayn*.
EI^2:2:415
Ṣifat al-ṣafwa:1:342–9
Ziriklī:3:74–5

Zufar b. al-Hadhīl al-ᶜAnbārī
7B

58 – 110/677–7 – 728–9.
A student of Abū Ḥanīfa who, before joining him, supported the School which refers to Hadith more than Abū Ḥanīfa's School of Analogy.
Luknawī:76
Quṭlūbugha:28
Ziriklī:3:78

IV
Copies of Manuscripts used in the study & translation of the Niṣāb

1. SELLY OAK COLLEGES LIBRARY, BIRMINGHAM.
MS no. Mingana 707
Date: Dhū al-ḥijja AH 1076
Length: 92 folios
Lines per page: 25
Author: ᶜUmar b. Muḥammad b. ᶜIwaḍ al-S.nāmī
Copyist: Muḥammad b. ᶜAlī b. Aḥmad al-Ḥanafī, a native of Tripoli
- No index attached.

2. PRINCETON UNIVERSITY LIBRARY, GARRETT COLLECTION.
MS no. 1775
Date: unknown
Length: 112 folios
Lines per page: 17
Author: ᶜUmar b. Muḥammad b. ᶜIwaḍ al-S.nāmī
Copyist: Aḥmad b. Muḥammad al-Qūsawī
– One of the owners' names can be read as Fāṭima bint Ḥamza Effendī and appears with the date 1079. The manuscript contains numerous marginal comments and corrections. It was originally part of the Bārūdī collection, but was later removed from Beirut.[1]

3. DEUTSCHE STAATSBIBLIOTHEK, BERLIN.
MS no. 4804 (Sprenger 657)
Date: Unknown
Length: 149 pages
Lines per page: 13
Author: ᶜAlī b. Muḥammad b. ᶜIwaḍ al-Sāmī
Copyist: unknown.
– Many errors. No index.

4. MS no. 4805 (Wetzstein ii 1417)
Date: unknown

1 P.K. Hitti *et al. Catalogue of the Garrett collection of Arabic Manuscripts* (Princeton, 1938): 528.

Length: 75 folios
Lines per page: 21
Author: ᶜUmar b. Muḥammad b. ᶜUwaḍ al-Shāmī
Copyist: unknown
– Index attached. A previous owner's name appears on the last leaf, with the date AH 1239.

5. MS no. 4805 (Petermann 1 578, fol. 48–142)
Date: Friday, end of Rajab 1097
Length: 94 folios
Lines per page: 17
Author: ᶜUmar b. Muḥammad b. ᶜUwaḍ al-Shāmī (corrected to *S.nāmī*)
Copyist: Aḥmad Effendī
– Index supplied in a European hand. The same hand glosses the word *muḥtasib* in German.

6. MS no. 4805 (Landberg 26)
Date: unknown
Length: 149 folios
Lines per page: 21
Author: ᶜUmar b. Muḥammad b.ᶜIwaḍ al-Sinnāmī
(with *shadda* over the *nūn*)
Copyist: unknown
– Not many mistakes occur in this copy. It is written in two different hands and the first seven chapters appear to be much more recent than the rest of the manuscript.

7. RIJKSUNIVERSITEIT BIBLIOTHEEK, LEIDEN.
MS no. Or 11686
Date: AH 1060
Length: 83 folios
Lines per page: 21
Author: ᶜUmar b. Muḥammad b.ᶜIwaḍ al-S.nāmī
Copyist: unknown
– Contains many marginal comments and explains Sunām as the name of a mountain between Baṣra and Yamāma.

8. The Calcutta edition, printed in the 1830s.
British Museum (catalogue number 14528 b.19)

9. INDIA OFFICE LIBRARY, LONDON
MS no. Arabic 1693. Levy
Date: 1241 A.H.
Length: 135 folios
Lines per page: 14
Author: ᶜUmar b. Muḥammad b.ᶜIwaḍ al-S.nāmī
Copyist: Muḥammad b. ᶜAṭā' Allāh b. Huẓūr Allāh
– Scattered marginal comments. Rubricated headings.
Index of chapters attached.

10. MS no. Arabic 1694. Levy
Date: nineteenth century, according to the library catalogue, although there is no evidence of date in the manuscript itself.
Length: 142 folios
Lines per page: 15
Author: not mentioned
Copyist: unknown
– This manuscript lacks the preface and commences with Chapter one.

11. MS no. Arabic 1695. Levy
Date: Seventeenth century, according to the library catalogue, although there is no evidence of date in the manuscript itself.
Length: 150 folios
Lines per page: 17
Author: ᶜUmar b. Muḥammad b.ᶜIwad al-Sunāmī
Copyist: not mentioned; however, the name Durr al-Ḥaqq Muḥammad Farīd appears on the fly-leaf and may be the name of the copyist.
– Some indistinct words on the fly-leaf might be read as *Delhi, Rajab al-murajjab...* The manuscript appears to be a conflation of other manuscripts.
An index is attached. Fol. 32–39 are damaged.

12. MS no. Arabic 277. Loth
Date: unknown
Length: 92 folios
Lines per page: 19
Author: ᶜUmar b. Muḥammad b.ᶜIwaḍ al-Sanāmī
Copyist: unknown

13. DAR AL-KUTUB AL-MIṢRIYYA, CAIRO
MS no. 32 (Fiqh Ḥanafī)

Date: Wednesday, Jumādā al-ākhira AH 1010
Length: 197 pages
Lines per page: 19
Author: ᶜUmar b. Muḥammad b. ᶜIwaḍ al-Sanāmī
Copyist: Shams al-Dīn b. Saᶜīd al-Dīn al-Ḥamawī
The copyist's seal appears on the fly-leaf. It was sold in the year AH 1088 to Ibrāhīm b. Ḥasan al-Ḥanafī. At the beginning of the manuscript the year 1009 is inscribed and this may be the date on which the copyist began his work. Written in a clear hand as far as p.120 and from there to p.140 in a different hand.

14. MS no. 618 (Ijtimāᶜ Ṭalᶜat)
Date: Friday, AH 1243
Length: 92 folios
Lines per page: 23
Author: ᶜUmar b. Muḥammad b. ᶜIwaḍ al-Sunāmī
Copyist: Al-Ḥājj Muḥammad Fāḍil
– The copyist states that he copied the manuscript for a Pasha called ᶜAbd al-Qādir Muḥammad Amīn. Very clear and neat script. No index attached.

15. MS no. 608 (Ijtimāᶜ Ṭalᶜat)
Date: the end of Dhū al-Qaᶜda AH 1084
Length: 80 folios
Lines per page: 22
Author: ᶜUmar b. Muḥammad b.ᶜIwaḍ al-Shāmī
(mentioned in the margin only)
Copyist: ᶜAlī of Qusṭanṭīniyya, in the Mosque of Sultan Aḥmad.

16. MS no. 607 (Ijtimāᶜ Ṭalᶜat)
Date: Sunday, Shawwāl AH 1075
Length: 115 folios
Lines per page: 17
Author: ᶜUmar b. Muḥammad b.ᶜIwaḍ al-Shāmī
Copyist: Muḥammad b. Manṣūr, of Oghlībāzār
– Index of chapters attached.

17. MS no. 233 (Fiqh Ḥanafī)
Date: 10th Dhū al-Ḥijja AH 1181
Length: 99 folios

Lines per page: 19
Author: ^{c}Umar b. Muḥammad b.^{c}Iwaḍ al-Shāmī al-Ḥanafī
Copyist: Muḥammad b. Ḥusayn
– This copy was donated as *waqf* by the Wāli Muḥammad ^{c}Alī

18. MS no. 89 (Ijtimā^{c} Taymūr)
Date: unknown
Length: 97 folios
Lines per page: 23
Author: ^{c}Umar b. Muḥammad b.^{c}Iwaḍ al-Shāmī
Copyist: unknown

19. MS no. 613 (Ijtimā^{c} Tal^{c}at)
Date: Muḥarram al-Ḥarām AH 1146
Length: 80 folios
Lines per page: 21
Author: ^{c}Umar b. Muḥammad b.^{c}Iwaḍ al-Shāmī
Copyist: unknown

20. MS no. 609 (Ijtimā^{c} Ṭal^{c}at)
Date: no date appears on the manuscript itself, although the library catalogue gives the date AH 1075
Length: 88 folios
Lines per page: 19
Author: ^{c}Umar b. Muḥammad b.^{c}Iwaḍ al-Nasāmī al-Shāmī
Copyist: unknown
– The title of the work appears as *Kitāb al-ḥisba wa-l-iḥtisāb.*

21. JOHN RYLANDS UNIVERSITY LIBRARY OF MANCHESTER
MS no. Arabic 183
Date: AH 1196
Length: 78 folios
Lines per page: 21
Author: ^{c}Umar b. Muḥammad b.^{c}Iwaḍ al-Sunnāmī
Copyist: Muḥammad Khādim Ahl Shar^{c} Allāh.
– Mingana only gave the date AH 1197,[2] which is in fact the date on which the manuscript was sold.

---

2 A. Mingana, *Catalogue of the Arabic Manuscripts in the John Rylands Library* (Manchester, 1934): 289.

The copyist's date AH 1196 is, however, very clear on the seal. Index attached.

22. IRAQI MUSEUM, BAGHDAD
MS. no. 5938
Date: 5th Shawwāl AH 1079
Length: 164 pages
Lines per page: 25
Author: ᶜUmar b. Muḥammad b. ᶜIwaḍ al-S.nāmī
Copyist: Aḥmad b. Shaykh ᶜAlī al-Maqnatī (or al-Muqnatī)
– Index attached.

23. MS no. 5939
Date: the middle of Dhu al-Ḥijja AH 1143
Length: 145 folios
Lines per page: 15
Author: ᶜUmar b. Muḥammad b. ᶜIwaḍ al-S.nāmī
Copyist: unknown.

24. ROYAL ASIATIC SOCIETY OF BENGAL, CALCUTTA
MS no. 472
Date: Thursday, Shaᶜbān AH 1121 during the reign of the Khāqān, son of Khāqān al-Mu'ayyad al-Manṣūr Abū al-Muẓaffar Muḥyī al-Dīn Muḥammad ᶜĀlim Kīr
Length: 151 pages
Lines per page: 17
Author: ᶜUmar b. Muḥammad b. ᶜIwaḍ al-Sunāmī
Copyist: Shaykh Muḥyī al-Dīn b. ᶜUmar
– Index attached.

25. KHUDA BAKHSH ORIENTAL PUBLIC LIBRARY, BANKIPORE
MS no. 1093
Date: AH 1245
Length: 233 pages
Lines per page: 19
Author: ᶜUmar b. Muḥammad b. ᶜIwaḍ al-Sināmī
Copyist: Anwār ᶜAlī

26. HYBERABAD STATE CENTRAL LIBRARY, HYBERABAD, DECCAN.
MS no. 2846 (Fiqh Ḥanafī)

Date: 10th Muḥarram al-Ḥarām AH 912
Length: 83 folios, plus fly-leaf and four unnumbered folios (see notes below)
Lines per page: 22
Author: ᶜUmar b. Muḥammad b.ᶜIwaḍ al-Shāmī
Copyist: Muṣṭafā b. ᶜAbd Allāh al-Kardawīyyāt
– Written in clear Indian *naskh*, with corrections and a few notes on the margins taken from other Ḥanafī sources. The fly-leaf bears the stamp of Īṣifiyya Library and the four unnumbered folios contain some quotations from other texts. One note on these folios reads, 'Written in the reign of Sultan Murād, the Conqueror of Baghdad,' and another indicates that the manuscript was once kept in the *dār al-khilāfa.* An index is also supplied in the unnumbered folios. Headings are in red (pale on microfilm). This manuscript appears to be the oldest copy of the *Niṣāb*. It contains the whole of chapter five, of which only a summary is found in the other copies. This chapter could have been added by the copyist from other sources, but the style appears to be that of al-Sunāmī and the references and people mentioned in the chapter do not indicate a later period than that of the rest of the text.

27. MS no. 101 (Fiqh Ḥanafī)
Date: AH 1133
Length: 62 folios
Lines per page: 23
Author: ᶜUmar b. Muḥammad b. ᶜIwaḍ al-Sināmī
Copyist: unknown

28. MS no. 396 (Fiqh Ḥanafī)
Date: unknown
Length: 94 folios
Lines per page: 19
Author: Sirāj al-Dīn ᶜUmar b. Muḥammad b. ᶜIwaḍ al-Sīnāmī (according to the preface).
Copyist: unknown
– Very unclear script. Many marginal comments.

Six manuscripts, together with the Calcutta printed edition, of the *Niṣāb* were used in establishing both the text and translation. They were selected from those listed above. The various copies were classed in six groups, from each of which one copy was selected. The six groups are presented below and in each group the manuscript selected is indicated by an asterisk.

A.	10.	India Office Library, MS no. Arabic 1694
	11.	India Office Library, MS no. Arabic 1695
	12.	India Office Library, MS no. Arabic 277
	*26.	Hyderabad State Central Library, MS no. 2846 (Fiqh Ḥanafī)
	28.	Hyderabad State Central Library, MS no. 396 (Fiqh Ḥanafī)
B.	3.	Deutsche Staatsbibliothek, MS no. 4804 (Sprenger 657)
	*5.	Deutsche Staatsbibliothek, MS no. 4805 (Petermann 1578)
	7.	Rijksuniversiteit Bibliotheek, MS no. Or. 11686
	27.	Hyderabad State Central Library, MS no. 101 (Fiqh Ḥanafī)
C.	*9.	India Office Library, MS no. Arabic 1693
	21.	John Rylands University Library of Manchester, MS no. Arabic 183
	24.	Royal Asiatic Society of Bengal, MS no. 472
D.	2.	Princeton University Library, Garrett Collection, MS no. 1775
	4.	Deutsche Staatsbibliothek, MS no. 4805 (Wetzstein ii 1417)
	*13.	Dār al-Kutub al-Miṣrīyya, MS no. 32 (Fiqh Ḥanafī)
	22.	Iraqi Museum, MS no. 5938
	23.	Iraqi Museum, MS no. 5939
E.	6.	Deutsche Staatsbibliothek MS no. 4805 (Landberg 26)
	*14.	Dār al-Kutub al-Miṣrīyya, MS no. 618 (Landberg 26)
	15.	Dār al-Kutub al-Miṣrīyya, MS no. 608 (Ijtimāᶜ Ṭalᶜat)
	16.	Dār al-Kutub al-Miṣrīyya, MS no. 607 (Ijtimāᶜ Ṭalᶜat)
	20.	Dār al-Kutub al-Miṣrīyya, MS no. 609 (Ijtimāᶜ Ṭalᶜat)
F.	*1.	Selly Oak Colleges Library, MS no. Mingana 707
	17.	Dār al-Kutub al-Miṣrīyya, MS no. 233 (Fiqh Ḥanafī)
	18.	Dār al-Kutub al-Miṣrīyya, MS no. 89 (Ijtimāᶜ Ṭalᶜat)
	19.	Dār al-Kutub al-Miṣrīyya, MS no. 613 (Ijtimāᶜ Ṭalᶜat)

Criteria for the above Classification

1. Similarity of general features.

Some manuscripts, e.g. nos. 6 and 14, have the same marginal notes and sometimes the same errors are found within the notes. There are many missing lines in no. 14, which are apparently dropped on account of homoioteleuton of lines in no.6.

Further, when comparing nos. 15 and 16, we find on 44B of the latter manuscript a very obscure line which may have resulted from some liquid having been dropped on it. In the other manuscript we find that the same line appears without dots, probably indicating that this line was copied from the first manuscript without the copyist being able to properly understand it.

There seems also to be no doubt that no. 23 has been copied from no. 22, for in both these manuscripts we find the same spelling mistakes and the same marginal comments, although the writing of no. 23 is very bad. Some times also the copyist has inserted marginal comments into the body of the text. An example off this occurs on 4B where the words have been incorporated into the text.

2. Harmony of variant readings.

This factor may be both useful and misleading; it is useful in comparing manuscripts and determining priority, providing that the results are supported by the dating of the documents. It can, however, be misleading if one considers that a manuscript may have been copied from more than one source. In such a case the manuscript will evidence the chracteristics of all the manuscripts against which it has been collated. No. 9 is a typical example. It has the basic features which may be considered sufficient to distinguish group C, yet it has some other features which are not represented in the manuscripts of group C, such as the chapter numbers. It has 65 instead of the characteristic 64, which has arisen on account of chapter 46 having been divided into two. This factor leads us to the conclusion that it has been collated against one or more other manuscripts. In fact, the manuscripts used by the copyist are probably indicated by the letters ـذ and ـز which appear in the margins (see e,g, fol. 42A, left-hand side).

Similar observations may also be made with regard to the Calcutta printed edition, which also seems to have been dependent on more than one manuscript, one of which may have been no. 9 in our listing, or alternatively one of those from which no. 9 was copied. There are several reasons for this supposition. On p. 216, for example, we find the words

وفي بعض النسخ indicating that more than one manuscript has been used in the preparation of the text. Apart from general similarities, there is also the identical numbering of chapters, the continuous use of the sign كك in abbreviation of كذلك (*sic* in Latin), and the obvious error of giving the title *Khulāṣat iftikhār* ᶜ*izz* to the work known as *Khulāṣat al-fatāwa*[3]

3. Dating by copyists

This factor helped in determining the priority of different manuscripts. The two manuscripts from the Iraqi Museum are good examples here. The dating of manuscripts lends support to the results already achieved through other evidence.

4. Provenance of manuscripts

This factor may in general be of importance in determining the relationship between different local texts of a given manuscript, but in this case it proved to be of little value, since manuscripts of similar provenance appear to represent different text types of *Niṣāb*. This is evidenced by a comparison of nos. 1 and 2 in our listing. The manuscripts in the Selly Oak College Library's collection and the Garrett Collection both derive from Lebanon; the Garrett manuscript comes from the Bārūdī Collection in Beirut and the Selly Oak College Library's manuscript was written by a native of Lebanese Tripoli, who also describes himself as a member of the Qādirīorder of Sufis. Notwithstanding the similarity of provenance, the manuscripts were found to differ in many features, so that I found it necessary to classify them in different groups.

It is necessary to remark here, that the textual divergence between the different groups was never of major proportions, perhaps because they all derive from similar manuscripts. Our conjectural text does not, in fact, depend entirely on one particular manuscript from among those examined; an ecletic text was found to be most satisfactory. However, I considered MS no. 2846 (fiqh Ḥanafi) of Hyderabad, as the main copy because I found it superior to the rest of the manuscripts in both the date and content.

Other Copies of the *Niṣāb* not referred to

1 Istanbul

Kurkīs ᶜAwwād gives the numbers of seven copies of the *Niṣāb* in Istanbul.[4] In spite of much effort, I have found it impossible to obtain

3 *Niṣāb* (Calcutta edition): p 60.

4 ᶜAwwād, *Niṣāb*; XVII (1942) p. 442.

copies of these manuscripts. I did, however, obtain a certain amount of information through the personal assistance of a friend, which seems in general agreement with the information given by ᶜAwwād. The complete list of manuscripts as ascertained so far is as follows:

1. MS no. 1230 Fiqh (Lālalī Library)
Date: 15th Shawwāl AH 1102
Length: 76 folios
Lines per page: 23
Author: ᶜUmar b. Muḥammad b.ᶜIwaḍ al-Sināmī
– Index attached. Rubrics. Some marginal comments and corrections.

2. MS no. 1045 (Bagdatli Vehbi Effendi)
Date: unknown
Length: 54 folios
Lines per page: 30
Author: ᶜUmar b. Muḥammad b.ᶜIwaḍ al-Shāmī
– Some missing pages

3. MS no. 1046 (Bagdatli Vehbi Effendi)
Date: unknown
Length: 108 folios
Lines per page: 22
Author: ᶜUmar b. Muḥammad b.ᶜIwaḍ al-Shāmī
– Occasional marginal comments.

4. MS no. 1024 Fiqh (Esad Effendi Library)
Date: AH 1335
Length: 149 folios
Lines per page: 20
Author: ᶜUmar b. Muḥammad b.ᶜIwaḍ al-Shāmī
– Many marginal comments. The name of the author is glossed as follows: 'The author's name (*nisba*) derives from Shibām, a village in Yemen near Ṣanᶜā'.'

5. MS no. 1581/2 (Esad Effendi Library)
Date: unknown
Length: 155 pages
Lines per page: 20
Author: ᶜUmar b. Muḥammad b.ᶜIwaḍ al-Shāmī

– This manuscript seems to have been copied from the previous one. The same gloss on the author's *nisba* is found here. Written by a very recent hand.

The above manuscripts appear to be the best available in Istanbul, all of them lacking the name of the copyist. Other Istanbul manuscripts are briefly listed below.

6. MS no. 248/1 (Fatih)
7. MS no. 78/3 (Givesün)
8. MS no. 1462/1/150 (Yaya Tavfik)
9. MS no. 303/1 (Haci Nesir Aga)
10. MS no. 160 (Halef Effendi)
11. MS no. 313 (Nasif Paša)
12. MS no. 406/1 (Reis ul Kuttāb)
13. MS no. 11/71 (Sevvez)
14. MS no. 685/Im (Süleymaniye)

2. Aleppo

1. Maktabat Aḥmadīyya, MS no. 610.
Date: AH 1103
2. Al-Takīyya al-Mawlawīyya, MS no. (?)[5]
3. Maktabat ᶜAbd al-Qādir al-Jābirī, MS no. (?)[6]

3. Mosul

1. Maktabat Jāmiᶜ al-Sulṭān ᶜAways, MS no. (?)
Date: AH 1095
2. Maktaba Ḥusaynīyya
Date: AH 1095
3. Madrasa Muḥamadīyya
Date: AH 1051[7]

4. Jedda

Maktabat Muḥammad Naṣīf
Date: AH 1135
Author: al-Shamī[8]

---

5 See M. Rāghib al-Ṭabbākh, *R.A.A.D.*, 18 (1944): 18:380.

6 *Majalla Maᶜhad al-Makhṭūṭāt al-ᶜArabīyya*, 2 (1956), p.251.

7 M. Rāghib al-Ṭabbākh, *R.A.A.D.* (1944): 18: 380.

8 *Majalla Maᶜhad al-Makhṭūṭāt al-ᶜArabīyya* (1955): 1:156.

5. Qatar
Dār al-Kutub al-Qaṭarīyya
Author: ᶜUmar b. Muḥammad b.ᶜIwaḍ al-Shāmī[9]

6. Tashkent
Institute of Oriental Studies[10]

7. Addenda
C. Brocklemann includes in his bibliography one or two additional copies of the manuscript, which I have not been able to consult. Brockelmann's cryptic bibliographical notes may be found in *GAL* Sup. II. 427.

---

9 *Ibid.*, (1963): 9:29.

10 *Ibid.*, (1960): 6:322.

Bibliography and Abbreviations

Abū al-Layth, *Bustān* (=*BA*)	Abū al-Layth, *Bustān al-ᶜārifīn*, Cairo, 1376/1966.
Abū al-Layth, *Tanbīh* (=*TGh*)	Abū al-Layth, *Tanbīh al-ghāfilīn*, Cairo, 1376/1966.
Afsar ud-Din, *Fatāwā*	Afsar Afzal ud-Din, *The Fatāwā-l-jahāndārī of Ziyā' ud-Dīn Baranī.* Translation with *introduction and notes*, Ph.D. thesis, School of Oriental and African studies, London, 1955.
AḥS	See Farrā', *Aḥkām.*
Arberry, *Muslim saints*	A.J. Arberry, *Muslim saints and mystics: Episodes from Tadhkirat al-awliyā' by Farīd al-Dīn al-ᶜAṭṭār*, London, 1966.
ᶜAwwād, *Ḥisba*	K. ᶜAwwād, '*Al-ḥisba fī khizānat al-kutub al-ᶜarabiyya*' *RAAD* 18 (1943).
ᶜAwwād, *Niṣāb*	K. ᶜAwwād, *Niṣāb al-iḥtisāb, RAAD* 17 (1942).
BA	See Abū al-Layth, *Bustān.*
Badawī, *Mu'allafāt*	A. Badawī, *Mu'allafāt al-Ghazālī*, Cairo, 1961.
Barthold, *Turkestan*	W. Barthold, *Turkestan down to the Mongol invasion* (GMS, N.S. V) London, 1928. Fourth edition 1977 (with additional chapter, further addenda and corrigenda etc. [included in third edition]).
BEO	*Bulletin d'Études Orientales. Institut Français de Damas.*

Bosworth, *Islamic Underworld*	C.E. Bosworth, *The Medieval Islamic Underworld: The Banū Sāsān in Arabic Society and Literature*, 2 vols, Leiden, 1976.
Chalmeta, *Zoco*	Pedro Chalmeta Gendrón, *"El señor del zoco" en Espana: edades media y moderna. Contribución al estudio de la historia del mercado*, Madrid, 1973.
Dihlawī, *Akhbār*	ᶜAbd al-Ḥaqq b. Sayf al-Dīn al-Dihlawī (d.1052/1642), *Akhbār al-akhyār*, MS no. Or221, Catalogue of Persian MSS in the B.M. (see Rieu, *Catalogue*).
Dozy, *Supplément*	R.P.A Dozy, *Supplément aux dictionnaires arabes*, 2 vols., Leiden, 2nd edition, 1927.
Dubois, *Hindu Manners*	Abbé J.A. Dubois, *Hindu Manners, Customs and Ceremonies*, tr. from the French by H. Beauchamp, Oxford, 1906.
EI[1]	*Encyclopaedia of Islam*, Leiden, 1913–1934.
EI[2]	*Encyclopaedia of Islam*, new edition, Leiden, 1960 – (in progress).
Faḍl al-iᶜtizāl	Abū al-Qāsim al-Balkhī, *Faḍl al-iᶜtizāl wa-ṭabaqāt al-Muᶜtazila*, ed. Fu'ād Sayyid, Tunis, 1393/1974.
Farrā', *Aḥkām* (=AḥS)	Muḥammad b. al-Ḥusayn Abū Yaᶜlā al-Farrā', *Al-aḥkām al-sulṭāniyya*, Cairo, 1357/1938–9.
Farrā', *Ṭabaqāt*	Abū al-Ḥusayn Muḥammad b. Abī Yaᶜlā al-Farrā', *Ṭabaqāt al-Ḥanābila*, ed. Muḥammad Ḥāmid al-Faqī, Cairo, 1952.
GAL	C. Brockelmann, *Geshchichte der arabischen Litteratur & Supplementbande*, 5 vols., Leiden, 1937–49.
Ghazālī, *Iḥyā'* (=Iḥ)	Muḥammad al-Ghazālī, *Iḥyā' ᶜulūm al-dīn*, cited by, Nadwī, M., *Tārīkh*.
GMS	"E.J.W. Gibb Memorial" Series.

H	See Marghinānī, *Hidāya.*
Hadiyyat al-ʿārifīn	Ismāʿīl Bāshā al-Baghdādī, *Hadiyyat al-ʿārifīn*, 2 vols., ed. S. Yatakaya & R. Bilge, Istanbul, 1941–43.
Haig	T.W. Haig, 'Five questions in the history of the Tughluq dynasty of Dihli', *JRAS*, 1922.
Ḥilyat al-awliyā'	Abū Nuʿaym Aḥmad b. ʿAbd Allāh al-Iṣbahānī, *Ḥilyat al-awliyā' wa-ṭabaqāt al-aṣfiyā',* 10 vols., Beirut, 1387/1967.
H.Kh., *Kashf*	Ḥājjī Khalīfa Kātib Čelebī, *Kashf al-ẓunūn ʿan asāmī al-kutub wa-l-funūn*, 2 vols., Istanbul, 1360/1941.
Hughes, *Dictionary*	T.P. Hughes, *A Dictionary of Islam.* London, 1935, (first published 1885).
Ḥujwīrī, *Kashf*	Al-Ḥujwirī, *Kashf al-maḥjūb*, ed. R.A. Nicholson, (GMS, N.S. XVII), Leiden, 1911.
Ibn ʿĀbidīn, *Baḥr*	Ibn ʿĀbidīn, *Al-baḥr al-rā'iq*, 7 vols., Cairo, 1311/1893–4.
Ibn al-Athīr, *Kāmil*	Ḍiyā' al-Dīn Nāṣr Allāh b. Muḥammad Ibn al-Athīr, *Al-kāmil fī al-tārīkh*, 13 vols, ed. C.J. Tornberg, Beirut, 1385–7/1965–7.
Ibn Bassām, *Nihāya*	Muḥammad b. Aḥmad Ibn Bassām, *Nihāyat al-rutba fī ṭalab al-ḥisba,* 13 vols., ed. Husām al-Sāmarrāī, Baghdad, 1387/1968.
Ibn Baṭṭūṭa (Gibb)	*The Travels of Ibn Baṭṭūṭa. A.D.1325–1354,* translated with revision and notes from the Arabic text, etc. by H.A.R. Gibb. Published for the Hakluyt Society at Cambridge University Press, Cambridge, 1958–71.
Ibn Baṭṭūṭa, *Riḥla*	Ibn Baṭṭūṭa, *Riḥlat Ibn Baṭṭūṭa,* Beirut, 1379/1960.

Ibn Ḥajar, *Durar*	Ibn Ḥajar al-ᶜAsqalānī, *Al-durar al-kāmina fī aᶜlām al-mi'a al-thāmina*, 5 vols., ed., S. Jād al-Ḥaqq, Cairo, 1966.
Ibn Ḥajar, *Lisān*	Ibn Ḥajar al-ᶜAsqalānī, *Lisān al-mīzān*, 7 vols., Hyderabad, 1912–1913.
Ibn Mājā, *Sunan*	Ibn Mājā, *Sunan Ibn Mājā,* 2 vols., ed. Fu'ād ᶜAbd al-Bāqī, Cairo, 1372/1952.
Ibn Qudāma, *Istibṣār*	Muwaffaq al-Dīn ᶜAbd Allāh b. Qudāma al-Maqdisī, *Al-istibṣār fī nasab al-Ṣaḥāba min al-Anṣār*, 9 vols., ed. ᶜAlī Nuwayhiḍ, Beirut, 1392/1972.
Ibn Saᶜd, *Ṭabaqāt*	Muḥammad al-Zuhrī Ibn Saᶜd, *Al-ṭabaqāt al-kubrā*, 9 vols., Beirut, 1957–8.
Ibn Taymiyya, *Ḥisba*	Taqī al-Dīn Aḥmad b. Taymiyya, *Al-ḥisba fī al-islām*, ed. Q. Muḥibb al-Dīn, Cairo, 1387/1967.
Ibn al-Ukhuwwa, *Maᶜālim*	Muḥammad b. Muḥammad al-Qurashī, Ibn al-Ukhuwwa, *Maᶜālim al-qurba fī aḥkām al-ḥisba*, ed. Reuben Levy (GMS N.S. XII), Cambridge, 1938.
Iḥ	See Ghazālī, *Iḥyā'*.
Īḍāh	Ismāᶜīl Bāshā al-Baghdādī, *Īḍāh al-maknūn fī al-dhayl ᶜalā Kashf al-ẓunūn*, 2 vols., ed. S. Yatakaya & R. Bilge, Istanbul, 1947.
Iṣāba	Shihāb al-Dīn Aḥmad b. Ḥajar al-ᶜAsqalānī, *Al-iṣāba fī tamyīz al-Ṣaḥāba*, 4 vols., ed. Aḥmad Shākir, Cairo, 1358/1939.
Jawālīqī, *Muᶜarrab*	Abū Manṣūr Mawhūb b. Aḥmad al-Jawālīqī, *Al-Muᶜarrab min al-kalām al-aᶜjamī*, ed. Aḥmad Muḥammad Shākir, Tehran, 1966.
JRAS	*The Journal of the Royal Asiatic Society of Great Britain and Ireland.*

Kaḥḥāla, *Aʿlam*	ʿU.R. Kaḥḥāla, *Aʿlām al-nisā'*, 5 vols., Damascus, 1379/1959.
Kaḥḥāla, *Muʿjam*	ʿU.R. Kaḥḥāla, *Muʿjam al-mu'allifīn* 15 vols., Damascus, 1376–1381/1957–1961.
Kifāya (=*KSh*)	Muḥammad b. ʿUmar Abū Jaʿfar, *Al-kifāya al-shaʿbiyya* or *Kifāyat al-shaʿbī,* MSS nos. 1698, 1699 in Lévy, *Catalogue.*
KSh	See *Kifāya.*
Al-kunā wa-l-alqāb	ʿAbbās al-Qummī, *Al-kunā wa-l-alqāb*, 3 vols., Najaf, 1389/1969–70.
Lévy, *Catalogue*	R. Lévy, *Catalogue of the Arabic manuscripts in the Library of the India Office,* London, 1973.
Lisān al-ʿArab	Muḥammad b. Mukarram Ibn Manẓūr, *Lisān al-ʿArab,* 20 vols., Būlāq, 1300–1303/1883–91.
Liqbāl, *Ḥisba*	Mūsā Liqbāl, *Al-ḥisba al-madhhabiyya fī bilād al-Maghrib al-ʿArabī,* Algiers, 1971.
Luknawī	Muḥammad ʿAbd al-Ḥayy al-Luknawī, *Al-fawā'id al-bahiyya fī tarājim al-Ḥanafiyya*, ed. Abū Firās al-Naʿsānī, Beirut, 1324/1975.
Mabs.	See Sarakhsī, *Mabsūṭ.*
Maqrīzī, *Khiṭaṭ*	Maqrīzī, *Al-khiṭaṭ al-Maqrīziyya,* 9 vols., Cairo, 1324–1326/1906–7 – 1908–9.
Marghinānī, *Hidāya* (=*H*)	Burhān al-Dīn al-Marghinānī, *Hidāyat al-muhtadī*, 4 vols. [in 2], Cairo, 1384/1965; trans. by C. Hamilton as *The Hedaya*, 2nd edition London, 1870, repr. Lahore 1957.

Māwardī, *Aḥkām*	ʿAlī b. Muḥammad b. Ḥabīb al-Māwardī, *Al-aḥkām al-sulṭāniyya,* Cairo, 1393/1973.
Milal	ʿAbd al-Karīm al-Shahrastānī, *Al-milal wa-l-niḥal,* 2 vols., Baghdad, 1321/1903–4.
Mīzān al-iʿtidāl	Shams al-Dīn Muḥammad b. ʿUthman al-Dhahabī, *Mīzān al-iʿtidāl fī naqd al-rijāl,* ed. S. al-Naʿsānī, Cairo, 1325/1907–8.
Mughrib (=*Mugh*)	Nāṣir b. ʿAbd al-Sayyid al-Muṭarrizī, *Al-Mughrib fī tartīb al-muʿrab*, Hyderabad, 1328/1910–11.
Mugh.	See *Mughrib.*
Muḥīṭ	Buṭrus al-Bustānī, *Muḥīṭ al-muḥīṭ*, 2 vols., Beirut, 1870.
Mujayladī, *Taysīr*	Aḥmad Saʿīd al-Mujayladī, *Kitāb al-taysīr fī aḥkām al-tasʿīr*, ed. Mūsā Liqbāl, Algiers, 1970.
Al-Muʿjam al-wasīṭ	I. Anīs *et al.*, *Al-Muʿjam al-wasīṭ*, Cairo 1380/1960.
Nadwī, *Nuzha*	ʿAbd al-Ḥayy al-Nadwī al-Ḥasanī, *Nuzhat al-khawāṭir wa-bahjat al-masāmiʿ wa-l-nawāẓir,* 8 vols., Hyderabad, 1378–1398/1959–1978.
Nadwī, M., *Tārīkh*	Masʿūd al-Nadwī, *Tārīkh al-daʿwa al-islāmiyya fī al-Hind,* Beirut,1370/1951.
Nicholson, *Mystics*	R.A. Nicholson, *The Mystics of Islam*, London, 1914.
Nizami, *Delhi sultanate*	Khaliq Ahmad Nizami and Mohammad Habib, *The Delhi Sultanate 1206–1526 AD. A Comprehensive history of India*, 5 vols., India, 1970.
N.S.	New Series.
Nūr al-qabas	Muḥammad b. ʿImrān al-Marzubānī Abū ʿUbayd Allāh, *Nūr al-qabas al-mukhtaṣar min al-muqtabas fī akhbār al-nuḥāt,* ed. R. Sellheim, Wiesbaden, 1964.

Qureshi, *Administration*	Ishtiaq Husain Qureshi, *The administration of the Sultanate of Delhi,* Karachi, 1958.
Qurṭubī, *Tafsīr*	Abū ʿAbd Allāh Muḥammad b. Aḥmad al-Qurṭubī, *Al-Jāmiʿ li-aḥkām al-Qur'ān*, or *Tafsīr al-Qurṭubī*, 20 vols. [in 10], Cairo, 1967.
Quṭlubughā	Ibn Quṭlubughā Qāsim Zayn al-Dīn, *Tāj al-tarājim fī ṭabaqāt al-Ḥanafiyya*, Baghdad, 1962.
RAAD	Revue de l'Académie Arabe de Damas.
Raḥmat Allāh, *Ḥāla*	Malīḥa Raḥmat Allāh, *Al-ḥāla al-ijtimāʿiyya fī al-ʿIrāq fī al-qarnayn al-thālith ʿashar wa-l-rābiʿ ʿashar baʿd al-Hijra*, Baghdad, 1970.
Rieu, *Catalogue*	Ch. Rieu, *Catalogue of Persian manuscripts in the British Museum,* London, 1879–1883; *Supplement*, London, 1894.
Rosenthal, *Herb*	F. Rosenthal, *The Herb: hashish versus medieval Muslim society*, Leiden, 1971.
RSO	*Rivista degli Studi Orientali.*
Samʿānī, *Ansāb*	Al-Samʿānī, *Al-Ansāb*, ed. D.S. Margoliouth, London, 1912.
Saqaṭī, *Ādāb*	Abū ʿAbd Allāh Muḥammad al-Saqaṭī, *Kitāb fī ādāb al-ḥisba*, ed. G.S. Colin and E. Lévi-Provençal, Paris, 1930.
Sarakhsī, *Mabsūṭ*	Abū Bakr Muḥammad b. Aḥmad Al-Sarakhsī, *Al-mabsūṭ fī al-furūʿ*, 30 vols., Cairo, 1324–31/1906–12.
Sarakhsī, *Sharḥ* (=*ShSK*)	Abū Bakr Muḥammad b. Aḥmad al-Sarakhsī, *Sharḥ kitāb al-siyar al-kabīr li-Muḥammad b. al-Ḥasan al-Shaybānī,* 5 vols., Cairo, 1971.
Sarkīs, *Muʿjam*	Yūsuf Ilyās Sarkīs, *Muʿjam al-maṭbūʿāt al-ʿArabiyya wa-l-muʿarraba*, 2 vols., Cairo, 1346/1928.

Schacht, *Introduction* — J. Schacht, *Introduction to Islamic law*, Oxford, 1964.

Schimmel, *Dimensions* — A.M. Schimmel, *Mystical Dimensions of Islam*, North Carolina, 1975.

Sharḥ adab al-qāḍī — Ḥusām al-Dīn ᶜUmar b. ᶜAbd al-ᶜAziz, *Sharḥ adab al-qāḍī*, MS no. 273. See Rieu, *Catalogue*.

Shayzarī, *Nihāya* — ᶜAbd al-Raḥmān b. Naṣr al-Shayzarī, *Nihāyat al-ruṭba fī ṭalab al-ḥisba*, ed. al-Sayyid al-Bāz al-ᶜArīnī, Cairo, 1365/1946.

Shabībī, *Ibn al-Fuwaṭī* — M. Riḍā al-Shābībī, *Mu'arrikh al-ᶜIrāq Ibn al-Fuwaṭī*, 2 vols., Baghdad, 1370–78/1950–58.

Ṣifat al-ṣafwa — Ibn al-Jawzī, *Ṣifat al-ṣafwa*, 4 vols., 2nd edition Hyderabad, 1388–1392/1968–1972.

S.M. Husain, *Sultans* — Syed Mashtaq Husain, *The Sultans of Delhi and their attitude towards religion (1206–1320 AD)*, M.A. thesis, University of Manchester, 1964.

S.M. Husain, *Indian Islam* — Syed Mashtaq Husain, *Some aspects of Indian Islam in the fourteenth century*, Ph.D. thesis, University of Manchester,1967.

S.M. Husain, *Studies in Islam* — Syed Mashtaq Husain, *Studies in Islam, Ahl al-Dhimma in the Sultanate of Delhi 1206–1320 AD*, 1967.

ShSK — See Sarakhsī, *Sharḥ*

Ṭabarī — Abū Jaᶜfar Muḥammad b. Jarīr al-Ṭabarī, *Tārīkh al-rusul wa-l-mulūk* ed. Muḥammad Abū al-Faḍl Ibrāhīm, 10 vols., Cairo, 1960.

Ṭabaqāt al-Muᶜtazila — Aḥmad b. Yaḥya b. al-Murtaḍā, *Ṭabaqāt al-Muᶜtazila*, ed. Susanna Diwald-Wilzer, Beirut-Wiesbaden, 1961.

Tadhkirat al-ḥuffāẓ — ᶜAbd Allāh Shams al-Dīn al-Dhahabī, *Tadhkirat al-ḥuffāẓ*, 4 vols., Hyderabad, 1955–1958.

Tahdhīb al-asmā' — Abū Zakariyya Muḥyī al-Dīn b. Sharaf al-Nawawī, *Tahdhib al-asmā' wa-l-lughāt*, Cairo, n.d..

Tahdhīb al-tahdhīb — Shihāb al-Dīn Aḥmad b. ᶜAlī al-ᶜAsqalānī, *Tahdhīb al-tahdhīb*, Beirut, 1968, reprint of Hyderabad edition AH 1325–1327.

Tarīkh Fershita — Mohamed Kasim Fershita, *Rise of Mahomedan power in India*, or *Tarikh Fershita*, trans. J. Briggs, Calcutta, 1966.

Tārīkh-i Fīrūz Shāhī — Ẓiyā' al-Dīn al-Baranī, *Tā'rīkh-i Fīrūz Shāhī* ed.S. Aḥmad, Calcutta, 1862.

Trimingham, *Sufi Orders* — J.S. Trimingham, *The Sufi orders in Islam*, Oxford, 1971.

Ṭurṭūshī, *Ḥawādith* — Abū Bakr Muḥammad al-Ṭurṭūshī, *Al-ḥawādith wa-l-bidaᶜ*, Tunis, 1959. See also Maribel Fierro's edition and translation into Spanish, Madrid, 1993.

ᶜUqbānī — A. Chenoufī (ed.), 'Un traité de ḥisba (*Tuḥfat an-nāẓir*) de Muḥammad al-ᶜUqbānī at-Tilmisanī [d.871/1467], édition critique', *BEO*, XIX (1965–66), 1967.

Watt, *Philosophy* — W.M. Watt, *Islamic philosophy and theology*, Edinburgh, 1962.

Wehr, *Dictionary* — Hans Wehr, *Dictionary of modern written Arabic*, New York, 1976.

Yaya, *Aḥkām* — Yaḥyā b. Umar, *Aḥkām al-sūq*, ed. Ḥasan Ḥusnī ᶜAbd al-Wahhāb, Tunis, 1975.

Yāqūt, *Muᶜjam* — Yāqūt al-Ḥamawī, *Muᶜjam al-buldān*, 5 vols., Beirut, 1955–7.

Zaydān, *Aḥkām al-dhimmiyyīn* — ᶜAbd al-Karīm Zaydān, *Aḥkām al-dhimmiyyīn wa-l-musta'minīn fī al-Islām*, Baghdad, 1382/1963.

ZDMG	*Zeitschrift der dutschen Morgenlandischen Gesellschaft*
Ziriklī	Khayr al-Dīn al-Ziriklī, *Al-aʿlām: qāmūs tarājim li-ashar al-rijāl*, 10 vols., Beirut, 1954-59. vols., Beirut, 1954–59.